Jacobean Private Theatre

Theatre Production Studies

General Editor
John Russell Brown
Associate of the National Theatre of Great Britain
and
Professor of Theatre Arts, State University of New York
at Stony Brook

Jacobean Private Theatre

Keith Sturgess

Routledge & Kegan Paul
London and New York

First published in 1987 by
Routledge & Kegan Paul Ltd
11 New Fetter Lane, London EC4P 4EE

Published in the USA by
Routledge & Kegan Paul Inc.
in association with Methuen Inc.
29 West 35th Street, New York, NY 10001

Phototypeset in Linotron Plantin
by Input Typesetting Ltd, London
and printed in Great Britain
by The Thetford Press
Thetford, Norfolk

Library of Congress Cataloging in Publication Data

Sturgess, Keith.
Jacobean private theatre.
(Theatre production studies)
Bibliography: p.
Includes index.
1. Theater—England—History—17th century.
2. English drama—17th century—History and criticism.
3. Theaters—England—History—17th century. I. Title.
II. Series.
PN2589.S78   1987   792'.0941   86–17877

British Library CIP Data also available
ISBN 0-7102-1017-5

To My Mother and Father

Contents

Illustrations

Plates

Figures

Preface and Acknowledgments

I have modernised all quotations, in spelling and punctuation, where taken from original or old spelling texts.

I should like to thank John Russell Brown for his creative advice in the early stages of planning this book and his rigorous criticism in the late stages of its writing; Margaret Eddershaw for constant encouragement and the painstaking reading of various versions; Lorna Gyngell, Fiona Knowles and Karen Clarke for their staunch efforts to cope with my 'foul papers'; and colleagues – both students and staff – at Lancaster University with whose skilful and enthusiastic co-operation I have directed productions of the major plays of Chapters 5, 6, 7 and 9 and reconstructed a full-scale, working model of the Blackfriars playhouse.

I am grateful for permission to reproduce illustrations to the following (with whom copyright remains): the Bodleian Library (Plates 1–3); the Trustee of the Will of the 8th Earl of Berkeley deceased (Plate 4); the Provost and Fellows of Worcester College, Oxford (Plates 5 and 6); the University Library, Utrecht (Plate 8); the Courtauld Institute of Art (Plates 9, 15, 21); the Ashmolean Museum, Oxford (Plate 10); the Duke of Buccleuch and Queensberry, K.T. (Plate 11); the British Library (Plate 12); the Royal Institute of British Architects (Plate 13); the Controller of Her Majesty's Stationery Office (Plate 14). I am also grateful to Bill Ellwood for making the models in Plate 7 and to Carlo Faulds for photographing them.

1 · Introduction: Jacobean Private Theatre

On 4 February 1596, James Burbage completed the purchase of rooms in the Upper Frater building of the old Blackfriars monastery in the south-west corner of the city of London. He paid £600 and his intention was to convert his new property into an indoors playhouse for the Lord Chamberlain's company whose lease at the Theatre (their regular playhouse in Shoreditch from 1576) was shortly to expire. The conversion was begun but in November inhabitants of the Blackfriars area sent a petition to the Privy Council asking that the project be stopped. They maintained that a playhouse in the precinct would be a general inconvenience and they rehearsed the time-honoured objections that playhouses attracted riff-raff and criminals and were a health hazard in times of plague. Particular to their case, they noted,

> the same playhouse is so near the Church that the noise of the drums and trumpets will greatly disturb and hinder both the ministers and parishioners in time of divine service and sermons.[1]

(The church was St Anne's and the trumpets and drums were presumably those customarily played outside a playhouse to draw patrons and signal the imminent beginning of a performance.) Then the trump card was played. The petitioners claimed

> that there hath not at any time heretofore been used any common playhouse within the same precinct, but that now all players being banished by the Lord Mayor . . . they now think to plant themselves in Liberties.

A 'liberty' is an area outside municipal authority and the Blackfriars was one by virtue of having been religious ground; in fact very shortly the city would control the area, but meanwhile the petitioners necessarily turned to the Privy Council.

The petition was evidently successful. In any case, the Lord Chamberlain's Men failed to get permission to perform at the new house and, shortly after, the company set about building the Globe on Bankside where they performed from 1599. Meanwhile the Blackfriars playhouse stood empty. James Burbage had died in 1597 and eventually, in 1600, his sons, intent on wresting some profit from the so far abortive venture, leased it at £40 a year to Henry Evans, manager of a children's troupe, the Children of the Chapel. The lease was to run for twenty-one years, so evidently the Burbages had given up hope of using the playhouse themselves in the short term. Evans's boys played there until 1608, presumably tolerated by the Blackfriars residents who had reacted so vigorously to the threat of an adult company in their midst.

By 1608, Evans's operation had run into severe difficulties and he was willing to let the Lord Chamberlain's Men, now prestigiously restyled the King's Men, repossess the Blackfriars. This time, perhaps because of their royal patronage, the company overcame any opposition to their occupancy of the playhouse and, having carried out repairs and refurbishment, they began playing there. Probably, because of interruptions through plague, their first full season was in 1610. From then until the closure of the theatres, they played the winter season each year at the Blackfriars, from October until March or April, and then transferred to the Globe for the summer, thus running the two houses in tandem.

With the King's Men finally installed at the Blackfriars begins the story proper of Jacobean Private Theatre and of this book.[2]

'Private' is a term that stands some scrutiny. It is absent from the Blackfriars petition, but one of its opposites is there – 'common': 'there hath not heretofore been used any common playhouse within the same precinct.' (Common's synonym is 'public'.) In fact, there had been a playhouse in the precinct, a first Blackfriars playhouse constructed in 1576, which was also an indoors conversion of an existing building. Its occupying company was the forerunner of Evans's troupe and either the 1596 petitioners were being disingenuous or they were ignoring it because, being an indoors, children's house, it was *not* 'common' but (though they do not use the word) 'private'.

Distinctions between 'private' and 'public' are clearly made in another petition of the Blackfriars residents against the playhouse, this one of 1618–19. Now, of course, the players are the adults of the King's Men and so the petitioners draw attention both to the Privy Council ruling of 1596 and to another, more general, directive of 1600 that there should only be two London playhouses *in toto;* and they then complain that 'contrary to the said orders, the owner of the said playhouse [the Blackfriars], under the name of a private house (respecting indeed private commodity only) convert the said house to a public playhouse'.[3]

No conversion was then in hand; the deed had been done a decade before, if this 'conversion' was the installation of the King's Men. But 'private house' evidently means what it says – in law, the domestic premises of a private individual, dedicated to his private advantage ('commodity'). But already, 'private house' also meant a private playhouse of the Blackfriars kind. Originally, perhaps, it denoted the playhouses occupied by boys and it first appears in print in that manner when Webster uses it in his 1604 Induction to *The Malcontent* where the Blackfriars itself is referred to. Dekker's *The Seven Deadly Sins* (1606) talks of a 'private playhouse' and quickly the term appears in regular usage to refer to the Blackfriars type of playhouse whether occupied by boys or adults and means, therefore, a small, enclosed playhouse as distinct from the larger, unroofed playhouses like the Globe.

W. J. Lawrence suggested that the managers of the boys companies first used 'private' to camouflage the fact that they were making capital out of the companies of choirboys under their charge by giving infrequent but profitable performances to paying customers.[4] The discretion of the operation and the fact that the boys played to a kind of club audience in enclosed premises allowed the authorities to turn a blind eye to the infringement of the Act of Common Council, 1572, which in fact allowed the performance of plays 'in the private house, dwelling, or lodging of any nobleman, citizen or gentleman . . . without public or common collection of money of the auditory'. Be that as it may, by the second decade of the seventeenth century, private/public meant primarily indoors/outdoors, and the King's Men had demonstrated the commercial viability of the indoors playhouse. British theatre would never be the same. The outdoor playhouse was not defunct – the Globe was worth rebuilding after fire in 1613 and the Fortune in 1621; and the Hope was a new theatre building in 1614 (though built, significantly, to double as an animal-baiting arena). But Beeston's Phoenix, converted from a cockpit in 1616 and the Salisbury Court playhouse of 1629 belonged to the new spirit of playhouse design and they would provide the model, with important refinements from the court theatre, for the Restoration playhouse building.

After the King's Men's move to the Blackfriars we can make a broad distinction between the 'private' and 'public' play. Many plays in the company's repertoire transferred easily from the Globe to the Blackfriars and vice versa according to the time of the year; and both acting personnel and, no doubt, commercial and artistic policy were broadly the same. Also, other companies found themselves first in a public house and then a private one and were dependent on largely the same repertory for both. But there rapidly were generated two kinds of audience, a process the boys companies had begun, and an essential difference developed between what we might see as a West End Theatre and a Bankside Theatre, and between a play aimed at an aristocratic and literary audience and a play aimed at a popular and low-brow audience. In effect, the audience determines the play, and the private playhouse became a club, an academy and an art-house, while its public counterpart became notable for rowdy behaviour and, on stage, an over-dependence on jigs, fighting and horseplay.

Such a polarizing of taste marks the cultural divide between an art or elitist theatre and a popular one, and it has been fashionable amongst drama historians to deplore that such a thing ever happened. Only in a truly popular theatre, received opinion would have it, might a great dramatist like Shakespeare develop, for cultural specialisation or class division in a social art-form like theatre leads to etiolation and decay. Alfred Harbage's seminal investigation of the private theatre's repertory, *Shakespeare and the Rival Traditions* (New York, 1952), makes much of this in demonstrating the loss in Jacobean drama of the robustness and clear-eyed, moral vigour which a popular culture alone promotes (where 'popular' means heterogeneous).

However, in the last twenty years, the stock of the 'decadent' Jacobean drama, specifically the 'private' plays (for few genuinely popular plays got into print), has risen enormously, particularly amongst theatre-makers and theatre-goers (the only true arbiters, dare we say it, of dramatic taste). Primed by lessons learned from 'Epic', 'Cruel' and 'Absurd' Theatre, actors and directors have found ways of playing the private theatre repertory and audiences of watching it, so that it constantly strikes us as aptly modern as well as challengingly ancient. This theatre, with its dramaturgies of discontinuity, its grotesque mixing of comic and tragic, its teasing strategies of characterisation and its existential preoccupation with problems of identity and authenticity, strikes us as a kind of dramatic expressionism we feel at home with. The playwrights that wrote it have all but extinguished the 'popular' Elizabethans, apart from Shakespeare, on the modern stage.

Our particular vantage point, then, enables a theatrical re-assessment of the group of plays – by Webster, Jonson, Middleton, Ford – that make up this alternative tradition to that which we associate with the Globe. Consequently, in this book our twentieth-century touchstones of theatrical style and practice – Brecht, Artaud *et al.* – are drawn on where appropriate and without apology to 'place' the theatrical events under discussion.

Primarily, though, the approach is necessarily historical: to rediscover the 'private' play-in-performance by treating it as an historical object. To that end, Chapters 2, 3 and 4 deal with the plays' auspices: audience, playhouse, performing company. There is no extended consideration of acting style here, largely because we still know little about it, though there are attempts to speculate about the changes in style imposed by the indoor playing conditions. In the chapters on the plays themselves (6, 7, 9 and 10) much use is made of the terms 'mannerist' and, to a lesser extent, 'baroque'. 'Mannerist' here is an epitome of the matrix of ideas, intuitions and aesthetic judgments prevailing in educated circles in Jacobean London which provided the intellectual climate in which the private theatre flourished. Some definitions of its usage here, and indeed a justification for it, seem called for.

Mannerism is a twentieth-century term used to describe the art of the post-Renaissance artists who flouted the rules deduced from classical art. Much of the rule-breaking, which presupposed an audience able to perceive the breaking itself, was an attempt to come to terms with a universe suddenly less explicable or less easily understood, for the old certainties were everywhere being challenged by new discoveries and new ways of thinking. For example, in 1610 when the King's Men played their first full season at the Blackfriars, Galileo published his earth-moving *Sidereus Nuncius*. This book described astronomical discoveries made with the telescope which demonstrated, by empirical observation, that the Ptolemaic model of the universe was wrong. (The idea was not new; the demonstration was.) On publication day, England's ambassador in Venice bought a copy, saw immediately its shattering import and promptly sent it to the English court. Within months Donne alluded to Galileo and his discoveries in his anonymous book *Ignatius his Conclave* (and the next year would write the famous lines beginning 'and new philosophy calls all in doubt'). In *The Duchess of Malfi*, played in 1613, Webster refers several times to Galileo, enigmatically but not at all casually (see p. 97), and a dozen years later, another Blackfriars play, Fletcher's *The Elder Brother*, can, this time with the casualness born of familiarity, make a passing joke about 'Galileo, the Italian star-wright'.

Thinkers like Machiavelli and Montaigne, similar in their scepticism and naturalism, turned metaphorical telescopes on the worlds of politics and moral values, making empirical discoveries as profound if less dramatic. These are thinkers of the 'Counter-Renaissance', that transitional stage in the general reformulation that would turn the old world into new,[5] and they occupied the thought-processes and even passages of the dialogue of the Jacobean playwrights. Shakespeare borrows Gonzalo's plantation speech in *The Tempest* from Montaigne, ideas relevant to Caliban, and, most strikingly, Prospero's reasoning that 'the rarer action is In virtue than in vengeance'; while whole sequences in Webster are excerpts from Montaigne lightly cast as dialogue. *'Que sais je?'* the French essayist took as his motto, and the habit of introspection and self-analysis, together with a relativist cast of thought, became the hallmark of every Jacobean hero.

Mannerism is the art equivalent of Counter-Renaissance. Montaigne's essays, unclassical, apparently spontaneous and improvised, catching the present moment, focused on the writer rather than on the nominal subject, are quintessentially mannerist. The term comes from Vasari, first biographer of the Renaissance painters, who used *maniera* to mean something like stylishness and an emphasis on style or a refined elegance is one aspect of the modern usage. The other is an emphasis on the artist's personal, often agonised, perception of reality and on an art which ignores or deconstructs conventional images of external nature. So mannerist art is often an art of imbalance and distortion: in painting, the human form is elongated, unrealistic and discordant colours are used, the canvas is crowded, often the nominal subject is displaced or not given a central accent and there is a tendency towards abstraction. Always, the mannerist perspective assumes an educated audience ready to respond to a challenge to its sensibility or to enjoy the flattery of a reference to its cultivation. For mannerism is not a popular but a coterie art; it developed at court and it asked questions and assumed standards of taste far different from those that prevail in popular art.[6]

The Reformation ensured that England had little sixteenth-century contact with mannerist pictorial art in its early phase in Italy, though Hilliard developed a genuine, native mannerism of his own in his miniature portraits with their jewel-like workmanship and the private, spontaneous expression of their sitters. Later, Inigo Jones copied mannerist fine-drawing from the Italian engravings he assiduously collected. But already by then the English experience in the fine arts had caught up apace.

Earlier, the 'metaphysical' poets, with their 'hard lines' and conceited style and their love of paradox and irony, had created a brand of literary mannerism which translated quickly and relatively easily into dramatic expression in the plays written by the likes of Marston and Middleton for the boys. The boys companies' whole endeavour was a paradox and a conceit: child actors aping the adult world and so twice removed from reality. Marston in the *Antonio* plays (1599) and in *The Malcontent* (1604) could exploit this to fine, ironic effect. But even on the adult stage, in Jonson's satires and Shakespeare's 'Problem Plays' (particularly *Troilus and Cressida*), a 'metaphysical' theatre was emerging which Fletcher's sense of style could refine into the characteristic Jacobean play, the tragicomedy (see Chapter 5).

In the Induction and parts of the play proper of *Bartholomew Fair* Jonson sniped away at the bold abstractions of Shakespeare's Late Plays, those 'tales, tempests and such like drolleries' which are themselves, in their unrealism, mannerist. (Prospero's best-known speech about transience, in its content and form, is a *locus classicus* of mannerist expression.)

But Jonson's classicism is only skin-deep and his debasing, cartoon theatre is a vehicle for the playwright's deeply pessimistic view of the social world which is also mannerist. In *Bartholomew Fair* he can create no character within the play with the moral authority to guarantee an ordered existence; the play's self-appointed moralists are simultaneously and justifiably restrained in the stocks.

In Webster's *The Duchess of Malfi* there is a continuous exercise in grotesque art and the cultivation of 'horrid' laughter learned from Marston. This is the highest reach of mannerist tragedy; the heroic notes of conventional tragedy have gone, for a pervasive irony forbids or deflates them; and we are left with a species of melodrama which mixes farce and sentiment in a challenging way.

At one point, in a passage often misunderstood, the heroine and audience see dead bodies which turn out to be mere artistic representations, a *trompe l'oeil* and so a joke played on the spectator. (It is the opposite effect of a similar passage in *A Winter's Tale;* where Shakespeare's trick is life-enhancing, Webster's is death-dealing.) 'Decadent' for this kind of radical presentation of an unholy world seems prudish and insensitive.[7]

'Jacobean' of the book's title is used to mean 'Jacobean and Caroline'. But as Jacobean changed into Caroline, the court culture, led by Henrietta Maria as much as Charles, re-discovered in part (these things are never simple) both heroism and optimism, and developed an English baroque. Some of this rubbed off on to the commercial theatre in the work of such as Ford and Davenant. If *'Tis Pity She's a Whore* (1633) is mannerist in its grotesque and uneasy collusion with the psychotic Giovanni, *The Broken Heart* (1633) achieves a fine baroque climax in the organ notes of Calantha's self-sacrifice to love. But it is in the masque that first James and then more confidently (or extravagantly) Charles cultivated a major baroque art-form. Here is that blending of art-forms so typical of baroque and a direct emotional appeal of theatrical illusionism; also an inflated, heroic view of the art's sponsors (here, the British monarchy) which is the English version of continental baroque. The texts (one of them is discussed in Chapter 10) are unrevivable, but they had an emphatic effect on the development of British theatre.

Alongside the masque, the court at Whitehall increasingly cultivated a range of theatrical activity which in turn, inevitably, had an effect on the commercial theatre of the day. Consequently, Part Three of the book centres on 'The King's Theatre' as a specific and important kind of Private Theatre. Here *Bartholomew Fair* is discussed, together with the argument, impossible to prove, that this play was written especially for court presentation.

Bartholomew Fair epitomises the subject-matter and the dangers of generalisation of this book. The play's emphasis on illicit sex, theft, urine and vomit should alert us, often it seems in vain, to the fact that a simple celebration of holiday festivities is far from Jonson's purpose. Yet the play opened at the public playhouse, the Hope, and played the next night at the Banqueting House at Whitehall. To Jonson, a classical tradition guaranteed the continuance of civilisation itself. But a popular culture in the sense of folk entertainment was anathema to him: his play has a puppet-show but he deplored the real thing, and his characters sing ballads but he despised them. Serious art lay elsewhere.

Part One

Private Theatre: Audiences, Buildings and Repertory

2 · The Audiences of the Jacobean Private Theatre

A theatre performance is a social event. In writing the script, the play-wright seeks to serve his audience as well as his muse, and the business of acting is only completed by the act of spectating. The play lies in the experience of the audience and to understand the play we must anatomise that audience as far as records allow.

The closest we get to a contemporary description of a private theatre audience is Henry Fitzgeoffrey's 'Notes from Blackfriars', satirical verse published in 1617 as part of his *Satires and Satirical Epigrams*.[1] The observing 'I' of the 'Notes' comments on a succession of personages as they enter the playhouse for an afternoon's performance. First there is the braggart soldier of 'reputation steel', who talks of 'basilisks, trenches, retires'. And then

> One we both know well,
> Sir Island Hunt, a traveller that will tell,
> Of stranger things than tatter'd Tom ever lied of,
> Than Pliny or Herodotus e'er writ of.

A Cheapside Dame comes next, identifiable by her headgear and evidently ready to be accosted, but 'she's bespoken for a box before'. She is followed by a fount of fashion who borrows from every nation, a giant hermaphro-dite, and a foppish lady's man who is all dance steps. From backstage in the tiring-house, his stool and cushion ordered, enters the prodigal, Tissue Slop:

> His year's revenues, I dare stand unto 't,
> Is not of worth to purchase such a suit.

A lady with a yellow fan comes next and she is followed by the author of *The Duchess of Malfi*, 'Crabbed Websterio, The playwright, cartwright', his mouth awry as he strains to bring forth his latest work.

So Fitzgeoffrey, a member of Lincoln's Inn, in these 'Fruits of the vacant hours of a vacation', reduces his gathering of playgoers to a collec-tion of freaks and caricatures. His intention is not objective observation but caricature, and his roll-call of humorous types has a somewhat clichéd look to it. We shall have to throw a wider net.

Professional theatre in the early Stuart period was largely a London phenomenon. Many aspects of London-based theatre work were seen in the provinces through the policy of summer touring by companies, but the history of 'private theatre' is confined largely to the development of small, roofed playhouses in the capital. Perhaps only in three towns in the provinces – Norwich, Bristol and York – were there sufficient numbers to provide regular audiences for repertory theatre in roofed playhouses, and Bristol appears to have had such a house for a while. But London, expanding rapidly through the Jacobean period to become Europe's largest city and ten times the size of the next largest English town, held a virtual monopoly. No accurate population figures exist, but with its suburbs and twin city of Westminster, London's inhabitants numbered about 200,000 out of a total population (England and Wales) of 5 million.

The story of London theatre, though, concerns not only born and bred Londoners. The city acted like a great magnet, attracting for short or long stay a regular influx of visitors. It was the centre of trade and the seat of national government, and it housed the King's court at Whitehall, Parliament, Westminster Hall and the Inns of Court (together with their associated Courts of Chancery). Many came to London on business or to pursue a career, others (in an age of litigation) to follow their legal interests, and swelling the ranks of these were the tourists, drawn by the capital's opportunity for pleasures, the latest fashions, imported luxury goods or society gossip. The London 'season' had arrived, in which for part or much of the winter and spring country gentry would leave their provincial responsibilities and reside in the capital.

The consequence of this new migration to London was a rapid growth of high-cost housing in what became the fashionable residential areas to the west of the dirty and congested city: along the Strand and Drury Lane, in the parishes of St Giles and St Martin-in-the-Fields, in Westminster and, during the 1630s, in Covent Garden.

The development of the Jacobean private theatre may be seen as part of this expansion westwards. The traditional playhouse areas had been north of the city or on the south bank of the Thames. The new private playhouses were situated in the westernmost part of the old city or in the western suburbs and so of easy access to courtiers, lawyers and the gentry families recently established in Westminster or along the Strand. The second Blackfriars playhouse was tucked inside the city wall to the west and its clients probably found a river approach convenient from Westminster and Whitehall. It especially, as we shall see, created traffic problems. The Phoenix, the first Drury Lane playhouse, lay in St Giles, adjacent to Lincoln's Inn Fields to its east and to the residences in the Strand and to the palace of St James. Benchers of Lincoln's Inn objected to its proximity. The Salisbury Court playhouse was situated between the Blackfriars and the Phoenix. It was in the grounds of Dorset House, close to the Inner and Middle Temples. Other private houses, though less successful, looked to the same 'West End' area. The Whitefriars playhouse was situated between Fleet Street and the Thames (a little to the west of where the Salisbury Court was later built). Its intended replacement, the Porter's Hall playhouse, was in Blackfriars, near Puddle Wharf. (See Figure 2.1 for these locations.)

This shift westwards was not universally approved. Noise and inconvenience were complained of by the residents of Blackfriars and Lincoln's Inn Fields. The watermen, whose business in part depended on the thousands daily who crossed the river to the south bank playhouses, petitioned the King in 1613 to ban the building of playhouses close to the city. In 1617, apprentices in their Shrovetide festivities sacked the recently opened Phoenix in what may well have been an objection to the moving of the theatre company of the Red Bull from north of the city to its new (and expensive) venue. But a trend had been set and it was motivated by the desire to transport a traditional form of city recreation to within easy reach of London's new, or newly housed, gentry.

The accepted model of the Elizabethan, public theatre audience is of a heterogeneous group broadly representative of the various social classes, but biased numerically towards the artisan.[2] The model has been modified of late[3] and we now see that audience as more predominantly bourgeois in composition. Nevertheless, a public playhouse like the Globe catered for a socially wide range of customers, and its commercial and physical structure recognised the ranking groups of a status-conscious society. A customer would choose his place carefully, according to his status and pocket: in the 'Lords' Rooms', private boxes adjacent to the stage, a seat cost a shilling; seats in the galleries (with some weather protection) were threepence and twopence; and in the unprotected pit, 'the groundling' stood and watched the performance for one penny.

From the King's Men's occupation of the second Blackfriars in 1608, a split in that heterogeneous audience of the public playhouse, anticipated already in the private houses of the boys companies, became a conspicuous feature of the London scene and two kinds of audience were created. The private playhouses hived off the more aristocratic patrons and created a coterie theatre for those able and inclined to pay more, leaving the public houses, like the Fortune and Red Bull, to provide popular theatre for a 'down-market' clientele.

Alone of the public houses, the Globe, by virtue of the high reputation

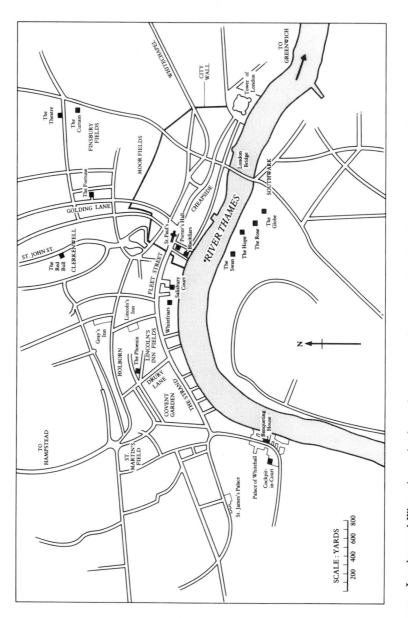

Figure 2.1: London and Westminster in the early seventeenth century, showing the approximate positions of the playhouses. Based on N. Brett-James, *The Growth of Stuart London*, London, 1935 and J. Q. Adams, *Shakespearean Playhouses*, Boston, 1917

of the King's Men and their plays, might continue to attract something of a heterogeneous audience during the summer months when their private house, the Blackfriars, was dark. But even there, the playwrights knew they must cater for a different clientele from that which they cultivated at the Blackfriars. Shirley's *The Doubtful Heir* (1640) was evidently intended for the private house but premiered at the Globe by an accident of timing and the author added a prologue disdainful of the public house audience's taste:

> Our author did not calculate this play
> For this meridian; the bankside, he knows,
> Are far more skilful at the ebbs and flows
> Of water than of wit; he does not mean
> For the elevation of your poles, this scene.
> No shows, no dance, and what you most delight in,
> Grave understanders, here's no target fighting
> Upon the stage, all work for cutters barred,
> No bawdry, nor no ballets; this goes hard.

Middleton's *A Game at Chess* (1624), a satire on Spanish politics, was played in summer at the Globe to hit the topical note. All the nobility left in London, Chamberlain noted, flocked to see it, but this was evidently very unusual. Three years earlier, Gondomar, the Spanish ambassador, principal object of satire in Middleton's play, had visited the Fortune. Chamberlain's account makes it clear that Gondomar was deliberately slumming.

With the rise of the private houses, the Red Bull and the Fortune became known for their vulgarity and noise both on and off stage. (The Hope, the last of the public houses, never achieved any kind of reputation that we know of.) The Fortune, originally 'the fairest playhouse in this town', became associated with cutpurses and with the jigs that made their trade easier. By 1632 it had declined, according to Alexander Gill, into a resort for 'prentices and apple wives' in contrast to the 'silks and plush' who favoured the Blackfriars. The Red Bull was noted for crowd disturbances and for a broad manner of playing. When *The White Devil* failed there, Webster grumbled at 'those ignorant asses' who visited that playhouse in pursuit of novelty, not quality.

The private theatre audience payed substantially more than its public theatre counterparts. A seat in the top gallery cost sixpence (and late in the period one shilling – the top price in the public playhouse); a seat in the middle or lower gallery cost one shilling; a seat in the pit (no standing) cost two shillings; a place on stage cost two shillings and sixpence, plus extra for a stool; and a seat in a box cost three shillings (or the whole box could be hired). For his money, the patron received various kinds of comfort and convenience not available in the public house. There was probably easier crowd control; acoustics were better; there was heating in winter; all customers sat; the stage was at least partly lit by candles; and, perhaps most important, an exclusivity of audience could virtually be guaranteed. For a visit to the private house by other than well-to-do professional people or monied gentry would be a luxury, perhaps a wild extravagance, and a social solecism to boot.

Many of the Blackfriars audience were positively wealthy. We may conclude this from the series of petitions to the city authorities and the Privy Council presented by the Blackfriars inhabitants between 1619 and 1633.[4] They consistently complained that the coaches of the theatre's patrons, setting down their passengers before the performance and waiting in the area for the end of the play in early evening, choked the narrow streets and thus inhibited the local citizens in their daily business or in their passage to the local church of St Anne's. Attention had already been drawn to the problem in 1615 when, as part of the attempt to halt the setting up of the Porter's Hall playhouse nearby, references had been made to the 'continual multitude' of coaches which frequented the Blackfriars playhouse.

The private coach was still a relative newcomer to the city's transport system. It first appeared in significant numbers in the 1580s and was still costly to buy and maintain in the early seventeenth century. Nevertheless, by 1617 a commentator (perhaps exaggerating somewhat) could claim 'there be few gentlemen of any account who have not their coaches, so as the streets of London are almost stopped with them'. In fact, some of the coaches offending the Blackfriars residents were hackney coaches on hire, as the 1619 petition makes clear, but hired coaches were expensive too. In 1633, the Privy Council, having abandoned the idea of removing the playhouse entirely, resolved that coaches should be banned from the immediate area, except for setting down. But this order was rescinded within weeks because of the discommodity done to 'divers persons of great quality, especially ladies and gentlewomen'.[5] Thereafter, the people of Blackfriars simply had to endure the nuisance.

How many coaches constituted the 'multitude' of the 1615 complaint is not known. The playhouse itself kept a piece of void ground valued at six pounds in which to turn coaches, and at an illegal performance at the Phoenix in 1648 there were sixty coaches parked and awaiting their passengers.[6] Clearly, many Blackfriars patrons maintained a coach and, we may infer, were therefore rich. At the end of the period (before 1642) a new form of transport made a contribution to playhouse visiting, the sedan chair; and this too was reserved for the wealthy.

A monied and socially elite audience was not an entirely new phenomenon in Jacobean London. Since the 1570s boys companies had played to such an audience, one performing in the earlier house in the monastic precinct of Blackfriars, the First Blackfriars, another in a house attached to St Paul's. The boys companies were, technically, troupes of choristers who were expected to perform plays at court for the Queen. Soon their masters smuggled in, under the pretext of open rehearsals, a regular (and profitable) playing to a select audience. The practice waned but then revived energetically in the 1590s when both the Second Blackfriars (converted initially for the King's Men) and St Paul's were so successful that the boys won (or won back) an audience at the expense of the London adult players (as *Hamlet* appears to record). The boys, in fact, attracted not only a commercially viable audience but most of the ambitious, young playwrights of the turn of the century: Jonson, Marston, Chapman, Beaumont and Middleton.

During the first decade of the seventeenth century, the boys lost favour and official support (though the taste for juvenile theatre never entirely disappeared). When the manager of the Chapel Children, at the Second Blackfriars, yielded the Blackfriars to the King's Men, he no doubt passed on, in part at least, an audience and a tradition of 'private' playgoing which was a strong factor in the composition of the Blackfriars clientele for some years.

The audiences for the boys at the Blackfriars and St Paul's was a select one, defined by the playwrights as genteel in education and behaviour. For a St Paul's play of 1601, for example, Marston wrote the following exchange:

FORTUNE   I saw the Children of Paul's last night.
PLANET   I' faith, I like that audience that frequenteth there
             With much applause; a man shall not be choked
             With the stench of garlic, nor be pasted
             To the barmy jacket of a beer-brewer.
BRABANT JR   'Tis a good, gentle audience.

Jonson, less confident, looks for a discerning audience at the Blackfriars for his play *Cynthia's Revels* in the same year:

> If gracious silence, sweet attention,
> Quick sight and quicker apprehension,
> The lights of judgment's throne, shine anywhere,
> Our doubtful author hopes this is the sphere.

The prologues and epilogues of plays in the Jacobean private theatre echo Marston and Jonson, flattering their audiences with references to their gentility, their discerning judgment and their powers of discrimination.

'Gentlemen' is the characteristic address of the private theatre prologue, and the 'gentle audience' is technically one composed of gentlemen. The gentry formed the top twentieth, numerically speaking, of the population at large. Two features confirmed their gentle status: they possessed sufficient wealth (in the form of real estate) to obviate the need for work; and they were willing to express a gentleman's life-style. Contemporary debate on what constituted a gentleman also laid stress on blood and descent, but personal qualities, attitudes and the possession of wealth were more important.

The gentry were seen by contemporary commentators as the first of four strata in society (the others being citizens, yeomen and artificers) and were themselves subdivided into greater gentry (the King, nobility and aristocracy) and minor gentry (knights, squires and simple gentlemen). Allowed into the rank of gentry were such professional people as doctors, dons and army officers, and it was widely maintained that the translation of wealthy merchant to gentleman was easy. Being a minor gentleman was partly a matter of descent, partly of wealth and partly of conviction. It conferred the right to bear arms and be called 'Master'.

Few in number, the gentry held almost all political and social power in the country. In London, they formed a higher proportion of the population than elsewhere, particularly during winter and spring. We might guess that the aggregate number in London of courtiers, lawyers and law students, Members of Parliament, doctors, army officers, merchant gentlemen, gallants and gentry tourists probably reached over 10,000. And it is from this group that the audiences at the Blackfriars, Phoenix and Salisbury Court were largely drawn.

They were led in the 1630s by the highest in the land. For Queen Henrietta Maria signalled the close sympathy between court and theatre by attending a number of what may have been command performances at the Phoenix and the Blackfriars, on one occasion at least accompanied by her husband. This was in 1634 when she and Charles attended a staging of Heywood's masque, *Love's Mistress*, which was in preparation for performance at court. In the same year, without the King, she saw Massinger's *Cleander* at the Blackfriars and in 1635 twice took there her nephew, Prince Elector of the Palatine, to see Carlell's *Arvirargus and Felicia* and the anonymous *Alphonsus, Emperor of Germany*. In 1638 she was there again, for Davenant's *The Unfortunate Lovers*. Other illustrious figures also frequented the private playhouses. The great Duke of Buckingham saw Heywood's *The Rape of Lucrece* at the Phoenix weeks before his murder in 1628, and Lady Newport, wife of the Earl of Newport, saw a play there in 1637. We hear of others in newsletters, often through their becoming embroiled in playhouse scuffles. Captain and Lady Essex quarrelled with Lord Thurles at the Blackfriars in 1632, and the Duke of Lennox (a cousin of the King) with the Lord Chamberlain in 1636. Prominent foreign visitors called at the private houses as part of the social round. Duke Philip of Stettin–Pomerania saw the Chapel Boys at Blackfriars in 1602 and Prince Otto von Hessen-Cassel visited the shortlived

Whitefriars in 1611. In 1625 the Duke of Brunswick visited the Black-friars possibly more than once and, as has been mentioned, the Prince Elector went there with his royal aunt in 1635. Just these few references make it clear that the private houses could regularly attract an audience glittering with the most exalted and powerful personages in the land.

It is inconceivable, of course, that the composition of the private theatre audience, in social rank, educational background and artistic taste, remained static and homogeneous for a whole generation between 1608 and 1642. Equally, it is likely that the three main houses each cultivated its own kind of audience. It is clear that Beeston, manager of the Phoenix, sought a more bourgeois audience for his playhouse, probably to encourage good summer houses. In a general way, over the whole period, there was probably a gradual shift from that early audience inherited from the boys, which had an intellectual, even radical bias (university men, Inns students, disenchanted seekers after court positions), to an increasingly cavalier, courtly and fashionable audience of the 1630s for whom theatre provided less the stimulation of provocation and debate, more a form of cultivated recreation.

That having been said, an Induction written for a play in 1638 probably outlines accurately some main audience groupings for the Jacobean and Caroline period. *The Careless Shepherdess*, premiered in 1618 (?), was revived at the Salisbury Court in 1638 when a 'Praeludium' was written for it in the audience-teasing manner of Jonson. (It was probably written by Brome, Jonson's protégé.)[7] The playlet introduces four (fictional) members of the audience, a door-keeper and three prologues in a piece of stage action lasting ten minutes before the play proper begins. The door-keeper is Bolt and the four patrons are Spruce (a courtier), Spark (an Inns of Court man), Landlord (a country gentleman), and Thrift (a citizen). Their tastes in theatre-going are precisely rendered.

The piece opens with Thrift, who is a shopkeeper, haggling with Bolt over the price of entry. He offers fourpence and Bolt demands, and finally gets, a shilling. Thrift is then engaged by Spruce and Spark in a discussion of dramatic style. The present play, he is told, does not contain a fool, which, Spruce and Spark maintain, is an outmoded comic device. So Thrift resolves to ask for his entrance fee back and leave:

> I'll to the Bull or Fortune, and there see
> A play for twopence, with a jig to boot.

In other words, by taste and by pocket, he is a likelier customer for the popular theatre of clowns and jigs at the Red Bull or Fortune.

Spruce, in his 'powdered hair and gaudy clothes', is a court dandy, intent as much on being seen as seeing. He and Spark intend, initially at least, to 'sit thus open on the stage to show their cloak and suit'. Later, however, they decide to sit with the ladies in 'some private room'. Spruce joins with Spark in deriding both Thrift's and Landlord's presumption in thinking they are fit to criticise the play, and he maintains that Thrift is unable to appreciate in general the poetic language of the contemporary, private theatre or discuss in detail the respective merits of individual playwrights. He, however, is an expert in these matters, a connoisseur.

Spark, Inns of Court man, is from the Temple. He values a playwright's wit above all and praises the poets of his day for purging the theatre of the crudities and 'loose lascivious mirth' of the previous age. He criticises Landlord for not being acquainted with the laws of drama or what goes to the fashioning of a superior plot. His financial resources, it is revealed, are more limited than his self-esteem, for he has been compelled to choose 'Rather to spend my money at a play than at the ordinary', and he and Spruce take sanctuary ''mongst the ladies, lest some creditor should spy them'. He takes comfort in the thought that 'if the play prove dull [Spruce's] company will satisfy my ears'.

Landlord, despite Spark and Spruce's mockery at his old-fashioned tastes in theatre, resolves to keep them company. To him a play's essential ingredient is the fool – 'I would have the fool in every act.' Nevertheless, he will stay to 'view the ladies' and listen with pleasure to the witty commentary of courtier and Inns of Court man. But in the cultural gap between him and them is something of the court/country split that would prove to be an important element in the English Revolution.

Spruce, Spark and Landlord were typical patrons (and Thrift an important absentee) of the private theatre. The courtier was a prominent figure in London life. James had created a magnificent but tainted court, and though Charles's was at first more sober and dignified, it became increasingly divorced from the culture and traditions of both city and country. Whitehall inevitably was a centre of sycophancy, privilege and graft, and the attractions of court life encouraged the nation's aristocrats and many an ambitious hopeful to take up temporary or permanent residency near it in the hope of preferment or notice. The idle, affected and even vicious courtier is a byword of the satirical literature of the age and its drama. He constantly gets into debt and altercations, is often drunk and libidinous, and yet cultivates an obsessive concern for personal honour.

The Palace of Whitehall was a cluster of ramshackle buildings, spread over 23 acres between the Thames and St James's Park, and mostly dating from the time of Henry VIII. Apart from Inigo Jones's Banqueting House (1619), it never received the face-lift successive monarchs planned for it. Courtiers, palace officers and servants numbered around 1,500. A minor courtier whose life-style was neither vicious nor ostentatious, will serve as a foil to Spruce and allow us to see, as nowhere else, the theatre-going habits of a Blackfriars patron over some years. Sir Humphrey Mildmay, in his forties for the decade concerned, came of a notable family. His grandfather had been Elizabeth's Chancellor of the Exchequer and two of his brothers held court appointments under Charles. He was accustomed to spending the summer on his estate in Danbury, Essex. In London, he frequented the court and saw masques and plays there but was not active in public affairs. His diary notes of the ten years from January 1632 record fifty-seven visits to London playhouses.[8]

In the notes, he only occasionally mentions the playhouse or play by name but the Blackfriars emerges as easily his favourite, with four times as many visits as all the other playhouses put together. It is named fourteen times and four other visits there can be identified by the play seen. In contrast, the Phoenix is named only three times and one other visit may be identified by the play. The Globe is specifically referred to four times, but each visit was made in the summer of 1613 when Mildmay remained in the capital longer than usual and the King's Men transferred earlier to their summer house. Unsurprisingly, there is no mention of the Red Bull of Fortune; but more surprisingly there is none of the Salisbury Court.

Mildmay's favourite theatre-going months were November, on his return to the capital, and May, after the Lent recess. He normally went in company (with his wife, one of his brothers or in a party) and the visits tended to cluster – once, four in six days. There seems little pattern. One gets the impression of spontaneous theatre-going according to mood, season or availability of company. He usually paid a shilling for an unostentatious seat in the gallery but sometimes joined the gallants in the pit.

He made an occasional, terse note on the play he had seen but shows none of the informed censoriousness of Spruce. He remarked if a play was new, three times described a play as 'foolish' and once as 'base', and only twelve times out of fifty-seven does he record a play's name and never its playwright. Only one named play receives an admiring note, and that is Shirley's *The Lady of Pleasure*, which he calls 'that rare play'. For the most part, it seems, for Mildmay a theatre visit was a social event, a civilised way of spending an afternoon in the company of acquaintances of similar taste and background. *The Lady of Pleasure* (see pp. 69–70) is a play about the excesses of the pleasurable life in the city and its moral dangers. One can see how it might earn a tribute from this evidently gentle, slightly puritanical patron of the Blackfriars.

Spark's real-life counterparts, the Inns of Court students, had long been considered inveterate theatre-goers. The four Inns constituted England's third university, originally set up to train the sons of gentlemen in the practices of Common Law but now welcoming the amateur student too. They provided accommodation and a working knowledge of legal processes useful in an age of litigation and real estate fluency. As importantly, they acted as finishing schools, providing students extra-curricularly with the opportunity to cultivate the polite arts of music, dancing and fencing and generally to acquire polish and civilised manners. Many students, like Spark, cultivated the courtiers, aping their fashions and identifying with them.

Though operational for rather less than half the year the Inns exerted a powerful effect on the cultural life of the capital. The students formed a well-educated group of young men, many from the universities, often with radical interests and trained, disputatious minds. They had the opportunity to engage in political intrigue and the pursuit of art and letters. Versifying was an Inns custom and the students' impact on literary fashion was considerable. Their penchant for verse satire was directly influential in the development of the satirical play.[9]

Moral and satirical literature emphasised the students' addiction to theatre. Study was not compulsory and the timetabling of curricular elements for morning and evening left the afternoons, the time of theatre performance, free. Dramatic entertainment had traditionally featured strongly at the Inns themselves (academic plays, masques, Christmas festivities) and many playwrights writing for the boys companies and, after, for the adult private theatre, were at one time themselves readers: Marston, Beaumont, Ford, Suckling, Carew. But the satirists saw theatre as just one more temptation – into idleness and debt – for the prodigal student:

> Your theatres he daily doth frequent
> (Except the intermitted time of Lent)
> Treasuring up within his memory
> The amorous toys of every comedy . . .
> The Cockpit [= the Phoenix] heretofore would serve
> his wit,
> But now upon the Friars stage he'll sit;
> It must be so, though this expensive fool
> Should pay an angel for a paltry stool.[10]

William Prynne, Puritan moralist and Lincoln's Inn bencher, grumbled of the Inns students:

This is one of the first things they learn as soon as they are admitted, to see stage plays and to take smoke at a play house, which they commonly make their study; where they quickly learn to follow all fashions.

Play-going and law study could in fact be happily combined. John

Greene, a Lincoln's Inn student, was the son of a judge and was called to the bar in 1639. A volume of his diary for 1635 gives details of his theatre-going of that year.[11] He records ten visits, though he in fact made only nine of them for two plays are mentioned for one occasion when his party divided. If we can identify the plays correctly, six of the visits were to the Blackfriars, three to the Phoenix and one to an unknown playhouse. Again (as with Mildmay), the King's Men are dominant and the public playhouses (and Salisbury Court) neglected. Four of the visits were made in February, only one in summer (to see Fletcher's *Wit Without Money* at the Phoenix). After his sister's wedding in November, he and 'all the bachelors' divided into two parties: one saw Killigrew's *The Conspiracy* at the Blackfriars, the other saw the Phoenix play admired by Mildmay a month later, *The Lady of Pleasure*.

More like the kind of Inns man deplored by Prynne was Edmund Heath, a student at the Inner Temple. In a year and a half from 1629-31, he made a prodigious forty-nine visits to the theatre. During the same period he purchased ten play books but made no other literary purchases.[12]

In their eagerness to self-advertise, Spruce and Spark represent that characteristic *habitué* of the seventeenth-century theatre, the gallant. Dekker's *The Gull's Hornbook*, published in 1609 and therefore referring probably to the period when the boys occupied the Blackfriars rather than the King's Men, gives a sustained analysis of the type.[13] He comes from the twelvepenny ordinary to the playhouse where he is enjoined (in the writer's ironic mode) to do everything in his power to draw the audience's attention to him so that 'you seem not to resort thither to taste vain pleasures with a hungry appetite, but only as a gentleman, to spend a foolish hour or two, because you can do nothing else'. He must arrive just before the play begins, enter the stage from the tiring house and call for a stool and a match for his pipe. Then he must loudly enquire who wrote the play. During the performance he must laugh in the serious places, and shortly before the end leave the stage, saluting 'all your gentle acquaintance, that are spread either on the rushes, or on stools about you, and draw what troupe you can from the stage after you'. Landlord in the 'Praeludium' suffers the contempt customarily reserved by London wits for country visitors. Many, no doubt, were old-fashioned in their tastes and appeared unworldly. Others, however, could not have been so. For example, during the parliamentary sessions they would have included the members themselves, up to 500 gentlemen, drawn from prominent landowning families and in touch with London affairs. A high proportion were barristers who, as Inns men, may previously have formed the theatre-going habit.

Visitors to London on business or for the law terms were often accompanied by their wives and families and the more wealthy of them acquired permanent London residences. Several hundred gentry families had done this by the 1630s. The less wealthy or more thrifty would go into lodgings. Such a phenomenon did the seasonal visitor become that there were nine royal proclamations against the practice between 1614 and 1627. Both James and Charles sought to curb the 'season' because of the crowding it brought to the capital and the neglect of country responsibilities it implied. In particular, they deplored the enthusiasm of country ladies who, intent on seeking out the latest fashions, bullied their menfolk into carrying them to London (on journeys made easier by the private coach) on expensive expeditions. (Lady Barnwell, in *The Lady of Pleasure* is just such a lady. See pp. 69–70.)

The country ladies allied themselves with the fashionable town ladies to form an increasingly significant sector of the private theatre audience. Foreigners had often remarked on the ease with which English women moved freely in public places, including playhouses. Prince Philip of Stettin–Pomerania had expressly noted the many respectable women at the Blackfriars in 1602. But it was no doubt always easier for ladies to visit private than public houses. The gathering of prostitutes at the latter was well known, while at the private houses, the audience was better controlled, the boxes became a kind of sanctuary, the coach made access comfortable and modesty was guaranteed, eventually, by the fashionable adoption of the mask. As we have seen, Henrietta Maria attended the theatre, and notably, in rescinding the ban on coaches at the Blackfriars, the Privy Council expressed specific concern for the well-being of the 'ladies and gentlewomen' who frequented there.

The ladies never took the final freedom of sitting on the stage. But playwrights increasingly recognised the importance of female patronage, and in a previously masculine-orientated theatre, the ladies' sensibility had to be flattered or accommodated, as prologues show. There is a growing tendency to fashion plays which may be said to have a feminine interest. The comedy of manners, developed in Fletcher and Shirley, recognises women as the arbiters and prime movers in important aspects of city and court life. A whole group of love-cult plays, neo-platonic in stance to flatter Henrietta Maria and her retinue, were written in the 1630s. And in Ford, the last great tragedian of the period, one woman's honour and another's broken heart form the two axes of his finest and most characteristic play.

There were never generally more than three private playhouses operating simultaneously during the pre-Commonwealth period, and their combined audience capacity was probably less than 3,000. But they were successful commercially and they developed a kind of theatre which alone would survive at the Restoration. When out-of-work players published *The Actors' Remonstrance* in 1643, they defended theatre only in terms of the private houses, talking of two kinds of audience, the rowdy gathering of butchers, cobblers, masons and pickpockets who frequent bear-baiting, and 'the best of the nobility and gentry' who alone come to 'our civil and well governed theatres'. Only the Blackfriars, the Phoenix and the Salisbury Court are named, no public houses.

The audience for which the private playhouses catered, it is argued here, was largely a gentry one. Where 'coterie' denotes a small group defined by a homogeneity of taste and cultural background and marked by a sense of exclusivity, the private theatre audience can properly be seen as a coterie audience. Indeed there may increasingly have been a closing of ranks. The 'I' of Fitzgeoffrey's 'Notes from Blackfriars' is encouraged to seduce a female patron because he can identify her as a citizen by her head-dress. No lady by her attire, she is marked down as fair game. No doubt others who could afford entry but were not of the gentry might also visit the private houses. Jonson in the commendatory verses to *The Faithful Shepherdess*, a Chapel Children play of 1608, notes with his divisive eye,

> Gamester, captain, Knight, Knight's man,
> Lady, or Pusill that wears a mask or fan,
> Velvet or taffeta cap, rank'd in the dark
> With the shop's foreman, or some such brave spark.

In the Induction to the Blackfriars' *The Magnetic Lady* (1632), he talks of 'the faeces or grounds of your people, that sit in the oblique caves and wedges of your house, your sinful, sixpenny mechanics'. The controlling irony and such words as 'brave spark' and 'sinful' suggest that foreman and mechanic should not have been there.

The world of the private theatres was an intimate one. Playwrights would be instantly recognisable (Fitzgeoffrey sees Webster enter) and so too would prominent audience members, so that the atmosphere partook both of an academy and a club. Shirley, major playwright himself, called the Beaumont and Fletcher plays

> the authentic wit that made Blackfriars an academy where the three
> hours' spectacle while Beaumont and Fletcher were presented was
> usually of more advantage to the hopeful young heir than a costly,
> dangerous, foreign travel, with the assistance of a governing
> monsieur or signor to boot.[14]

The club-like aspect is brought out by the story of 'Whitelocke's Coranto'.

Bulstrode Whitelocke was a parliamentarian, lawyer and politician, called to the bar of the Middle Temple in 1626. In 1634 he was put in charge of the music for the great masque donated by the Inns to their sovereign, *The Triumph of Peace*. A well-educated, art-loving cavalier not rare in London, he had amongst his other accomplishments the distinction of having written, at about the time of the masque, a coranto, a dance tune. This, he tells us,

> being cried up, was first played publicly, by the Blackfriars music [the playhouse orchestra], who were then esteemed the best of common musicians in London. Whenever I came to that house (as I did sometimes in those days), though not often, to see a play, the musicians would presently play *Whitelocke's Coranto*, and it was so often called for, that they would have played it twice or thrice in an afternoon.[15]

The story highlights the club-like atmosphere for, as G. E. Bentley observes, 'not only did the musicians have to recognise him, but they had to expect various members of the audience to recognise him too, in order for the gesture to be telling.'[16] Nothing more clearly suggests the intimate and artful atmosphere of the club theatre in which the private playhouse plays were designed to make their special impact.

3 · Jacobean Private Playhouses

James Wright's *Historia Histrionica*, 1699, as its title declares, is a history of the theatre. It was published anonymously and is cast as a dialogue between two interlocutors, Lovewit and Truman. Truman is 'an old cavalier', and he claims a first-hand knowledge of the theatre of the 1630s which Wright, an antiquary and playbook collector, must have gleaned from reliable sources (he himself was not born until 1643). Truman, self-confessed admirer of the pre-Commonwealth stage, explains to Lovewit the major differences between private and public playhouses:

> TRUMAN   The Blackfriars, Cockpit, and Salisbury Court were very
> small to what we see now [presumably 1699]. The Cockpit
> was standing since the Restoration, and Rhodes' company
> acted there for some time.
> LOVEWIT   I have seen that.
> TRUMAN   Then you have seen the other two, in effect; for they were
> all three built almost exactly alike in form and bigness.
> Here they had pits for the gentry, and acted by candle-
> light. The Globe, Fortune and [Red] Bull were very large
> houses, and lay partly open to the weather.

Truman thus identifies the three main private houses of the pre-Common-wealth stage and he notes four crucial differences between them and the public houses: they were smaller; they had pits for the gentry; they were roofed; and performances in them were given by candlelight. With these differences modern scholarship concurs.

The private/public distinction reflects two separate traditions that lay behind the development of Elizabethan playhouse forms. On the one hand, the Tudor acting companies had regularly played in innyards, sporting arenas, baiting houses, fairgrounds and other open-air, public places of recreation. On the other hand, the same companies had performed in various kinds of private hall – in manor houses, colleges,

Inns of Court and royal palaces. The first public playhouse, the Theatre, which was built by James Burbage in 1576, derived from the first tradition. It took the form of an amphitheatre, with a frame of three tiers of galleries surrounding a yard and a stage. The first 'Wooden O', it became the prototype of the public house for the next forty years and its erection was a bold, innovative step. So satisfactory did its form prove that it was, in effect, dismantled and reassembled as the Globe in 1598.[1]

Simultaneous with the building of the Theatre, the first commercial houses derived from the second tradition appeared. In 1575, the Paul's Choristers began to perform plays to a paying audience in a hall connected with St Paul's Church; and in 1576, the Children of the Chapel, another chorister troupe, started performing in the Buttery of a former monastery, the Blackfriars, between Ludgate and the Thames. Thus the Paul's playhouse, used intermittently between 1575 and 1608, and the First Blackfriars (there was to be a second house in the precinct), used from 1576 to 1584, were the first private playhouses. They charged high prices, initially performed only once a week and generated an exclusive audience.[2]

In 1596, James Burbage bought the upstairs hall of the Upper Frater building in the Blackfriars range and converted it into a playhouse, the Second Blackfriars. He intended the Lord Chamberlain's Men to occupy it, perhaps in anticipation of the expiry of the lease of the Theatre. But the company (adults) was forbidden to perform there (virtually in the city itself) by the Privy Council, and so the house was leased to the Chapel Children who evidently enjoyed privileges denied to their adult competitors. Meanwhile, the Lord Chamberlain's Men built the Globe on the Bankside. In 1608, in a new and evidently more propitious era, Burbage's company, now the King's Men, bought back the lease from the juvenile company and occupied the Blackfriars as their winter home. Here they performed each year until the closure from October until March or April, then transferring to the Globe for the evidently less remunerative summer season.

Other companies sought to follow suit and the activities of Philip Henslowe, entrepreneur and theatre impresario, demonstrate both the desirability and difficulty of establishing adult companies in private houses. He had financed the building of the Rose (1587) and the Fortune (1600) for the Admiral's Men, both public houses; and in 1614 he built the Hope on Bankside, where *Bartholomew Fair* was given its first production. With the Hope, the last public house to be built, he hedged his bets by designing a building which would double as playhouse and baiting-house. (A removable stage was part of the equipment.) Meanwhile, he was also attempting to establish a private house for the amalgamated company of the Children of the Queen's Revels and Lady Elizabeth's Men. They performed first at the Whitefriars, a playhouse about which we know very little. When the Whitefriars lease expired at the end of 1614, Henslowe undertook to provide a replacement house in the same area. A staying order prevented that and so he then financed the building of the Porter's Hall playhouse in Puddle Wharf. There was considerable opposition to this too from local residents, but when Henslowe died in 1616, his son-in-law, Edward Alleyn, continued the project. Finally, a Privy Council order halted the whole operation, at which point Alleyn claimed, no doubt with some exaggeration, that the considerable sum of £1500 had been expended on it (£100 more than the rebuilding of the Globe in 1613–14).[3]

Whether Porter's Hall was intended to run in tandem with the Hope (or the Swan where the Lady Elizabeth's Men also performed) is not clear. But it is evident that soon after 1608, an acting company's best interests might be served by their gaining access, at least for the winter season, to a private house. This evidently was the motivation for Christopher Beeston, actor turned manager. In 1616, he converted a cockpit near Drury Lane as a private house for his company, Queen Anne's Men, and then managed a succession of companies that he formed to play there until his death in 1638. He called the playhouse the Phoenix (perhaps after its restoration in 1617 when it had been ransacked in Shrove Tuesday riots).

In 1629, the third of the successful private houses was established, the Salisbury Court. This was built with the active backing of Sir Henry Herbert, Master of the Revels, and operated under the part-managership of William Blagrave, his deputy. When an Oxford diarist described the London theatre scene in 1634 he noted these three houses together with the Red Bull and the Fortune, the public playhouses. But the Globe, so dear to modern scholarship, rated no mention at all, so eclipsed had it been by the Blackfriars.[4]

From 1608 to 1642 there were six private playhouses in and around London used by adult companies. The Whitefriars remains almost a total mystery to us. Porter's Hall was dismantled before going into regular use. The Second Blackfriars, the Phoenix and the Salisbury Court were all conversions (as private houses always were) of existing buildings – specifically the upper floor of the Upper Frater, a cockpit and a large barn. (The Phoenix in fact continued to be called the Cockpit.) All were producing houses with resident performing companies (and their locations are discussed on pp. 12–13; see Figure 2.1. To these we must add what is in effect the most exclusive of the private playhouses, the Cockpit-in-Court at the palace of Whitehall. Originally built as a cockpit for Henry VIII, the building was used intermittently for plays during the Jacobean period and concerted into a permanent playhouse by Inigo Jones in 1629 (the same year as the establishment of the Salisbury Court). It differed from the other houses in that it was a receiving house for incoming shows, not a producing house; it was not operated commercially but as a focus for the dramatic entertainment of the royal house (and as such is discussed in Chapter 8).

There are few visual records of the private playhouses (as indeed there are of the public) and some identifications are clearly wrong.[5] The Upper Frater Building in which was the Second Blackfriars has been located twice over in topographical views by Hollar,[6] and an engaging although probably erroneous attempt has been made to see a representation of the Blackfriars stage-end in a picture of a 'memory' theatre by Robert Fludd in his *Art of Memory*, 1617.[7] Important witnesses to indoor playhouse construction (though they may not be independent of each other) are the title page vignettes of *Roxana*, 1632, and *Messalina*, 1640 (see Plates 1 and 2). *Messalina* was played at the Salisbury Court. Another intriguing representation of an indoor playhouse is the frontispiece of *The Wits*, 1662 (see Plate 3). This evidently records a performance at a fit-up playhouse during the closure but carries significant information.

In contrast, an abundance of visual information survives for the Cock-pit-in-Court. The Agas map of 1570 shows its original external plan, a Danckerts painting of 'Whitehall and St James's Park, Time of Charles II' records its appearance after Jones's conversion (see Plate 4) and the building is manifest again on a Hollar portrait of Charles II. Most important, however, is a set of drawings in Worcester College Library, Oxford, showing the interior. They are a ground plan of the whole (Plate 5a), an elevation of the stage facade (Plate 5b), and a plan of the stage alone. The drawings are evidently in the hand of Inigo Jones's assistant, John Webb, and they may have been prepared by him in 1660 for the large-scale restoration of the playhouse put in hand at that time. But they almost certainly record, with a little ambiguity, the playhouse of Jones's conversion of 1629.

Most compelling of all the visual records of private playhouses is a second set of drawings, also at Worcester College, and in the hand of Inigo Jones himself. These represent a small, unnamed, free-standing, roofed playhouse. The set comprises two transverse sections of the interior, one looking towards the house-end, one the stage-end, a groundplan and an exterior elevation of the house-end (see Plate 6).[8]

These drawings may be exhibition designs for a playhouse never built, even never intended to be built. But they have been dated on grounds of draughtsmanship and style to the period 1616–18, encouraging us to connect them with either Beeston's Phoenix conversion or the Porter's Hall venture. (Jones's patron, Lord Arundel, counted Edward Alleyn as a friend and, by January 1615, he and Jones had returned from a continental tour. Later that year a patent was issued for Porter's Hall.) But the Phoenix connection is the more likely. It has been persuasively argued that the semi-circular auditorium is based on half the original (and circular) cockpit, and that the stage-end is a rebuilding in a squared-off shape of the other half to provide stage, side galleries and backstage area. Other evidence now exists to tie the designs to the Phoenix.[9]

What the designs show is an attractive but unusual building, apsidal-ended, with heavy brick walls supported by slender buttresses and a tiled roof. Staircases at either end but positioned outside the main walls give access to the upper floor. The whole structure is church-like (and curiously was the model for Peter Harrison's Jewish Synagogue built in Newport, United States, 1759). Externally and internally, the style is simple, even austere (Jones would have said 'masculine') though the stage façade has 'classical' decoration in the form of statues in niches, swags, an open pediment above the central arched window and a cartouche over the central doorway. But all is rendered in a restrained Palladianism.

If these drawings represent the Phoenix, and they probably do, then practical constraints imposed by the existing building and a ready sense of improvisation account largely for what we might otherwise be tempted to see as Vitruvian experimentation. Jones's Italian tour of 1614 had taken in Palladio's Teatro Olympico at Vicenza and Scamozzi's playhouse at Sabbioneta, both of which had (and have) 'Roman' curved auditoria with stepped seating not unlike Jones's. Both had been designed as scenic theatres with perspective scenery providing, in a standing scene, a vista or vistas behind a proscenium and Jones himself, for ten years before 1616, had been developing sophisticated movable scenery in the masque. But the Worcester designs show an open stage in front of a neutral façade. There are three entrances, two side doors and a central arch, and above is a gallery which appears to be a continuation of the side balconies of the auditorium and is broken by a window. There is no provision for scenery here. Jones has evidently been content to reproduce the non-scenic facilities associated with the public playhouses. Suitably curtained, the central arch would provide a 'discovery space'.

This apparent conservatism of stage architecture is echoed by the Cock-pit-in-Court designs. Here, despite the more elaborate classicism of the facade, Jones had again created an essentially Elizabethan stage and auditorium. The stage is markedly shallow and curved, presumably because the façade necessarily incorporates load bearing columns. But again we are shown a non-scenic, open stage with audience seating on three sides. The façade here had four square-headed entrances flanking a larger central opening above which there appears to be a practical window. The four-sided auditorium follows the original, octagonal shape of the building and provides a pit with stepped seating angled to the stage and surrounded

1   Vignette of an indoors stage; from the
frontispiece to William Alabaster's
Roxana, 1632

2   Vignette of an indoors stage; from the
frontispiece to Nathaneal Richards's
Messalina, 1640

Changling

Simpleto[n]

French Dancing M[r]

S[r] I Falstafe

Hostes

Clauſe

3   An indoors theatre; the frontispiece to Francis Kirkman's *The Wits*, 1662

WHITEHALL & ST. JAMES'S PARK, TIME OF CHARLES II. BY DANCKER.

4 Danckert's painting of 'Whitehall and St James's Park, Time of Charles II', showing the Cockpit-in-Court on the right (with lantern) and the second Jacobean Banqueting House (by Inigo Jones) on the left

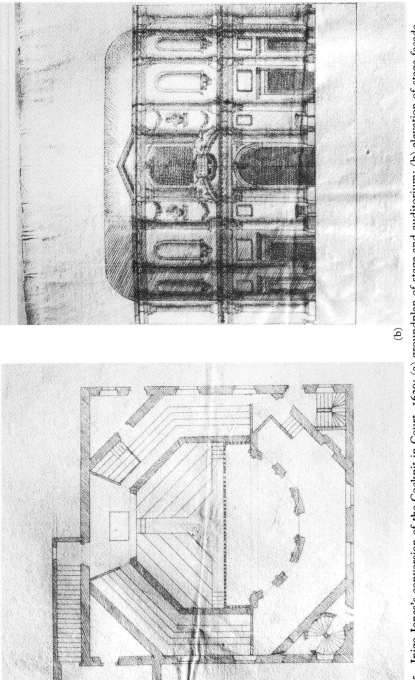

(b)

(a)

5 Inigo Jones's conversion of the Cockpit-in-Court, 1629; (a) groundplan of stage and auditorium; (b) elevation of stage facade. Drawings by John Webb, c. 1660

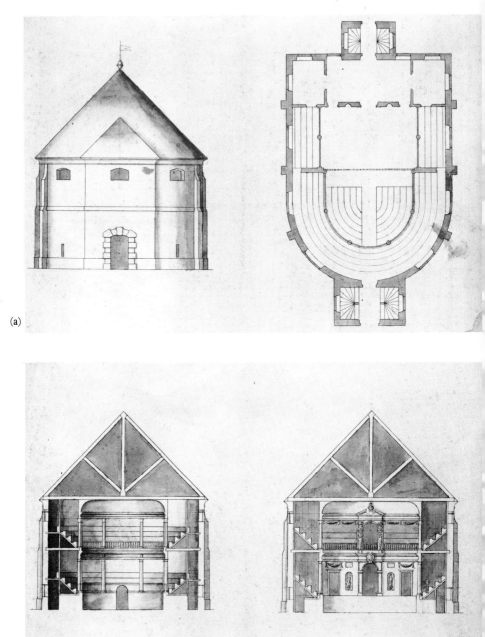

(a)

(b)

6   Designs by Inigo Jones for an unnamed playhouse, probably Beeston's
    conversion of the Cockpit/Phoenix, 1616: (a) groundplan and external
    elevation of the house-end; (b) internal elevations of the house-end and the
    stage-end

by galleries. Opposite the stage, and evidently the reason for the design of the pit-seating, is the King's State. Whether this is at stage level, so that its set of private stairs to the right of the plan descend to it, or at second gallery level, so that the stairs ascend to it, is not clear. Probably it is at stage level.[10]

The evidence then from the two design sets which represent probably a commercial house of 1616 and certainly a royal house of 1629 points to a continuation of the kind of staging associated with the earliest public playhouses. The unnamed playhouse has been described as 'the missing link' between the Swan and the Cockpit-in-Court. The plans bear witness against the notion, previously popular, that the indoor theatres provided players and playwrights with the opportunity to avail themselves of scenic innovations developed in the court masque and commonly practised in continental theatre. Separate studies of the repertories of the three main commercial houses, the Blackfriars, the Phoenix and the Salisbury Court, confirm this.[11] All that the plays require for their staging is an open stage, a tiring-house facade with three entrances, a gallery providing limited playing-space above and some provision for a 'music room'. Stage machinery demanded is never more than a simple, bucket-in-a-well flying device for a throne or the like and a stage trap.

In fact, as plays regularly transferred from public to private houses (at least those of the King's Men) and from the private houses to the Cockpit-in-Court we should expect a standardised (and therefore conservative) practice of staging. Masque insets and masque-like events in private playhouse plays like *The Tempest* did not draw on the scenic methods of the Jacobean Masque but were contrived out of the basic elements of its Elizabethan forerunner: music, costume, procession and dance. There was evidently no 'inner stage' (or embryonic proscenium arch) and the time-honoured practice continued of carrying out large properties on stage to establish place or facilitate stage business where necessary. 'Scenes' were still stretches of continuous stage activity bounded by actors' entrances and exits, and the stage was predominantly a neutral playing area or platform. The private theatre, like the public, was an actor's and playwright's theatre, not a scene-painter's theatre. Wright (*Historia Histrionica*) supports this view emphatically, claiming through Truman that the plays and actors of the pre-Restoration stage were clearly superior to those of his own time because 'they could support themselves merely from their own merit – the weight, the matter and goodness of the action – without scenes and machines'.

Nevertheless, there may have been (surprising had there not) a limited experimentation in scenic presentation in the playhouses late in the period. It is argued that a Jones design inscribed 'for the Cockpit for my Lord Chamberlain, 1639' may have been intended for the Phoenix. Stage directions in the Salisbury Court play *Microcosmus*, 1637, may also imply scenic staging and there is other, though non-conclusive, evidence as well. Certainly, at least one scenic playhouse was planned before the closure. In 1639, William Davenant, who led the way in scenic theatre at the Restoration, obtained a licence to erect a Fleet Street house to provide a baroque theatre of music and 'scenes'. But four factors ensured that Jacobean theatre remained non-scenic: a deep conservatism typical of most periods of theatre history; cost; the constant turn-round necessary for daily performances of a huge repertory; and the fact that in the Jacobean mind, scenic display was connected not with the play proper but with the masque and its continental cousin, the court pastoral. 'Shows' were for masques and masques were not plays.[12]

Truman tells Lovewit that the second Blackfriars, the Phoenix and the Salisbury Court were 'almost exactly alike for form and bigness'. The Blackfriars, it is reliably assumed, was constructed out of a large hall on the first floor of the fourteenth-century Upper Frater building. The building itself was tall, gabled and 110 feet long. The hall had served from time to time as a Parliament chamber and in 1529 was the scene of the trial of the marriage of Henry VIII and Queen Katherine.[13] After the dissolution, the range of buildings of which the Upper Frater was part was sold off piecemeal and the hall itself was divided into several rooms. It was this that Burbage converted to theatrical use in 1596.[14]

The hall was reached by a great pair of winding stairs at its north end. A legal deposition of 1609 tells us, what we would expect, that the playhouse had a stage, galleries and seats. Leonard Digges's commendatory verses to the Shakespeare Second Folio mentions a pit and boxes, and that these boxes were contiguous with the stage is implied by a newsletter reporting a quarrel in the house when a stage-sitter obstructed the view of a spectator in a box. Another letter yields the information that the boxes were lockable.[15] We do not know how many galleries there were. Three was the standard number in the public houses and there was sufficient height in the hall; but Jones's unnamed playhouse has two, and it is assumed that the Cockpit-in-Court did too (though the plans do not show them).

The 1609 deposition gives the overall dimensions of the playhouse as 66 feet by 46 feet internally. However, we have no information on the size of individual parts of the playhouse, including its stage. In particular, we cannot be certain about the location of the tiring-house, that is, whether this was included in the 66 feet length or whether 66 feet refers only to the stage and auditorium. Reconstructors are divided, but most probably the tiring-house facade, like that in Jones's playhouse, was a screen, not a structural wall; and so auditorium, stage and tiring-house were contained in the 66 feet.[16]

Assuming this to be so, the Second Blackfriars had a total ground area (internal) of 3,036 square feet, compared to that of the Fortune public house's ground area of 6,400 square feet (including external walls). The Globe, the King's Men's other house, probably had a ground area of about 8,000 square feet. Jones's Phoenix designs (assuming that is what they are) show a playhouse 52 feet by 37 feet, with a ground area (including the two projecting staircases) of about 2,000 square feet. The Salisbury Court was built on a plot 42 feet wide and its internal width can have been no more than 40 feet. Contemporary references, in fact, suggest it was smaller than its rivals. The Cockpit-in-Court, originally octagonal (and squared by Jones to make extra access points),[17] is on the Webb plans 58 feet across, and it has a ground area of 3,364. But there is generous backstage room here in a house not intent on providing maximum audience capacity. Overall, then, in approximate terms, the private houses were half or less than half the size of the public houses.

A comparison of known stage sizes shows the same disparity. Jones's designs for the Phoenix (?) show a stage 23½ feet by 15 feet, an area of 252½ square feet. The Cockpit-in-Court's unusually curved stage is 35 feet across and 16 feet at its deepest, approximately 400 square feet. If we read the building contract aright, the Fortune stage measured 43 feet by 27½ feet, giving 1,183 square feet (and it is often assumed that the Globe stage on which it was based was the same size). The Blackfriars stage, fitted as it was into a larger area than that of the Phoenix, the Salisbury Court and the Cockpit-in-Court, was probably the largest of the private stages but would certainly have been much smaller than the Globe stage, approximately half its size.

If we now venture tentatively into a reconstruction of the internal lay-out of the Second Blackfriars, we must bear in mind that the results, however precise they look, rest on no more than informed guesses.

We can begin with the balconies. Those at the Fortune were 15 feet deep, at the Cockpit-in-Court 11 feet deep, and in the Jones playhouse 7 feet 6 inches at the house-end, 6 feet 9 inches at the stage-end. At the Cockpit-in-Court there are three rows of seating for spectators with a gangway behind and in front, in the Jones design, three rows with a gangway behind the house-end and balcony. At the Blackfriars, we may guess, there were balconies 8 feet deep, and the stage boxes were a continuation of the lower side balconies. This means that the pit does not extend narrow arms along either side of the stage as it did in the public

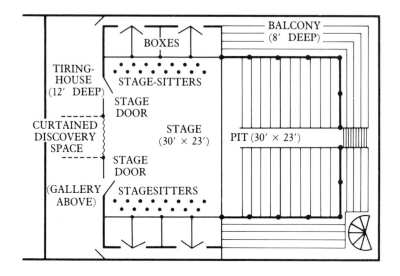

Figure 3.1: Hypothetical reconstruction of the Second Blackfriars (a groundplan) assuming that the tiring-house is contained within the 66-feet overall length of the playhouse

houses and as it evidently does in *The Wits* frontispiece and in the *Roxana* and *Messalina* illustrations.

Thus we have a Blackfriars stage of 30 feet in width (46 feet less two rows of boxes each 8 feet deep). Assuming that the tiring-house behind the facade is part of the 66 feet overall length and that it is (somewhat arbitrarily) 12 feet deep, pit and stage together are 46 feet (66 feet minus tiring-house and house-end gallery). The Fortune stage (and probably the Globe's) extended halfway across the yard so an actor at the centre of the downstage edge of the stage stood at the centre of the house. If this were so at the Blackfriars, and it makes aesthetic sense, this gives us a stage 23 feet deep. We now have a stage 30 feet by 23 feet, a little over half the size of the Fortune stage and half as big again as that of the Jones playhouse. Its height from the playhouse floor (and the height of the first gallery) was probably either the 4 feet of the Jones design or the 4½ feet of the Cockpit-in-Court.

The pit, 30 feet by 23 feet, was set with benched seating and may have been raked, like that of the Jones playhouse (though this is not indicated in the house-end elevation) and of the Cockpit-in-Court. In fact, benches on a flat floor would have provided adequate sightlines. For models of the Jones playhouse and this reconstructed Blackfriars see Plate 7.

The audience capacity of the private playhouses was probably no more than a third of that of their public counterparts. De Witt tells us that the Swan held 3,000 spectators and the Globe probably had a similar capacity (the Spanish Ambassador claimed over 3,000 a day saw *A Game at Chess*). It has been estimated that the Jones playhouse could hold 500 and estimates for the Blackfriars, assuming three galleries, have varied from 500 to just under 1,000.[18] Spectators, of course, were allowed much less legroom than their modern counterparts (and needed less), and we can assume there was little concern for the wide gangways and multiple access points required by modern safety regulations. Also, the seating rows in the Jones designs are only 18 inches wide. It is probable therefore that the Blackfriars, even with only two balconies, would have seated upwards of 1,000 spectators and this figure is confirmed by commendatory verses for *The Faithful Shepherdess*, a Blackfriars play of 1608, which warn that 'a thousand men in judgement sit'. The Blackfriars probably had the largest capacity of the private houses. But even here, the reduction from 3,000 to 1,000 makes this, with other factors, a different playspace in kind from the public playhouses.

A small but significant part of the private theatre audience was accommodated on the stage itself, sprawled on the stage rushes or perched on stools. We can assume that they sat at the sides of the stage in front of the boxes, perhaps ten or more on each side. There they were a notable feature of the performance itself whether they sat still or engaged, as some of them must have, in the distracting behaviour of Dekker's gull (see p. 23): they contributed significantly to others' experience of the play. Jonson waged war on them in prologues and inductions and complained (*The Devil is an Ass*, Blackfriars, 1616) that they forced the actors to play 'in compass of a cheese-trencher'. But they were tolerated because they were an important element in playhouse income, so that when they were banned by royal decree from the Salisbury Court stage, the manager there, Heton, had to compensate the players 'in consideration of the want of stools on the stage'.

The stage-sitters, as Jonson complains, would necessarily reduce the width of the acting area. On our hypothetical Blackfriars stage the reduction might be from 30 feet to 23 feet, so creating a square playing space. But if the side balconies ran over the boxes, as we assume, the sides of the stage were in fact inferior acting areas because of poor sightlines. In effect, and provided they did not stray, the stage-sitters occupied two 'dead' areas of the stage. But they must have acted as a special form of stage-dressing, operating a kind of 'alienating' effect by which other spectators were reminded that they were witnessing a play event, and thus they had an influence on the kind of stage illusion it was possible to generate: they broke the picture-frame by their presence and

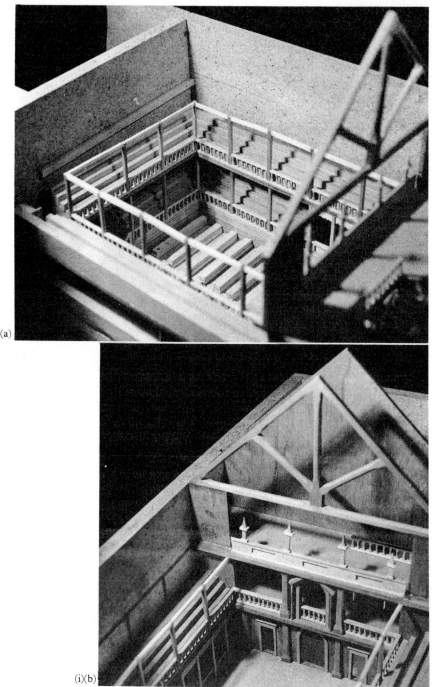

(i)(a)

(i)(b)

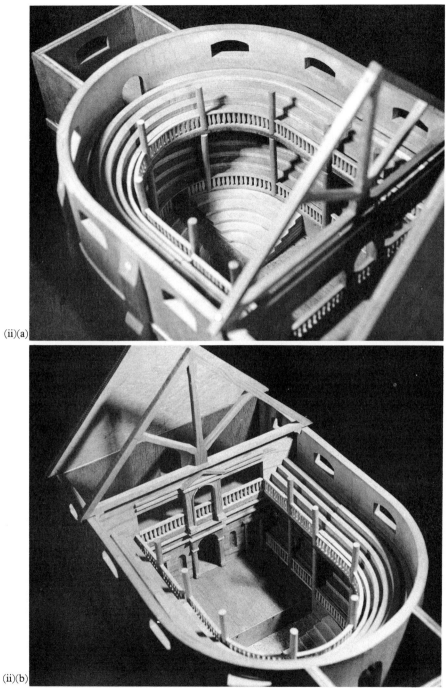

7 (i) Model of a hypothetical reconstruction of the Blackfriars Playhouse: (a) looking towards the house-end; (b) looking towards the stage-end (ii) Model based on Inigo Jones's drawings, probably the Cockpit/Phoenix: (a) looking towards the house-end; (b) looking towards the stage-end

in turn invited the players to do so also. (It is generally assumed that there were no stage-sitters in the public houses. They certainly have left no record and their presence would have severely obstructed the viewing of the groundlings.)

Wright's third characteristic of the private playhouses is the provision of artificial lighting: 'Here they . . . acted by candlelight', in contrast to the public houses were 'they always acted by daylight'. The Duke of Stettin-Pomerania reports, of his 1602 visit to the Blackfriars, *'alle bei Lichte agiret, welches ein gross Ansehen macht'*. But this is crucially ambiguous, for it might mean either 'all was played by artificial light, which made a great spectacle'; or 'the performance was given wholly in artificial light, which [etc.]'.[19] We know that candles were used for lighting in private playhouses; we do not know if they were used instead of daylight (as Wright implies) or in conjunction with daylight. Nor do we know if it was possible to use lighting for special stage effects.

On even the most overcast days, daylight entering the playhouse would be so much brighter than candlelight as virtually to obliterate it, at least until early evening in winter. But the Blackfriars and The Phoenix evidently gave command performances at night and were able to light a play, and the house, artificially. The poem in praise of *The Faithful Shepherdess*, quoted earlier with reference to audience capacity, goes so far as to imply that the quality of candles might make or mar a performance. When the boys were at the Blackfriars, there is a suggestion in Dekker's *The Seven Deadly Sins of London* (1606) that only certain kinds of play, namely nocturnals (whatever they were) and tragedies, were played by candlelight alone 'when the windows were clapped down'. (The Blackfriars, in fact, had wooden shutters, as their state of disrepair is referred to in the 1609 deposition, and the windows of the building of the First Blackfriars had been spoiled by the conversion.)

The Jones playhouse designs show no artificial lighting and neither do the drawings of the Cockpit-in-Court. However, the Office of Works Accounts for 1630–1, talking of repairs in the cockpit, refers to fifteen candlesticks (candelabra?) which lit the stage and auditorium, 'whereof ten smaller and two greater than the other [are] about the stage'. In the accounts for the previous year, we learn that the window panes in the lantern which had illuminated the cockpit from above had been painted out.[20] But this, of course, was a house which tended to play at night. On the other hand, Jones's designs for the Phoenix clearly show provision for a very limited amount of daylighting: slit windows at ground floor level to provide light for the walkways under the first gallery; and six oddly-shaped, first floor windows which would give light to the upper gallery and also diffused, clerestory lighting for the auditorium. But no direct lighting could reach the stage.

The frontispiece of *The Wits*, perhaps representing an indoors performance during the closure, shows shadows thrown by actors as though from daylight from a steep angle to the left. But this is probably a convention of the draughtsmanship. There are two kinds of artificial stage illumination shown in the same illustration: two eight-branched candelabra over the stage, and a line of six, twin-wick floats or oil lamps serving as footlights. (There is, in fact, no pre-Restoration reference to footlights.) The two candelabra may be anticipated in the Cockpit-in-Court's 'two greater than the other' and also in a passage in Overbury's *Characters* (sixth edition of 1615) describing a gallant who sits onstage: at the end of the play his rising is 'a kind of walking epilogue between the two candles [candelabra], to know if his suit may pass for current'. Heton, manager at the Salisbury Court, claimed that half the charge for lights 'both wax and tallow . . . all winter is near 5s. a day'. Ten shillings, it is estimated, would have bought him ten wax candles and thirty tallow of sufficient size to last a performance. We might imagine there were ten wax candles in two candelabra lighting the downstage area, while thirty tallow candles in twos were disposed along the tiring-house facade, above the boxes at the sides of the stage and around the auditorium above the first gallery.

This whole matter of lighting is of more than academic interest. It is part of the audience's experiencing of the performance, not merely a means to that experiencing. Candlelight is extremely low-level illumination compared with electric lighting and the number of candles suggested above would light the stage very inadequately by modern standards and leave the auditorium in relative gloom. Consequently, we might expect private playhouses to make all possible use of daylight. However, when daytime performances of plays were given for royalty in colleges and elsewhere, it was customary to board up windows and play by artificial light. Similarly, the ground floor windows of Jones's Banqueting House were walled up, allowing only top lighting to filter down to illuminate daytime, royal events otherwise candlelit. It is important to remember that brightness and gloom as perceived by the eye and not the light-meter are largely a matter of contrast; and commentators could boast that artificial light at court for masques and plays converted darkest night to brightest day. Jonson and others built into the inductions of several plays of the private theatre the lighting of stage candles by the tiremen (or stagehands). So, at the beginning of *The Staple of News* (1626), tiremen enter with 'a torch in their hands, to give light to the business'.

It seems impossible not to conclude that it was frequently the practice, certainly in winter and perhaps particularly for certain kinds of play, for private theatre performances to be given wholly by candlelight. It would be folly to light the candles at the beginning of a performance if they were likely to do no work until the last scenes of the play when the evening drew in. On the other hand, the shuttering of windows and consequent exclusion of daylight would undoubtedly have enhanced the indoor privacy of playhouses very different in kind to the open-air public houses.

Such a conclusion about the regular, exclusive use of artificial light involves other considerations. If both auditorium and stage were candlelit, then the auditorium was probably noticeably darker than the stage, giving something of the stage emphasis that today's lighting regularly and markedly creates. Nevertheless, the actual level of stage lighting would be generally lower than the daylighting of the public houses and this must be taken into account in a consideration of acting style. Also, to light the actors even moderately well, the overstage candelabra (probably hung further downstage than *The Wits'* illustration suggests) would need to be suspended at a height not greatly above the actors' heads because candles have very little 'throw'. The result of this would be that the candelabra would be a dazzling, somewhat distracting, part of the stage picture, especially inconvenient for spectators alongside the stage on the second gallery (and even more for those in the third gallery, if there were one) who would have to look at the actors for much of the time through the flickering candles themselves.[21] Indeed, it is conceivable that the nuisance value of the candelabra contributed to making the pit of the private house the favoured auditorium area for the gentry, consequently determining a different seating arrangement and financial structure from what pertained in the public houses. Finally, the exclusion of daylight might have made possible a precise control of lighting for stage effects.

A measure of lighting control, it is often claimed, was a distinct advantage enjoyed by the private over the public playhouse. If candles or lamps could be rapidly shaded or extinguished at a precise moment and as rapidly revealed or lit, levels of stage lighting might be altered for the realistic representation of night and day, and other illusionistic effects could be achieved. It is persuasively argued, for example, that in *The Duchess of Malfi*, IV, i, when a dead man's hand is given to the Duchess, only the plunging of the stage into relative darkness on Ferdinand's command to remove the lights could avoid bathos. Another lighting effect is employed later in the play, it is claimed, when Antonio remarks (V,iii) that 'on a sudden a clear light Presented me a face folded in sorrows'.[22]

However, there are very few references of this latter kind in the plays and no direct mention of lighting equipment or of lighting effects. Neither are there specific requirements in stage directions, other than the standard one (public as well as private) of squibs and powdered resin for lightning, for the kind of special lighting effects developed in the masque. Even there, lighting had mostly to do with scenery. On the other hand, it is evident from stage directions that lamps and tapers held by actors continued conventionally, as they did in the public tradition, to signal to an audience that a scene takes place by night. On the whole, therefore, it seems that the lighting design was non-existent or extremely rudimentary in the private theatre.

A likely side-effect of the use of candlelight for private theatre performance was the development of the act interval to allow the intermittent tending of candles during performance. In turn, the act interval promoted what was certainly a pronounced performance feature, the use of *entr'acte* music which was part of the generous provision of music in the private theatre. Incidental music effects used naturalistically (such as fanfares and songs) had always featured in the public playhouse. But the juvenile companies of the first private playhouses generally made great use of their particular skills in song and dance and the playhouses had employed theatre orchestras to provide pre-show, *entr'acte* and incidental music. The Duke of Stettin-Pomerania enthused about such things at the Blackfriars of the boys, and the tradition continued with the King's Men. It was at the pre-show concert that Whitelocke's coranto was played (see p. 26), and according to the flattered composer the musicians were 'esteemed the best of common musicians in London'. The excellence evidently continued till the closure. *The Actors' Remonstrance* (1643) lamented the demise of the private playhouse musicians, 'our music, that was held so delectable and precious'.

In fact, the playhouse bands did more than decorate a play round its edges. The size of their contribution to the performance must have varied considerably, but Marston shows in the plays he wrote for the boys at the Blackfriars such as *The Malcontent* (1604) and *Sophonisba* (1605) what was possible. In both, the music plays an integrated part in the action, underscoring narrative effects, defining the emotional responses of the audience and exploring thematic ideas. Normally, perhaps, the printed text of the play conceals the part played by the music, but at the end of the first edition of *Sophonisba* (1606), the playwright appears to apologise for including information about the music customarily omitted in the printing. *The Malcontent*, when it was acquired (or stolen) from the boys' repertory at the Blackfriars in 1604 by the King's Men to play at the Globe, had to be padded out with extra dialogue to compensate, so the induction says, for 'the not received custom of music in our [= public] theatre'.

The provision of music in the private theatre invited the playwrights to write less dialogue and, more importantly, to experiment in bold, multi-media effects. The plays Shakespeare wrote after the King's Men moved to the Blackfriars – *Cymbeline*, *The Winter's Tale* and *The Tempest*, together with *The Two Noble Kinsmen*, probably composed in tandem with Fletcher – all make plentiful use of song. *The Tempest* is a kind of music play, a melodrama, presenting both narrative events and abstract ideas about magic and metamorphosis through a consistent use of song and instrumental piece. The masque inset is the most sustained and complex musical effect in a play which constantly seeks to express things beyond the reach of dialogue and character, for 'the isle is full of noises' (see pp. 82–4).

The musicians in the bands played a variety of instruments and would need a proper space in which to perform. The 'music room' was evidently located behind the facade and above (from where music is often summoned by characters on stage). Jasper Mayne commended Jonson, in 1638, because 'Thou laidst no sieges to the music room'. On or behind the gallery above the stage, the 'music room' occupied the position of the musician's gallery in the Tudor hall. The Jones design and the Cockpit-in-Court both have a central, practical window which might serve for actors or the band. In a boys' private play at St Paul's, 1599, the areas either side of the practical window are evidently referred to when a stage direction calls for a ghost to be placed 'betwixt the music houses' (*Antonio's Revenge*).

Music 'above' was generally available to the private theatre playwright. It contributed more powerfully to the play-in-performance than printed texts indicate. And it provided an aspect of that atmosphere of artful cultivation that marked private from public.

A public theatre performance in a large amphitheatre 100 feet across with an audience of 3,000, many standing, and with the auditorium open to sky and weather, would have been a markedly different experience from a private theatre performance in an enclosed hall, with a seated audience of 500 to 1,000, shut off from the outside world, with candles flickering and music playing. At the first, however attentive they are, the spectators form a crowd; at the second, an audience. At the first, the spectators assist in a community celebration which takes the form of a traditional, city entertainment. Here, the performer demands attention by the force of his personality and the bravura of his performance – his glamour – but the spectators consistently alter the content of the play-in-performance by their overt participation. At the second, the play is less ritual and more art. The performers – in that subtly shifting interdependence – are now less important (comparatively speaking) than their material and the audience, a group of value-sharing individuals, validates the performance by its appreciation. Its participation is less obtrusive (despite the stage-sitters) but more pervasive in that an awareness of its critical acumen is built into the play and its production.

The difference is partly one of sheer scale. The Globe, 100 feet across, 33 feet high, held a mass audience (mass particularly in the days when crowds were discouraged or heavily organised for political reasons). We have nothing to compare with this now except perhaps a popular music concert or certain sporting events. The 'feel' of the private playhouses we can partly get at the Georgian playhouse at Richmond, Yorkshire (despite its accommodation of scenery). Auditorium and stage there are roughly 61 feet by 28 feet, and the stage occupies half the available space. Closer to the dimensions of the Blackfriars is the Cottesloe Theatre in the National Theatre complex (London). This is a flexible, 'studio' theatre, often used in a Blackfriars configuration, with a pit surrounded on three sides by galleries and with a raised end-stage on the fourth side; its overall measurements are 66 feet by 56 feet (compare the Blackfriars' 66 feet by 46 feet). While it was being developed it was described in these felicitous terms:

> In form and scale it feels like a Georgian playhouse while having an indoor Elizabethan quality that favours the non-scenic production. When it is lined by an audience it could well be an exciting cockpit for experimental productions.[23]

Of course, the King's Men when they moved to the Blackfriars were not experimenting aesthetically, only commercially. At court and on tour, they were perfectly accustomed to performing in halls the size of their own house and with something, perhaps most, of the new facilities. They would have experienced few practical difficulties in adapting their performance style to the new playhouse conditions and were used, as a part of their professional expertise, to modifying their playing in accordance with whatever conditions they met. A flexibility of approach was part of their trade. So their leading player of the first decade at the new house, Richard Burbage, had been star of the Globe and continued to be star of the Blackfriars. Nevertheless, playing conditions were very different and so must have been the acting style or styles. Though there is still little agreement upon, or understanding of, what an Elizabethan acting style actually was, we should be able to speculate on some differences encouraged by the private house playing conditions.

Most obviously, the playing space, as we have seen, was much smaller, the Blackfriars stage being half the size of that of the Globe. Shirley's playwrighting career related almost entirely to the private houses – first the Phoenix, then Ogilby's Dublin playhouse and finally the Blackfriars. When his play *The Doubtful Heir* was premiered at the Globe in 1640, he wrote a prologue which asked the audience to 'pardon our vast stage'. Compare this with Jonson's 'cheese-trencher' grumble about the Blackfriars. By modern standards, and especially as an open stage, the Globe's platform was vast and it inevitably called for a large style of playing from the actors. The actor was obliged to fill the space with energetic movement and large gestures or he would be dwarfed by it. In particular, he would tend to keep a generous, unnaturally large space between himself and the other actors; he would try to avoid tight groupings (which would, in any case, be bad for sightlines); and he would cut out small and fussy moves. Everything, usually, would be expansive. The 'actors' on the public stage of De Witt's Swan show this clearly (see Plate 8). A boy-actress sits stage centre on an unnecessarily long bench, her spread arms and skirt giving her substantial presence. A boy-actress in attendance stands upstage and to one side, with arms again widely spread. And a man with a staff stands several metres downstage of the seated 'lady' and some distance to the other side, in a straddle-legged gesture of (apparent) obeisance. The whole grouping of only three actors, even allowing for De Witt's usual liberties with proportion, contrives to occupy a good deal of the key acting area downstage of the stage pillars; it stretches in both dimensions as though to fill as much available space as possible. Compare this with the *The Wits'* illustration of a small, indoor stage (Plate 3). Represented here simultaneously (as they would not be in actual performance) are all the characters of a comic medley. But if we concentrate on one real grouping, that of Falstaff and the Hostess, we see something very different from the Swan stagecraft. The two are pressed as far downstage as possible and, engaged evidently in some stage business over a wine cup, have taken up positions 'naturally' close to each other; they occupy realistic space (and the horizontals are not accentuated as they are at the Swan). Only the cup is exaggerated in size, presumably a comic prop. The Falstaff actor, far from filling space, appears to be playing as small as possible in exchanging a sidelong look with the audience members at his feet. Without wishing to press evidence from the two pictures too far, we might presume that one represents public acting, the other private. But this difference is one of size not kind.

As a less expansive style of physical gesture would be the norm in the private theatre, so too would a restrained vocal style. The enclosed and smaller volume of the Blackfriars or Phoenix would have created very different acoustical conditions from those pertaining at the Globe. The actor had a smaller space to fill with his voice and his words would be in no danger of escaping to the skies. Also, unlike in the public houses, there would have been little or at least less competition from noises either from outside (street sounds or the weather) or from inside (from the audience, which in a public house was both much larger and partly promenade). Shirley's prologue to *The Doubtful Heir* comments on this

8   A copy of De Witt's sketch of the Swan Playhouse, c. 1596

too: quiet is requested from the Globe audience 'Because we have no heart to break our lungs'.

However, a factor working against better audibility in the private play-houses was the generally lower level of lighting. In life and on stage, a part of verbal communication is done by the visible shapes made by the face: words can be seen even though not properly heard. An audience that cannot see properly cannot, or thinks it cannot, hear clearly. Never-theless, on balance, we should expect the indoor acoustics to be much better, if only because, quite simply, the actor worked closer to the majority of his audience, At the Globe, the longest carry (from, say, upstage right or left to an audience member in the third gallery diagonally opposite) was about 90 feet. At the Blackfriars, the furthest carry was 60 feet and in Jones's Phoenix (no third gallery), 50 feet. So at the Black-friars, less than the length of a cricket pitch or the width of a tennis court could at most separate an onstage actor from any member of the audience.

It would clearly be a mistake to assume that in moving to the private playhouses, the adult actors were encouraged to adopt a naturalistic style that sharply contrasted with their practice on the outdoor stages. We do not know enough about the acting style in the period to make such an assumption; nor is 'naturalistic' an absolute or even unambiguous term when attached to playing. What we can say is that the actors were able to strain less after effect and had less need to develop the battery of personal mannerisms and bravura techniques employed by the popular artist to impose himself on a large or inattentive gathering. In general, we might expect the private houses to encourage a greater fidelity to the script and to the role (note how the broad, improvisational comics popular in the 1580s and 1590s disappear), and also a tendency towards a more ensemble style of playing. Some such notion may lie behind Carew's praise of the King's Men in his commendatory verses for Davenant's *The Just Italian* (1630). They are 'the true brood of actors, that alone keep natural unstrained action in her throne'. (But he may just have meant that they were better actors than the rest.)

Generally an advantage to the actors, one might expect the smaller playing space in the private theatre to be dramaturgically restricting to the playwrights. Changes of dramaturgy would only emerge slowly after 1609 and show most clearly in playwrights like Massinger, Ford and Shirley, whose working lives related wholly or almost wholly to the private playhouses. But what is clear in an analysis of, for example, numbers of characters on stage at any one time is that there is little obvious change. Because of the special restrictions of focus and sightlines on a thrust stage such as the Globe's, it was seldom filled with speaking characters. However many extras or supernumaries there might be in a particular scene, mostly left upstage and therefore out of the way, the majority of scenes in Shakespeare require five speaking actors or less on stage at any one time.[24] And so there had to be little adaptation of practice for the smaller, private stage. As the history play went out of fashion at the turn of the century, so the most elaborate of conventional scenes, the 'alarms and excursions', sieges and pitched battles of chronicle drama, naturally died away in any case. Jasper Mayne's praise for Jonson, that he did not lay siege to the music room, shows that some contemporaries showed the anxiety about dramatic illusion of *Henry V*'s Prologue (even if Shakespeare did not). But such scenes did not disappear entirely on the smaller stages. City walls and castle ramparts scenes occur, for example, in Ford's *Perkin Warbeck* (before 1633) at the Phoenix, in Shirley's *The Maid's Revenge* (1626) also at the Phoenix, and in the same writer's *The Politician* (1639) at the Salisbury Court. A generous suspension of disbelief could still be counted on.

Nevertheless, the more populous scenes usually have some ceremonious or ritual quality so that they are easily managed on a limiting stage. The crowd scene again and again takes the form of the favourite Jacobean device of the masque, dance or banquet, or it has the structuring principle of a formal procession, a court pageant or a legal ceremony. So the Loretto scene of *The Duchess of Malfi*, III, which required at least fifteen actors on stage simultaneously, is a kind of double dumbshow, with commentary supplied by the two pilgrims, and its action is centred on the shrine of Our Lady (upstage centre) which serves as a focal point for the blocking of the scene. In the wedding celebration of *The Broken Heart*, V, ii, thirteen characters are present at an elaborate dance which fills the Black-friars stage with a patterned activity interrupted three times over by the arrival of bad news. Though stage-sitters may get jostled, the action itself remains shapely, coherently organised by narrative and by dialogue.

For the most part, though, private theatre scenes are much less crowded than this and the smaller stage and auditorium generally encouraged the presentation of intimate scenes and quiet exchanges amongst few characters. In *The Duchess of Malfi*, the most violent and the most poignant scenes are those with two or three characters on stage; and for all the formal power of the last three scenes of *The Broken Heart* (including the dance scene), Ford's best and most intense writing is in the series of two-hander exchanges that characterise the particular quality of that play. It is impossible to imagine Ford developing his special kind of theatre at the Globe or the Swan: he seems almost to write with television in mind.

Granville Barker summarises, with characteristic insight, the long-term influences of the indoor stages on the writers who composed for them:

The plots of new plays might well grow more elaborate and their writing more diffuse, for it would be easier to keep an audience attentive and see that no points were missed. If violence is still the thing, noise will not be. The old clattering battles may gradually go out of favour; but processions will look finer than ever, and apparitions and the like will be twice as effective. Rhetoric will lose hold a little . . . and sentiment will become as telling as passion.[25]

One likely influence of the private playhouse on playing style lay in its predominantly end-stage effect. In the public amphitheatre, the audience surrounded the performer in a wide arc of up to 300°. His dominant position was near the downstage edge of the platform, almost at the midpoint of the yard where he was literally the centre of attention. In the private playhouse, two factors served to shift the bulk of the audience to a position more clearly in front of the stage: the oblong shape of the house (even where the auditorium itself is curved as at the Phoenix), and the adoption by the gentry of the pit. The effect of these two factors was to create (far more obviously than in the Wooden O), a house-end and a stage-end, and Jones's elevations for the Phoenix show this distinction working in the mind of the playhouse architect. In a royal theatre like the Cockpit-in-Court, the effect is further emphasised by the position of the state (the King's position) directly opposite the stage. Again, this was nothing new. In the private hall, the players had customarily performed with their backs to the buttery screen and with the high table, where the important spectators sat, in front of them on the opposite short wall. In the Phoenix design, it has been estimated that 112 spectators sat on either side of the stage (in the two balconies) while more than three times that many, 360, sat in front of the stage; and the proportion of audience in front would increase in a larger auditorium (such as the Blackfriars). The effect of the shift of audience numbers in front would be to move the dominant position of the actor upstage and to encourage him to adopt a more front-on than in-the-round manner of acting. He begins inevitably to be concerned about upstaging.

It is a fallacy of course (though not uncommon) to see an end-stage as an embryonic or failed proscenium stage. The stage is open and is architecturally part of the same space as the auditorium; actor and spectator are in one room. Also, entrances are still on the upstage facade, and the actor works in depth, not laterally as the proscenium arch encourages: the stage pictures are three-dimensional. Nevertheless, the end-stage especially favours tableau-like effects, such as the last two scenes of *The Broken Heart*, the Loretto scene of *The Duchess of Malfi* and the chess-game at the end of *The Tempest:* a succession of eloquent stage pictures best seen from the front.

Finally, an important difference from the Cottesloe or from other modern 'studio' theatres with which the Jacobean private playhouses can be seen to share important practical features was that this was not a 'poor' theatre, in the way that experimental theatres after Grotowski tend to be. Today's studio reacts to the gilt and plush of the conventional proscenium theatre with a virtuous show of unplastered walls, spartan seating and a conspicuous display of such functional elements as lighting bars and so on. Jones's designs for the Phoenix and the Cockpit-in-Court, however, suggest a far different ambiance. Even the public playhouses seemed opulent and richly adorned to the foreign visitor. The private playhouses must have been more so. They were decorously furnished for their genteel clients with tapestries, paintwork and statuary. The decor of the Cockpit-in-Court is indicated in the Office of Works Accounts for 1629–32. The walls were predominantly blue and the candlesticks, other decorative features and the pillars of the facade were picked out in gold. The ceiling over the stage, which concealed a folding throne which could be flown in, was finished in blue calico and embellished with silver stars. The seating of the pit was covered in matting and round about the walls of the auditorium were precious art-works: the twelve Caesars, painted by Titian, 'two great pieces of painted work done by Palma', and several statues especially carved (perhaps those shown on the elevation of the facade).[26]

The Blackfriars, the Phoenix and the Salisbury Court may not have been so richly decorated as that. But the second of those was probably designed not by a jobbing carpenter but by a major visual artist of international stature (i.e. Inigo Jones). The music, playhouse furnishings and the audience itself undoubtedly created an atmosphere of high culture for the private theatre play-in-performance.

4 · The Private Theatre Companies, their Playwrights and their Repertory[1]

The 'arm's-length' control of the capital' theatre operated by Elizabeth was changed immediately on James's accession into direct and powerful royal patronage; and an Act of Parliament soon confirmed this development by forbidding the traditional patronage of acting companies by peers of the realm. The Lord Chamberlain's Company was translated into the King's Men, the Lord Admiral's Company into Prince Henry's Men, and the Earl of Worcester's Men into Queen Anne's Men. One aspect of the growing split between private and public theatre, this development must have given the favoured companies a new sense of privilege and may have enabled the King's Men just five years later to do what they failed to do in 1596, occupy the Blackfriars. During the reigns of James and Charles, the court showed a consistent interest in professional theatre, supporting it through the Privy Council against the City authorities and influencing its development and style of repertory.

James himself was not passionately interested in stage plays; his real enthusiasm was for dancing and the hunt. But his consort and his first son, the precocious Henry, were theatre enthusiasts, and they cultivated the actors as friends. If the unnamed Jones playhouse is the Phoenix, it may have been planned in part with command performances in mind, for the awkwardly curved seating in the pit makes sense only if we imagine a royal box opposite the stage at the rear of the house (which is, however, not represented on the house-end elevation). Certainly, Charles and Henrietta Maria were to visit the private playhouses on several occasions. And Charles showed a continual interest in theatre. He read plays in manuscript before performance, arbitrated in disputes over licensing, and even suggested plots for new plays.

Henrietta Maria's preoccupation with theatre also extended beyond enthusiastic spectating. With her interest in drama developed at the French court, she not only performed in masques (which she and Charles might properly do in the way of court ceremonial) but also, and sensationally, in two pastorals at court. The first earned a raised eyebrow from Chamberlain: 'I have known when this would have seemed a strange sight, to see a Queen act in a play, but *tempora mutantur et nos.*' After the second production, for which the queen and her fellow thespians who were ladies-in-waiting had been coached in their performances by the King's Man, Joseph Taylor, Henrietta Maria saw, what was probably not intended, a personal attack on her in print by William Prynne. The hapless Prynne suffered dire punishments and when James Shirley ironically dedicated his latest comedy to him, the playwright was rewarded by being taken into Henrietta Maria's household.

The Queen maintained contact with the stage in other ways, too. Centre of a platonic-love cult, she commissioned the play *The Platonic Lovers* from William Davenant. She donated costumes from the pastoral that led to Prynne's punishment to Taylor to use in the King's Men's revival of *The Faithful Shepherdess*. She gave her name and support to the company which, from 1625, was the chief rival of the King's Men. And generally she viewed the Caroline stage, amateur and professional, as what it undoubtedly was, an adornment of court life.

The career of Thomas Heywood clearly charts a change of complexion from Elizabethan popular theatre to a Caroline theatre increasingly concerned to cater to the court. The playwright's life in theatre spanned four decades, and long before the end he could claim to 'have had either an entire hand, or at the least a main finger' in 220 plays. His most distinctive achievements in the eyes of posterity are dramas of a bourgeois and domestic character written in a plain unpretentious style. Yet the high point of his career, and the last play he wrote, was *Love's Mistress* (1634), a masque-like allegory, in part on the subject of the queen's favourite theme of platonic love and incidentally attacking Prynne. It was presented three times in eight days before the King and Queen, once at the Phoenix and then twice, now with sets by Jones, at Denmark House. A professional theatre person's aim is to please his audience – and that audience had become Charles, his Queen and their court.

The King's Men, both with regard to their status at court and in terms of their financial and artistic success, were consistently the premier troupe from the accession of James to the closure of the theatre in 1642. Their innovatory move to the Blackfriars was an astute and decisive one and they hedged their bets by continuing to play at the Globe in the summer, thus gaining for themselves a unique place in the public and private theatre worlds. And besides, or because of, developing the best playhouse in London, the King's Men maintained a superiority both in acting and in play-scripts over their rivals. So for the period 1603–17, of 299 known plays given at court, 177 were by the King's Men.[2] Only for a short time in the 1630s were they seriously challenged by another company, Henrietta Maria's Men. And even then, we find that in the 1630–1 season at court, the King's Men performed twenty-one plays to the Queen's Men's sixteen. We have already seen (p. 21) that Sir Humphrey Mildmay made four times as many visits to the Blackfriars as to all the other playhouses put together.

Troupes other than the King's Men who were granted royal patronage in 1603 flourished for a while and then declined, to be replaced by new companies able to find sponsorship with the royal family. At Henry's death in 1612, his company passed under the protection of the Elector Palatine who was shortly to marry James's daughter. Never enjoying the prominence of the Admiral's Men before them, they suffered severe losses (including that of their play books) when the Fortune burned down in 1621, and though reformed in 1626 as the King and Queen of Bohemia's Company they never achieved great status thereafter. Queen Anne's men were successful for a time, becoming the first resident company at the Phoenix. But when the queen died in 1619 they appear to have dwindled into a provincial touring company. Lady Elizabeth's Men, formed in 1611, was a troupe which Henslowe strove to house in a permanent private playhouse (see pp. 28–9). In part a juvenile company, it supplied a number of important actors to the King's Men. Prince Charles's Company, created in 1610 and restyled the Prince's Men after Henry's death, was amalgamated with Lady Elizabeth's Men and the combined company, having premiered *Bartholomew Fair*, eventually replaced Queen Anne's Men at the Phoenix. They disbanded on Charles's accession.

Henrietta Maria lent her name to a company formed in 1625 partly out of Lady Elizabeth's players and former members of Queen Anne's Men. This company enjoyed a successful decade at the Phoenix but were then reformed to play till the closure at the Salisbury Court (1637–42). First at the Salisbury Court, and the last of the prominent companies, was a juvenile troupe formed to be a nursery theatre for the Blackfriars. Known as the King's Revels, they survived only a few years.

The King's Men had the best actors. Until his death in 1619, Burbage's prestige remained unrivalled. To Cokes in *Bartholomew Fair* his name signifies 'best actor'. If the identification is correct he is the model of 'An Excellent Actor' supplied by Webster for Overbury's *Characters*, 'for by a full and significant action of body he charms our attention'. At his death he was replaced in the King's Men by the highly experienced Joseph Taylor from Prince Charles's Men (and, before that, Lady Elizabeth's Company). He took over, amongst other Burbage parts, Ferdinand in *The Duchess of Malfi* and possibly Prospero. John Lowin was another leading actor with the company, a stalwart member from before its move to the Blackfriars until the closure. He played Falstaff and Henry VIII amongst his Shakespeare roles, Volpone and Mammon in Jonson, and Melantius and Bellur in Fletcher (that last, we are told, 'most naturally'). Amongst the prominent female impersonators were Richard Robinson, highly praised by Jonson (and referred to in *The Devil Is an Ass*), who graduated to being a second-string adult actor, Richard Sharpe who played the Duchess in *The Duchess of Malfi* and, despite an early death, became a leading adult performer, and Stephen Hammerton who played the female lead in Fletcher's *The Wild Goose Chase* in 1632 before also becoming an adult actor.

However, as important as the individual and collective quality of the company's acting, and no doubt contributing to it, was the striking continuity of company personnel through the whole period. A good living could be made as a King's Man and with general high unemployment in the acting profession there was no incentive for a player to move to another company. Actors today are mobile people, constantly seeking better remuneration or fresh artistic challenge. But the turnover of King's Men's players between 1608 and 1642 was minimal, certainly amongst the patented actors who formed the heart of the company and took the principal roles. Their number was fixed at twelve and changes in the team occurred only when a member died or retired. Through three decades, replacements of this kind were made at a rate of little more than one a year. Recruitment was often through the company itself, the best of the boy actors and apprentices graduating to patent status. Or occasionally other actors were drafted in from the juvenile or hybrid troupes such as the Lady Elizabeth's Men. For the period 1616–42, Bentley lists seventy-six King's Men actors in all.[3] Many of these were boys and hired men, the latter never taking principal roles. The patented actors were half that number.

The slow turnover of company personnel becomes sharply evident if we compare actor lists for specific plays. A cast list for *The Custom of the Country*, Fletcher's play first performed in 1619, has eight names for the principal roles: Taylor, Lowin, Underwood, Benfield, Eccleston, Sharpe and Holcombe. The last two of these were boys who played female roles. A comparable list of ten years later for Massinger's *The Picture* has seven names. Of these, four survive from the earlier list: Taylor, Lowin, Benfield and Sharpe, but Sharpe has progressed in the interim to male roles. Of the four missing, all had died (Tooley in 1623, Underwood in 1624, Eccleston probably in 1622 and Holcombe in 1625). Of the three new actors in the second list, two had already been members of the company at the time of the earlier play and in all probability played minor roles in it. These were Pollard, originally a boy actor in the company who by 1929 had graduated to adult roles, and Shank, the principal comedian of the company who had been a King's Man from 1612. The only actor in the 1629 cast-list not with the company in 1619 was Swanston who had replaced Underwood in 1624. Of the seven named actors of *The Picture*, Sharpe was to die in 1632 and Shank in 1636; but the remaining five were still performing with the King's Men at the closure thirteen years later. These included Taylor, Lowin and Benfield who had performed *The Custom of the Country* twenty-three years previously.

This astonishing continuity must have been a hugely important factor in the success of the company's repertory work, and in a number of different ways. Probably no company in the history of theatre has been in a position to develop such loyalty in its audience members, and it is a special and legitimate pleasure of repertory theatre work for an audience to watch actors, with whose work and style they are familiar, taking on new roles. What an audience sees in this situation is not simply a part being played, or even a part being played together with an actor playing it, but a part, the actor and other parts he has played.

Continuity would lead, too, to a very strong sense of ensemble playing. Often, acting in theatre, even during the performance itself, is a highly competitive business; but in a stable repertory system a sense of co-operative endeavour would inevitably emerge. More important, a marked house style and a fluent pattern of staging, significant in a theatre in which today's detailed and lengthy rehearsal process was impossible, would be increasingly developed.

'Lines', too, would be maintained. In the nature of the system, a great deal of type-casting took place and a part once created by an actor would remain with him through future revivals, often over a very long period. When an actor left the company, it was obviously convenient, where possible, to replace him with someone who could take on most of his parts. So, as we have seen, Taylor inherited many of the Burbage roles. But the effect, again, would be to reinforce the continuity and stability of the company and its playing.

Continuity and stability also marked the choice of repertory. The company habitually performed about four new plays a year but, as had been customary in earlier times, guaranteed a constant appeal to their audience by retaining in their repertory a large number of plays (we might guess thirty to forty at one time) from which a daily changing programme might be constructed. We do not have, for the King's Men, the detailed information about daily performances that exists for the Admiral's Men at the Rose playhouse in the 1590s, and so we are only able to make fairly general guesses about how the programme was actually operated. But we can say something about the overall composition of the repertoire.

In 1641, the King's Men obtained protection from the Lord Chamberlain against the publication of sixty-one, unprinted plays available for playing (and valuable copyright material therefore). Most are identifiable by name and author. From all sources, and for the period 1616–42, a list of 170 King's Men's plays has been compiled,[4] a total probably not far short of all the plays the company played during those twenty-six years. If we narrow down our scrutiny to the decade of the 1630s, we would expect about forty new plays to come into the repertory during that period, many written by the house poets, some given or sold to the company by freelance writers and amateurs. (There are, in fact, about twenty plays from the period 1630–41 in the 1641 list.) But we find references to the continued currency of many other plays, some of the preceding decade (which we would expect) but many from much earlier, including no less than thirty-two plays from 1610 (the King's Men's first full season at the Blackfriars) and before. Some of these plays were Elizabethan dramas, forty years old.

Twelve of the thirty-two are by Shakespeare and they cover almost the whole period of his writing. They are: *Pericles, A Winter's Tale, A Midsummer Night's Dream, Richard III, The Taming of the Shrew, Cymbeline, Othello, Hamlet, Julius Caesar, The Merry Wives of Windsor, Richard II* and *Henry IV*. There is no *Twelfth Night* here, no *Macbeth* or *King Lear*, and no *The Tempest*. But the full range of Shakespeare's writing is well represented, and if we clear our minds of the unique status of Shakespeare in subsequent theatre history we will be impressed that a third of the canon, some of it first on stage forty years before, was still being revived for the Blackfriars audience. Indeed, thirty to forty years old will prove the most dangerous age for a play in subsequent years – old-fashioned but not yet a period piece (i.e. revered for its age).

Also in the 1630s repertory of the King's Men, the early Jonson plays survived well, for there were revivals of *Volpone, Epicoene, The Alchemist* and even the Elizabethan *Every Man in His Humour* (and just escaping the 1610 cut-off is *Catiline*). Revived, too, were Marston's *The Malcontent* (1604) which the King's Men revamped when they took it over from the boys, Chapman's *Bussy D'Ambois* (originally performed in 1610) and, most oddly to our eyes, the collaborative play, *Sir John Oldcastle*, first performed in 1599. Less surprisingly, in view of his domination of the King's Men repertory, Fletcher is well represented by early plays from his workshop – *The Tamer Tamed* (1604), *The Coxcomb* and *Valentinian* (1610), and even *The Faithful Shepherdess* (1608), damned on its first performance but now, in a more receptive age, sumptuously reproduced. Finally, making up the thirty-two plays from an earlier age still performed in the 1630s is the anonymous but evergreen *The Merry Devil of Edmonton* (1603).

There were, then, almost as many very old plays in the repertoire as new ones, and well tried plays of up to ten years old greatly outnumbered the recent acquisitions. Plays survived on merit – most of the thirty-two are still greatly admired now – and the King's Men, over a lengthy period, had evidently built up a classical repertory in which the revival was a vital feature, even if the play-script might be freshened up or heavily revised for production. In a list of twenty-one plays presented by the King's men at court in 1630–1, three plays, one an 'Induction for the House', were evidently new, and the average age of the others was nineteen years. Again, then, as in company personnel and the playing of individual roles, the watchword is continuity, even perhaps conservatism.

The King's Men were not alone in playing 'classic' texts in the 1630s. Queen Henrietta's Men revived Marlowe's *The Jew of Malta* (1589) in 1633, Middleton's *A Mad World My Masters* (1605) was played at the Salisbury Court, and a list of plays belonging to the King and Queen's Young Company in 1639 included *George a Greene* (1593), *The Knight of the Burning Pestle* (1607) and Webster's *Apius and Virginia* (1608). A generation after the almost frantic attempts by Elizabethan playwrights to furnish their theatre with enough plays to satisfy a need for constant novelty, the Caroline period shows a slower tempo, an appreciation of the best of the earlier writing and the development of a classic repertoire.

The King's Men were successful commercially as well as artistically. They modelled their business venture at the Blackfriars on their continuing and efficient operation at the Globe (and probably before that at the Curtain). The company's stock and the playhouse lease were owned by two (substantially overlapping) groups of sharers, a majority of whom were patented company members who were principal actors. The business manager, if there were such an officer, was also one of the patented members, and he may have shed acting duties as he assumed the role. So Heminges filled this position from 1616–30 and he was succeeded by Lowin (who was evidently aided by Taylor). There is a strong sense here of a co-operative venture, with only a minimum of specialisation of roles.

However, the business arrangements of the companies at the Phoenix and the Salisbury Court were very different. The Phoenix and the companies that performed there were managed by Christopher Beeston who also owned the playhouse. His position was innovatory and would be a pattern for the immediate and long-term future of British theatre. He was a product of the development of private theatre and had an important influence upon it, and for two decades from the erection of the Phoenix (1617) he was probably the single most important man in London theatre.

He had begun his career as an actor with the Lord Chamberlain's Men and, shrewdly as it would turn out, he transferred in 1601 to Worcester's Men who became Queen Anne's Men two years later. When the company's actor-manager, Thomas Greene, died in 1612, Beeston took over the leadership of the company and his control became complete five years later when he converted the Cockpit into the Phoenix and installed the company there. Now he was a new kind of theatre impresario, combining the roles of a Heminges and a Henslowe. He was styled 'governor' in official papers and commanded the Phoenix operation in a high-handed, perhaps ruthless, manner, always ready to dismiss companies from his playhouse if it were advantageous for him to do so. In all, he managed five Phoenix companies: Queen Anne's (1617–19), Prince Charles's (1619–22), Lady Elizabeth's (1622–5), Henrietta Maria's (1625–37) and the King and Queen's Young Company, also known as 'Beeston's Boys' (1637–42).

Beeston's example may well have been followed at the Salisbury Court. Richard Gunnell, ex-actor, and William Blagrave, deputy to the Master of the Revels, financed the building of the playhouse and set up there a company of boys, the King's Revels, which they intended partly to operate as a nursery theatre for the Blackfriars.[5] By or after Gunnell's death in 1635, the company had ceased to be a wholly juvenile troupe and contained a number of adult actors. The management of both building and company passed to Richard Heton and the lease was now rented by housekeepers. Little is known about Heton, but some idea of his style of management can be gleaned from three documents of 1639 which record his dealings with the King's Revels and the housekeepers. In the first, Heton evidently seeks to ensure a stable company at the Salisbury Court after recent upheavals. The second is a 'draft of his patent' by which he tries to establish his legal standing both inside and outside the company. And in the third are recorded details of agreements between him and the housekeepers over production costs, benefits and so on. What is exposed is Heton's pressing need to reorganise a complicated commercial operation on sound financial and legal lines. He must have looked across with envy at the King's Men's old-fashioned but immensely stable organisation at Blackfriars.[6]

One other of this new breed of theatre managers created by the private theatre development deserves mention – William Davenant. Christopher Beeston's son, William, succeeded his father at the Phoenix in 1638 but in 1640 he was imprisoned for mounting a seditious play and Davenant was made governor. His management lasted less than a year as he was caught up in the political manoeuvring that heralded the Civil War and was forced to flee London. Before his spell at the Phoenix, he had become an important theatrical figure as dramatist and masque writer, and in 1639 he had obtained a patent to build a large playhouse in Fleet Street (though the project proved abortive). He returned briefly to the Phoenix during the republic to play *The Siege of Rhodes* (1659) and at the Restoration succeeded in obtaining the patent for one of the two monopoly companies. His important, though brief, career belongs thereafter to the history of Restoration theatre.

We may speculate that there is a natural growth cycle in theatre: comedian – dramatic poet – tragedian – manager. So the age of Tarlton is succeeded, at the bidding of Marlowe and Shakespeare, by the age of Burbage, and after him comes Beeston and Davenant. The progress is, in part, from popular to private, the comic on the bare boards to the manager developing a coterie or courtly, baroque theatre.

In the private theatre, the playwright is a key figure of the repertory system. A literate, educated audience values a literary play and we have seen (p. 20) that Spruce and Spark bring their critical faculties to the script as well as to the playing. In popular theatre the player is more important than what he plays; his personality transcends his material, bravura acting counts more than the words uttered, the performer's personality outweighs the character he plays. A theatre of clowns, jigs and target practice, which is what the theatre at the Fortune and the Red Bull became, asks little of the scriptwriter. But the private theatre favoured wit in the dialogue, poetry in the passion and artful plotting: to an extent, it was a writer's theatre. The house poet was paid fifty pounds a year for three plays. Or, like Brome who left the Salisbury Court and went to the Phoenix, he might get even more elsewhere. If not princely, the rewards for the writer were very good.

Three kinds of dramatist served the private theatre: regular professionals contracted to a company, freelance writers who negotiated the sale of individual plays to companies of their choice but often had other means of support and, an increasing phenomenon, the amateur, often a court acolyte, who offered the occasional play to the professional theatre (inevitably the private sector) for the pleasure of seeing it performed.

In terms of new writing, the King's Men were served, for the most part, by the best writers. When they moved to the Blackfriars, Shakespeare was still the house poet but close to retirement. Of his plays, *The Winter's Tale* and *The Tempest* were certainly written after the move, and it has been argued that *Cymbeline* anticipates the Blackfriars playing conditions and the audience of the private theatre.[7] After Shakespeare's retirement about 1611, his place as principal (and contracted) playwright was taken by Fletcher whose importance in the development of seventeenth-century theatre has never been properly acknowledged or assessed. He wrote exclusively for the King's Men from the time of their move to Blackfriars until his death in 1625 and his collected works (in which the collaboration with such writers as Beaumont and Massinger is generally recognised but impossible now, as it evidently was then, to detail) contain fifty-two plays. (Of the sixty-one plays protected in 1641, twenty-one were by Fletcher.)

After Fletcher, the King's Men employed Massinger as principal playwright. About seventeen of his solo plays are extant, but many Fletcher plays evidently survive in a form given them subsequently by the later playwright. At Massinger's death, in 1640, the prolific James Shirley, who had written for Beeston at the Phoenix and then for the new theatre in Dublin, was engaged as house poet. Before the closure, he had written half a dozen plays for the King's Men, including his own favourite and most frequently anthologised tragedy, *The Cardinal* (1641).

A list of plays by Shakespeare, Fletcher, Massinger and Shirley would give us the central stock of repertory material for the period 1608–42 but would by no means exhaust the range of new work coming in. Jonson plays appeared sporadically – *The Alchemist* (1610), *The Devil Is An Ass* (1616), *The Staple of News* (1626), *The New Inn* (1629) and *The Magnetic Lady* (1632). *The Duchess of Malfi* was premiered at the Blackfriars in 1614. Several Middleton plays were written for the King's Men (including *Women Beware Women*) and three Ford plays, the lost *Beauty in a Trance* (?1630), *The Lover's Melancholy* (1628) and *The Broken Heart*.

Davenant contributed eight plays to the Blackfriars repertory (as well as the Globe play, *News from Plymouth*, 1635). He is a halfway figure between the professionals on one side and the group of amateur writers, dubbed the cavalier playwrights, on the other. The cavaliers wrote a small but significant group of plays performed at the Blackfriars (sometimes after premieres at court) in the 1620s and 1630s. They include Suckling (whose *Aglaura* is the most celebrated composition by this group), Carlell (the most prolific, with six King's Men's plays), Habington and Berkeley.

At the Phoenix, Christopher Beeston also built up a fine repertory. Characteristically, the plays which were performed at the Phoenix appear not to have been copyrighted to the particular company that first performed them but to Beeston himself who made them available to each succeeding company. He inherited, as house poet to Queen Anne's Men, the prolific Heywood who, we have seen, was well able to cater for a now socially superior audience. But the major playwrights associated with the Phoenix were Ford and Shirley.

Ford contributed five plays to the repertory, four premiered by Henrietta Maria's Men and the fifth, *The Lady's Trial* (1639), by Beeston's Boys. He is, in the judgment of history, the most important dramatist who wrote for the Phoenix. Shirley was contracted poet from 1625 when *Love Tricks* was licensed for performance until 1636 when, with playing interrupted by the plague and Beeston taking the opportunity to regroup, he went to Dublin to write for the new theatre there. During his Phoenix years he wrote about twenty plays, most of them extant.

Two notable Phoenix plays were Massinger's *A New Way to Pay Old Debts* (1622) and Jonson's *A Tale of a Tub* (1633). Among non-Phoenix plays annexed for the Phoenix companies from companies who played there were Webster's *The White Devil* (1612) and Middleton and Rowley's *The Changeling* (1622).

At the Salisbury Court, the major writer was Richard Brome, disciple and one-time servant of Jonson (in which capacity he is mentioned in the Induction of *Bartholomew Fair*). Brome had already written both for the Red Bull and the Blackfriars when he contracted to be house poet to the Salisbury Court. There he furnished six plays for the King's Revels before moving on to join Beeston.

In the extant plays of the dramatists writing for the private theatre between 1608 and 1642, there is, quite naturally, a broad range of material: comedy, tragedy, social observation and satire, fantasy, moral allegory and the compliment of courtly masque. Companies throve in part on an ability to ring the changes and made a corresponding demand on their poets. However, from the combined output of the most prolific and successful of the professional dramatists – Fletcher, Massinger and Shirley – it is evident that the staple diet of that long period is the romantic tragicomedy or heroic romance, the kind of play fashioned in those very years, 1608–11, when the King's Men were establishing themselves at the Blackfriars and producing such plays as *Cymbeline*, *The Winter's Tale*, *Philaster* and *A King and No King*. Fletcher, following Guarini, provided a critical description of the genre:

> A tragicomedy is not so called in respect of mirth and killing, but in respect it wants deaths, which is enough to make it no tragedy, yet brings some near it, which is enough to make it no comedy.[8]

Simultaneously, there develops alongside the tragicomedy its mirror image and first cousin, the comedy of manners with its characteristically urbane and satirical exposé of high life in a realistically depicted London setting. In both the tragicomedy and the comedy of manners, love and sexual relations are foregrounded and so a dramatic world is constructed in which women characters and their actions are at the heart of the play. Often, the romance plot and the comedy of manners were allied in a single drama. The tragedy proper does not disappear, but it often, now, looks like a tragicomedy except that the disastrous end is not averted, although an audience might be led to believe it could be.

The Fletcher canon is classifiable as follows: there are eighteen comedies (several of them comedies of manners, of which *The Wild Goose Chase* is the best example, its Paris setting being a thinly disguised London); twelve tragedies; two plays which cannot be classified; and the remainder, the largest group, are tragicomedies. Massinger's bent too is tragicomic and his work is often indistinguishable from that of Fletcher. Of his seventeen surviving plays, four are comedies (the best known, *A New Way to Pay Old Debts* not being entirely typical), five are tragedies and eight are tragicomedies. In Shirley, too, there is a marked tragicomic bias (*The Young Admiral*, for example, is written strictly to a Fletcherian formula), but the comedy of manners is also strongly represented in his work. In Davenant and the cavalier dramatists Fletcherian romance is again the model, and even in Ford its features are plainly discernible.

Mildmay's notes on his theatre-going, discussed in Chapter 2, provide a shortlist of plays at the Blackfriars and court in the 1630s, a sampling chosen, as it were, by a contemporary. There are twelve identifiable plays by six playwrights. Four are by Fletcher – *Rollo* (?1617), *The Elder Brother* (1625), *The Lover's Progress* (1623) and *The Mad Lover* (?1616); three are by Jonson – *Catiline* (1611), *Volpone* (1606) and *The Alchemist* (1610); two are by Davenant – *The Wits* (1633) and *Love and Honour* (1630); and there are one each by Shakespeare, Shirley and Carlell – *Othello* (1604), *The Lady of Pleasure* (1635) and *The Spartan Ladies* (1634). The last is lost. It was quite new when Mildmay saw it, as also were the Davenant plays and Shirley's. The rest are old repertory pieces, *Rollo* and *The Lover's Progress* recently revised by Massinger.

Four of the twelve (if we include *The Spartan Ladies*) are tragedies and the three surviving were included in Rymer's 1667 choice of the six best tragedies of the previous age. Five of the twelve are comedies, Jonson's being city satires, the others, *The Elder Brother*, *The Wits* and *The Lady of Pleasure*, comedies of manners. The remaining three, *The Lover's Progress*, *The Mad Lover* and *Love and Honour*, are tragicomedies. These plays tell us much about the development of the private theatre repertory from 1616 (*The Mad Lover*) to 1635 (*The Lady of Pleasure*).

Fletcher is the last of the major Jacobean dramatists to be rediscovered. Even now, a prevailing view maintains that he was a mere entertainer to a bored, sensation-seeking audience. Yet on the publication of his collected plays in 1647, Shirley could claim that the book was

> without flattery, the greatest monument of the scene that time and humanity have produced, and must live, not only the crown and sole reputation of our own, but the stain of all other nations and languages.

This is no mere inflation appropriate to this kind of puff material. Fletcher's plays (and their influence) had dominated the thirty years of adult private theatre before the closure. In the King's Men's plays at court in 1630–1, eight out of twenty-one were his, in 1636, nine out of twenty-two.

The four Fletcher plays in Mildmay, written between 1616 and 1625, represent the range of his dramatic work: social comedy (*The Elder Brother*) through tragicomedy (*The Lover's Progress*, *The Mad Lover*) to full-blown tragedy (*Rollo*). Each shows a characteristically Fletcherian mingling of tones in which the Jacobean grotesque is muted. The audience is addressed by a refined sensibility that insulates the harsh or brutal through an arch knowingness and cultivates a melodramatic concern for the softer sentiments of love, pity and sorrow.

Rollo was a highly popular play. Its date of composition is unknown (?1617) but it was revised by Massinger in 1630 and it enjoyed a series of revivals. Mildmay saw it in 1633 when Taylor played the lead and Lowin the supporting role (probably written for him). Rymer thought the play owed its success to the comic episodes, but he missed the consistently serious discussion of political morality it contains and took for granted Fletcher's facility in contriving scenes of immediate, theatrical impact.

Seriousness, in fact, is a feature not generally associated with Fletcher: the romance elements of his plays locate them often in a never-never-land where the laws of probability are suspended. But his characters debate important issues of the day and in a concerned manner calculated to engage the interest of a Blackfriars audience. In particular, his plays show a constant concern, obsessively shared by many of the audience, with the theme of personal honour. A sense of injured honour is the mainspring of the action of *The Elder Brother*, and *The Lover's Progress* contains an elaborate critique of the duel fought for honour's sake. In a general way, *The Elder Brother* is concerned with the fashioning of a gentleman (the two brothers of the play go through an educative process) and reminds us that Fletcher's wit 'made Blackfriars an academy' for the young gentleman auditor.

Wit is in the language and the plotting, and it is the latter, seen as theatrical virtuosity, that has caught the eye of the twentieth-century critic. But a sophisticated sense of narrative design impressed also Fletcher's own century. Writing in the 1647 collected edition, William Cartwright praised the elegant, *trompe l'oeil* effect of Fletcher's dramaturgy and did so in lines studded with mannerist touchstones – 'fancy', 'cheat', 'shadows', 'lights', 'design':

> None can prevent [= forsee] the fancy, and see through
> At the first opening: all stand wond'ring how
> The thing will be, until it is; which thence,
> With fresh delight still cheats, still takes the sense;

> The whole design, the shadows, the lights, such
> That none can say he hides or shows too much.

The Lover's Progress's teasing dramaturgy and convoluted structure, too complicated to summarise here but handled with great ease, show Fletcher's tragicomic wit at its best. This is perhaps no play for today, but its writerly skills are abundantly evident and all sentiment is braced by irony.

Davenant's theatre is simpler than Fletcher's and essentially courtly and Caroline. In him, mannerism shades into baroque, and in the tragicomedies an heroic strain is evident, in *Love and Honour* linked with a large element of sentimentality. *The Wits* and *Love and Honour* were written during a busy three years, 1633–5, in which the King's Men played four new plays by him. *Love and Honour* was licensed in 1634 and Mildmay saw it in that year. It was played at court in 1637 and continued to look actable property so that the King's Men blocked its publication in 1641. It tells a story of courageous and selfless love and the maids of its subtitle, 'The Matchless Maids', are as strong in their idealism as the men. There is a clear neo-platonic strain here and a flattery of Henrietta Maria's court and its sentiments. At the end, a tragic outcome is averted by a preposterous but predictable dénouement, arbitrary in the Fletcher mode.

To a modern eye, *The Wits* is much more attractive. It is a comedy of manners with labelling character names suggesting also a line of descent from Jonson. (A central plot motif in which the heroine, Lady Ample, feigns death to smoke out would-be inheritors clearly derives from *Volpone*.) But the satire is light of touch and the ending, in which Lady Ample's financially attractive hand is won in marriage by the Elder Pallatine, is genial, though not festive in the Shakesperian way. Lady Ample and her husband-to-be's younger brother each win their financial freedom by comic intrigue and are the true-wits of the play.

This is, indeed, a comedy of wit, and so a mirror image of *Love and Honour*, sense as opposed to sensibility. It is an open-eyed, realistic play about love and marriage choices in a world where financial considerations are primary. In Lady Ample many of the features of the Restoration comic heroine are discernible. Her younger sister, a Commonwealth away, is Millamant, and in creating her Davenant achieved his best private theatre work.

Mildmay saw *The Lady of Pleasure* in December 1635 and accorded it the brief, appreciative note, 'that rare play'. He may have admired the interweaving of a comedy-of-manners main plot centred on Lady Bornwell with a romance subplot centred on Celestine. Lady Bornwell is a careful portrait of the contemporary phenomenon, the woman who drags her husband to London and wastes the family fortune and her personal honour in a crass pursuit of luxury and novelty. She is framed by a detailed and realistic picture of the London of the pleasure-seeking class that made up a significant part of the audience.

The two heroines are initially presented in parallel terms but are then developed quite differently. Lady Bornwell's career leads to a moral chastening and at the end she returns to the country with her long-suffering husband. Celestine, on the other hand, demonstrates a strong sense of moral values in two striking scenes with Lord A in which he seeks to seduce her. At the same time, she shows a spirited independence and a disaffection with men that again anticipate the Restoration heroine, and she remains resolutely unmarried at the end of the play.

The Lady of Pleasure has both comic and serious strengths (its comedy is serious) and deserved Mildmay's admiration. To us Shirley's tragedies and tragicomedies appear now undistinguished. But in the best of his comedies, a comic-moral tradition from both Shakespeare and Jonson is energised by new ideas, and the plays show that dramatic vigour had not deserted the London stage of the 1630s. New directions were available to good professionals like Shirley even if society and theatre itself were in a state of crisis.

Part Two

Blackfriars Plays

5 · 'A Quaint Device': *The Tempest* at the Blackfriars

In Act III, scene iii of *The Tempest*, Ariel, costumed as a harpy, bursts on to stage and causes a banquet set out before the court party of Alonso and the others to disappear. The stage direction tells us that this is done 'with a quaint device', where 'quaint' means ingenious and thereby pleasing. It is a word Prospero uses elsewhere of Ariel himself, to praise the spirit's appearance as a water nymph (I,ii,319).[1] The disappearing banquet is a sleight of hand. It is a conjuror's trick, real magic to the courtiers and a stage illusion to the audience. An experiment in meta-theatre, the whole play explores the baffling territory marked out by 'magic', 'illusion' and 'trick'. The staging of the play is both device and meaning. Design, not narrative, is *The Tempest*'s major impulse and its structure is architectural, not dynamic. So far as we can tell it was a success on stage. Strange as it is (and 'strange' is a word much used in the play), Hemmings and Condell placed it first in the First Folio. Para-doxical and enigmatic, it occupies a special place too in theatre history and dramatic criticism. It is both a summation of Shakespeare's writing career and a radically experimental, new departure. Especially, it seems a 'quaintly' fashioned play appropriate to the Blackfriars.

The writing and first production of *The Tempest* can be dated reasonably accurately. Shakespeare derived a number of features of the story from the various accounts of Sir George Somers's ill-fated voyage to Virginia in 1609–10.[2] The accounts circulated in England in the last months of 1610 and the play itself was performed at Whitehall on 1 November 1611. Meanwhile, Simon Forman, an astrologer, likely to be interested in the play and perhaps himself a part model for Prospero, mentions having seen *Cymbeline* and *The Winter's Tale* at the Globe in the early summer of 1611 but not *The Tempest*. Either *The Tempest* was first played at the Blackfriars in the winter of 1610/11 but not acted at the Globe in the following summer, or, more likely, the play was premiered at the Black-friars season of autumn 1611 and was still quite new when it was played at court. We know of another court performance: as part of the festivities organised around the betrothal of Princess Elizabeth and the Elector Palatine in May 1613. But in 1670, Dryden wrote in the published edition of his adaptation of Shakespeare's play that the original 'had formerly been acted with success in the Blackfriars'. Dryden's collaborator was Davenant who should have known. On internal grounds, one would readily identify *The Tempest* as a 'private theatre' play for the Blackfriars and court. And it is the Blackfriars production that is the theme of this account.

In 1611, *The Tempest* had considerable topical interest for a Blackfriars audience. Members of the Virginia Company who had organised Somers's expedition and others who were investors in it were a part of that audience. Shakespeare himself was personally acquainted with prominent figures in the Council, and he had access to a letter about the wreck and the providential escape by those on board which had been written by William Strachey in Virginia on 15 July 1610 and was not available in print until 1625. Strachey soon followed his letter home and was himself living in Blackfriars by December 1611.

No single narrative source fits the whole play, but the Bermuda shipwreck and associated ideas concerning 'plantation' and New World natives provide a plausible starting-point for Shakespeare's composition. This then brought to mind, we may imagine, Montaigne's handling of similar topics in the essay 'Of the Cannibals', where Gonzalo's Utopia speech of II,i,139–64 finds its origin. Montaigne unironically paints an ideal version of the natural life free of the debilitating effects of sophisticated society. And this in turn suggests to Shakespeare Caliban (probably anagrammatised from 'Cannibal') who provides an antithetical comment on Montaigne's naturalism.

The plot is more or less completed by the magician motif, which itself was of topical, even Blackfriars, interest. Jonson's *The Alchemist* had been performed by Shakespeare's company in 1610. Its Dr Subtle, Aubrey thought, was based on the astrologer, mathematician and, it was reputed, necromancer, Dr John Dee. Dee, who died in 1608, had had connections with Western travel, coined the expression 'the British Empire', and advised navigators on technical matters. Forman, too, we have suggested, connects with Prospero. In September 1611 (two months before the play was certainly in production) he had predicted his own death while in good health and expired suddenly five days later. He, too, was interested in 'Plantation' and was a well-known figure in theatre circles (he rated a mention in *Epicoene* and would be referred to again after his death in *Bartholomew Fair*). He had also treated Shakespeare's landlady, both medically and astrologically. For the playwright and his audience, the mage was a noted contemporary – part scientist, part neo-platonist. Shakespeare's own plays provided models for Prospero's other features: as usurped monarch (*Much Ado about Nothing*), magical operator (*A Midsummer Night's Dream*) and abdicated ruler conducting a controlled experiment on his subjects (*Measure for Measure*).

The play's dramatic power is not developed through the conventional means of character conflict. Only Prospero, a 'god of power', can take significant action. The plot in effect is his, and the other *personae*, caught out of contingent time and confined by his experiment, can only react. Even the love story is developed within the master plan conceived and executed by Prospero.

The role was almost certainly written for Burbage. In 1611 he was at the height of his powers, the greatest actor of his generation, aged 37 or 38, who had played most of Shakespeare's tragic leads. Something of the character of Lear, whom he had first acted about five years earlier – banished king with faithful daughter – could be drawn on to endue the role with an epic quality which Shakespeare only sketches lightly in the later play – righteous anger dependent on a personally authentic sense of sovereignty. For Prospero is enigmatic where Lear is painfully transparent. His inner life remains largely hidden from the audience and he is aloof and magisterial in his relationship with the other characters. Indeed, his purpose in shipwrecking the court party is never clarified until the beginning of the final sequence (V,i,28–30). Until then we know there is a design; the play is his handiwork; he organises it with clock-watching precision and constantly dispatches Ariel to fashion its individual parts. But several times (I,ii, 320,498) the command is whispered so that the audience might not hear (not only the others on stage, note, for elsewhere in the play the convention of inaudibility is employed). Twice he refers to his 'project' (V,i, 1 and Epilogue, 1.12) and Ariel does so once (II,i, 294). But for four acts he maintains an elusiveness of intent (as opposed to a complexity of motivation) uncharacteristic of Shakespeare's leading characters. Vincentio in *Measure for Measure*, for example, explains his purpose even if underlying, unconscious motivations are only half-expressed. But Prospero is as detached from us as from the other characters. He evidently feels deeply, but we are not expected to feel with him. The modern actor, who, playing Prospero, tries to explain the enigma takes a different line from that of Burbage.

Burbage, however, brought something else. For it was he, in all probability, who had played Jonson's Dr Subtle a year earlier. *The Alchemist*, remaining in the repertory (like *The Tempest* it was played at court in 1613) would inevitably colour not only Burbage's playing but also an audience's reception of Shakespeare's play about a conjuror. Subtle is the other side of the coin – magician as charlatan. He is an illusionist whose art is cheating not charming and he is exiled from his little empire at the end of the play, not welcomed home in triumph. Prospero is a 'projector' too and his solemn intensity was in part permitted by the shadow figure of the comic magician of the earlier play remaining in Burbage's portrayal. A Blackfriars audience at *The Tempest* would not only see a Burbage-Lear-Prospero stage figure but also a Burbage-Subtle-Prospero stage figure.[3]

Prospero's is the dominant role in *The Tempest* in all important respects. He has over 600 lines of a short play (the second shortest in the canon), and the next biggest part, Ariel's, tops 200 lines only if we add in (as we probably may) Ceres' lines as well. (At IV,i, 167 Ariel explains that he played Ceres in the masque.) In fact, ten of the seventeen speaking (and singing) roles only have between 100 and 200 lines, so that character development outside Prospero is flattened out in an unusual manner. Only Pericles, elsewhere in Shakespeare, and possibly Hamlet, so out-talk their fellow characters.

The casting of the play by the King's Men would have caused little difficulty (and granted, perhaps, small satisfaction). There are thirteen parts for adult actors and four for boys if we assume, as we should, that Ariel was played by a boy. There was no doubling, because all the adult male characters are on stage together at the end of the play and all four characters for boys appear together. (The King's Men normally had four boy actors and so the doubling of Ariel and Ceres, or something like it, becomes inevitable; Shakespeare makes a virtue of necessity by referring to it in the play.) The Master's is a strange role – three lines in scene i when he abdicates responsibility (and the stage) to the Boatswain, and no word on his other appearance at the end when, by rank, he might be expected to relate the events on board ship. (It is tempting to see this as a Hitchcockian cameo for Shakespeare himself in his last play.) All other parts, including the three very minor ones of Adrian, Francisco and the Boatswain, have something clear and theatrically emphatic to do at some point of the play, even though it is rightly maintained by critics and experienced by actors that, apart from Ariel and Caliban, they are handled in a perfunctory and flat manner. They lack an individual language and sharp personality and are subordinated to the overall design.

Beside the speaking roles, the play calls for a squad of supernumaries who people the spirit world. The company would normally provide extras from the backstage staff to play walk-ons like the mariners of I,i. But something more organised is needed for the Shapes (III,iii), the dance team of Nymphs and Reapers (IV,i) and the hunting dogs (also IV,i). Especially in the masque scene the normal company personnel would be overstretched, though actors of other roles might here have doubled the roles of Reapers. For none of these episodes does Shakespeare specify an exact number of spirits, though only three dogs are named in the hunting.

But in that characteristic self-reflexivity of the play, Prospero demands that to the masque Ariel 'bring a corollary, Rather than want a spirit', and the outer play would benefit from the same generous treatment. Evidently, the King's Men could draw on a number of trained extras to fill the ranks. For *The Winter's Tale* of the previous year, a scene required on stage six principals, shepherds and shepherdesses to make up a dance, and then a troupe of twelve satyrs. Perhaps the Chapel Royal, now without a regular playing operation of their own, might have supplied these choreographed (and in I,ii singing) extras. They would need to be well trained.

Who filled the other roles is mere (though interesting) speculation. Ariel, we have assumed, was played by a boy. Prospero, whether affectionate or vexed, treats him like a child, certainly as someone small of stature: he calls him 'delicate', 'dainty' and 'chick'. The spirit adopts for much of the play the costume of a sea-nymph and he evidently plays the part of Ceres in the masque. William Poel, whose instincts in these matters were often right, evidently thought he was played by an adult. But an Elizabethan boy actor would not bring to his playing of Ariel the kind of naive charm that a child actor of today would, and his training would provide the physical and musical skills necessary for the part. Richard Robinson was the principal company juvenile at the time, but, an experienced female impersonator, he may well have played Miranda rather than Ariel.

Lowin customarily played the second leads. In this play devoid of major supporting roles, that of Caliban might well have gone to him, although Shakespeare developed the part oddly. For, as Caliban begins as a strong protagonist set in opposition to Prospero, he features increasingly as a comic foil for Trinculo and Stephano. Nevertheless, a figure of physical menace and no longer youthful, Caliban would need to be played by a mature actor capable of both the passion and the poetry of the part. Lowin may well have been cast here, his large frame made suitably grotesque by the tiremen.

Trinculo would presumably be played by the King's Men's regular comedian, Robert Armin. Armin had played Shakespeare's other professional fools, Touchstone, Feste and probably the Fool in *King Lear*. But this fool is kept away from the ranking characters in the play and is forced to expend his wit on a man-monster and a drunken butler. Rather than providing a stalking-horse for the playwright's satire, he becomes the comic butt of the true wit of the play, Ariel. Outside the characters of Prospero and to a limited extent Ariel and Caliban, there is little challenge here for the King's Men's actors. It is not, in fact, an actor's play.

In a specialised sense, *The Tempest* is a designer's play. Short of conflict and rounded characterisation, it has always been staged in a spectacularly visual way. At the Restoration, rewritten by Dryden and Shadwell, it was rapidly converted into a baroque melodrama, complete with elaborate, moveable scenery and complex flying effects. When restored to Shakespeare's script in the nineteenth century, *The Tempest* was still the excuse for a lavish display of pantomime stage effects. A reviewer of Beerbohm Tree's production at His Majesty's in 1904 observed that Tree had 'stage-managed Shakespeare out of sight'.[4] Meanwhile, William Poel's non-scenic, 'Elizabethan' production of the play in 1897 encouraged Bernard Shaw to see the special gains of simple staging:

> It requires the nicest judgment to know exactly how much help the imagination wants. There is no general rule, not even for any particular author. You can do best without scenery in *The Tempest* and *A Midsummer Night's Dream*, because the best scenery you can get will only destroy the illusion created by the poetry.[5]

Much earlier, Coleridge, talking of *The Tempest*, had argued against 'the complicated machinery and decorations of modern times' which in Shakesperian productions distracted 'the moved and sympathetic imagination' of the audience from the true focus, 'the spiritual vision' of the play.[6] It is all about delusion versus illusion, the 'glistering apparel' set before Caliban and his crew versus 'the most majestic vision' presented to Ferdinand and Miranda. The play at large is constantly concerned with the matter and so must have been the Blackfriars production and its audience.

The Blackfriars playhouse where, according to Dryden, *The Tempest* was a popular success, was non-scenic (see Chapter 3). The stage was a platform for the actors, not a locale realistically presented through flats, borders and curtains. The 'scene' is the architectural, upstage wall providing entrances, discovery-space and gallery over; and stage left and right the action is closed in by the stage-sitters. 'Design' for the play will concern actors, properly costumed and carefully blocked, together with a few, simple properties. And it will create a series of shows, which is largely the substance of the play.

It is worth referring here to the persuasive argument that in its court performance in the Banqueting Hall, Hallowmas night, 1611, the play might have been decked out with stock scenic elements built for, and left over from, previous masques. A whole topography for the play, it is argued, can be assembled out of the timber and canvas realisation of masques such as *Oberon* (ten months earlier) and others: a seashore, rocks, clouds, a cave and a wood.[7] But it is difficult to imagine that a play intended for the Blackfriars repertory should receive a radically different staging at court; and though 'canvas for the booths and other necessaries' were provided for *Bartholomew Fair* at court in 1614 (see p. 181) and Inigo Jones built scenery for *The Faithful Shepherdess* for its court revival in 1634, on economic grounds alone it is unlikely that plays were regularly produced in this way at Whitehall. The King's Men themselves gave twenty-two plays at court between 31 October 1611 and 26 April 1612.

Nevertheless, it is clear that in *The Tempest* Shakespeare was experimenting with graphic kinds of stage imagery. A special poetry is developed in place of the verbal richness of the earlier plays.[8] The audience is given a series of stage pictures which, like the visions in a dream, have a sharp-edged clarity and a sense of careful composition. They seem, again as in a dream, to be both emblematic and not readily accessible to simple interpretation. For the play moves in a masque-like way, proceeding by way of a series of counterpointed events that act like revelations or epiphanies. Again, the relation to dream is insistent, and the characters themselves suspect they are inhabiting a dream. But the shows are not dream-work but a species of art-work, created by artist Prospero.

In a special way, it is imperative that the magic island should not be scenically realised. To the different characters it becomes a different place; they each impose on it a construction that comes from their personality and their moral bias. Though fictively 'real' (it exists prior to Prospero's discovery of it), it is a symbolic landscape: for Gonzalo, a Utopia; for Ferdinand, a new Garden of Eden where Adam re-meets Eve; for Antonio and Sebastian, a desert place; for Caliban, an empire and possession; for Ariel, a prison; for Prospero, a 'poor isle' where he refinds his dukedom and loses his daughter. The realistic topography is amply created by the one most concerned to live in and by it, Caliban. His densely specific poetry realises a world of plants, animals and fish, rocks and springs, and the attendant diseases and discomforts of nature in the raw. But the island is essentially a pastoral, unreal world incapable of being imaged concretely. What the actors had was the 'magic' space of the Blackfriars stage, unlocalised, where they might 'enact [Shakespeare's] present fancies'.

Legitimate visual display derives partly from the action, partly from the characterisation. For the latter, to an unremarkable extent it concerns the conventional Elizabethan emphasis on costume denoting the man and his function. For much of the play, Prospero wears his 'magic garment' over normal clothes (we might assume a robe covered in cabalastic signs, the badge of the magician) and he carries a staff. But at the climax of the play he changes costume onstage to mark his resumption of his true role as duke: 'I will discase me, and myself present As I was sometime Milan' (V,i,85–6). And so his rapier and hat are brought out, his robe taken away. We should expect Trinculo to wear the Fool's outfit of suit of motley and coxcomb. Perhaps he carried a bauble. Stephano would have been costumed as Butler to the King to make his assumption of regal power the more ridiculous. His and Trinculo's final appearance in their 'stolen apparel' is an apt comment. The court party's clothes too would describe their wearers in social terms, and it is interesting that Shake-speare insists, twice over, that they are unspoiled by the sea-drenching they have received. Indeed they are 'rather new-dyed than stained with salt water' (II,i,61–2). For the courtiers are not firstly shipwrecked survivors; they are aristocrats and rulers of men exiled from their preferred surroundings into a pastoral world.

So far, then, there is nothing unduly taxing for the keeper of the King's Men's wardrobe, all stock commodities. But in Ariel and Caliban, the company confronted a significant design challenge, perhaps the most crucial in the whole of Shakespeare. In a play which moves easily within a nexus of ideas we recognise as neo-platonic, by their very appearance these two non-realistic figures necessarily impose a large element of the play's meaning. We shall return to them.

Visual display which derives from the play's action is present at every turn in a composition almost excessively full of variety and invention. Five episodes in particular, each a spectacular *coup de théâtre*, show Shake-speare's confidence in the staging ability of the Blackfriars company, though each works through simple theatrical means contrived from actors, their costume and careful blocking. These are the shipwreck of I,i, Ferdi-nand's meeting with Miranda in I,ii, the banquet of III,iii, the masque of IV,i and the chess game of V,i. (It is worth mentioning here that the first printing of the text, in the First Folio, contains unusually detailed and impressionistic stage directions. They might be Shakespeare's or those of an eye-witness. Either way, they enable the 'reconstruction' of several of these episodes with more confidence than we might normally allow.)

In Act I, scene i, Shakespeare writes the first of two prologues for the play, the 'dramatic' one[9] which will make possible the leisurely, recap-ping, story-so-far that occupies a good deal of scene ii. The location is shipboard, the action is tempest at sea and, at the moment, the audience is not aware of Prospero's control through his agent, Ariel. Later productions have sometimes shown Prospero's hand too early. It is important that to the audience, as to those aboard, it is a 'real' storm. For a Jacobean audience and for us, the initial 'meaning' is human frailty confronted by the elemental powers in nature.

The first effect is aural. No dimming of the houselights, of course, but in the enclosed (roofed) space at the Blackfriars, an emphatic opening: '*A tempestuous noise of thunder and lightning is heard.*' The comic illogicality (the noise of lightning?) happily catches the notion of cosmic chaos and the play will exploit at other moments a richly combined assault upon the senses of the audience. Squibs from the upper level of the Blackfriars facade or a resin box provided the lighting and the thunder was mimicked by drums in the tiring-house or music room or by cannonballs rolled in a thunder run, perhaps a combination of the two. And offstage sound effects from a sea machine (small pebbles revolved in a drum) and a wind machine (a loose length of canvas turned on a wheel) would complete a compelling storm sequence, probably enhanced by an echo from the high roof-space over the auditorium. Jonson deplored this kind of thing. He preferred his own kind of naturalistic theatre where

> [No] nimble squib is seen to make afear'd
> The gentlewomen; nor roll'd thunder heard
> To say, it thunders; nor tempestuous drum
> Rumbles, to tell you when the storm doth come.[10]

Shakespeare and Prospero were not so purist. They both had greater faith in the power of theatrical illusion.

The ship itself is largely presented through dialogue and action. The first, carefully placed word is 'Boatswain' (is this the major function of the Master?) and the next eight lines, nautically technical but explicit to the layman, deftly present ship, storm, nearness of land and imminence of shipwreck. Shipboard scenes are frequent in Elizabethan drama and more ambitious stage action is required in other plays than here. With confidence, the playwright expects the actors to create and sustain the illusion. '*Enter mariners wet*' (after l. 50) is a graphic piece of theatre shorthand, and the offstage voices – '*A cry within*' (l. 35) and '*A confused noise within*' (l. 58) – combine with onstage shouting and a good deal of frantic rushing about to present a little world of fear and disaster at sea. A. C. Sprague, describing the New Mermaid production of 1951, bears testimony to the effectiveness with which this scene will work when staged in a simple, 'Elizabethan' manner:

> The scene began with a clap of thunder and howling wind. In each of the two windows [above the stage, on the 'gallery'] a ship's lantern swung back and forth. Ropes and a ladder were lowered from somewhere above the gallery. A trapdoor opened and became a hatchway; the upper stage, the upper deck. Sailors, shouting orders, clung for support to the pillars, or swarmed up the tackling. It was as if the ship were there before our eyes! Yet, as crew and passengers departed and the ropes dropped out of sight through the trap, it was gone again in an instant.[11]

And so it must, for the play structurally makes much of abrupt transitions and the opening of scene ii 'explains' and completes scene i. We hear straightway of Prospero's Art (insistently capitalised throughout the

First Folio) and it is that art that controls nature, evoking a harmless 'tempest' first 'believed in' by the audience. Miranda knows that the tempest is Prospero's but she does not know how it was done (nor, indeed, that it is harmless). But Ariel's entrance, in a little while, clarifies the matter finely, for he 'perform'd to point the tempest' (l.194) as his master had bade him; or, in other words, the tempest was a theatrical illusion, a device or trick. Scene i is a brief masterpiece, possible to stage at the Globe, but deriving from the enclosed and smaller Blackfriars greater affective power, and offering a literate audience an inconographic statement, bound up in conventional emblem book imagery, of human constancy in an inconstant world (Gonzalo's ironies about the Boatswain alerted the spectators to this).

The scenery of the first scene is in fact largely acoustical, and before an analysis of the other 'shows', it is appropriate to discuss the importance of sound effects generally in the play. The thunder will recur throughout. It opens II,ii – '*A noise of thunder heard*' – and is present again at Ariel's entrance as the Harpy in III,iii ('*Thunder and lightning*') and his exit ('*He vanishes in Thunder*'). Alonso hears the thunder, conscience-stricken as he is, pronounce Prospero's name (III,i, 97–8), and it is one of the devices in the list of magical powers that Prospero resolves to abandon (V,i 44–5). But noises of all kinds, as Caliban famously describes at III,ii, 133–41, fill the island, and Shakespeare scored these with a frequency that suggests an artist's pleasure in a new resource, new in its controllability.

The principal sound is music and *The Tempest* is Shakespeare's most musical play, a genuine melodrama. Music expresses both the functioning and the effect of Prospero's magic, the world of spirit, hallucination and dream, and it relates the group of ideas concerned with the harmony of the spheres and astral influences. But disharmonious sound is also prominent, sound effects which tell of chaos, pain and punishment. There is the thunder which surrounds the wicked with the promise of retribution, and the fear of the sailors in I,i, '*a confused noise within*'. 'Confused' is used again of the interrupted masque in IV,i when the masquers vanish '*to a strange, hollow and confused noise*'. Hollow, too (an effect of the roofed auditorium), would be the baying of the dogs as a prelude to the routing of Caliban and the others at the end of the same scene – '*a noise of hunters*' is heard, and then the pain of the hunted: 'Hark, they roar'. The characters' senses are heightened in the animistic world of the magic island and other sounds tug at the mind. Antonio claims to hear the roaring of bulls or lions in II,i, but Gonzalo, wakened by Ariel's song, remembers confusedly 'a humming, And that a stange one too'. Trinculo, taken up with simpler problems, hears the storm 'sing i' th' wind'. And Alonso, made mad by the Harpy's peroration, is accused by voices in the elements:

Methought the billows spoke, and told me of it;
The winds did sing it to me; and the thunder,
That deep and dreadful organ-pipe, pronounced
The name of Prosper.

(III,iii, 96–9)

As for the actual theatre music, Alonso's 'dreadful organ-pipe' may have been actually employed at the Blackfriars. In the play, song and instrumental pieces alternate in a rich score that exists now largely in the suggestive descriptions of the stage directions. There are nine songs in the play (three of them, all in II,ii, probably unaccompanied), six pieces of orchestral music and, most probably, four *entr'acte* sequences that Shakespeare's pedantic observation of a five-act structure gives opportunity for, or is deliberately accommodated by. Settings survive for 'Full Fathom Five' (I,ii) and 'Where the Bee Sucks' (V,i). They were written by the King's musician, lutenist Robert Johnson, and it is suggested they were composed for a court revival. But Johnson wrote music for several King's Men's plays (including the madmen's song in *The Duchess of Malfi*) and he may well have played in the Blackfriars orchestra. Perhaps he composed the whole score for the original production; certainly something more is required than a rehashing of popular melodies.

The orchestra might well have been a broken consort of strings and woodwind. But this was probably augmented by an organ to produce the sonorous and unearthly music the play requires. For though music in *The Tempest* evidently provides a continuum of localising references and a prompting of sensuous impressions that makes it the play's true scenery, in particular, and at the various climaxes except the last, music enacts Prospero's magic power – drawing Ferdinand to his meeting with Miranda, charming the court party asleep and rousing them again, accompanying the dance of the Shapes around the banquet and finally leading the court party, 'spell-stopped', into the magic circle where their brains are unscrambled by 'A solemn air, and the best comforter to an unsettled fancy'. Only a full sympathy towards the Renaissance belief in the ethical, religious and therapeutic effects of music will release all the significance of what Shakespeare is doing in this music-theatre. But his (or his editor's) grace notes (in stage direction) help: 'solemn', 'solemn and strange', 'soft', 'soft', and 'solemn'. And to these we may add the character's responses: 'Sure, it waits upon some god o' th' island'; 'what harmony is this? . . . Marvellous, sweet music'; 'harmonious charmingly'; 'some heavenly music'. 'Charm' is the key word – meaning magical incantation, song (Latin *carmen*), and the mixed warbling of birds. The island is literally charming. And most musical of all is Prospero's own bird, Ariel, whose name and Folio description, 'an airy spirit', contain the pun on air (= ether and melody).

Ariel's whole being is expressed through the power of song. He plays pipe and tabor and probably also accompanied himself at the Blackfriars on the lute. And he tells Prospero, with pride, that he so lured Caliban and the others with his playing that

> they prick'd their ears,
> Advanc'd their eyelids, lifted up their noses,
> As they smelt music: so I charm'd their ears.
>
> (IV,i, 176–8)

The final sound of the play, rhythmic and life-enhancing like the music, and able, too, to effect a magical release, is also scored by Shakespeare. Prospero, in abrogating his magic powers, also gives up his music. So the play does not end with a festive dance to celebrate the forthcoming marriage. Instead, 'his charms o'erthrown', Prospero requests in the Epilogue that the audience will work its own magic to release him from the confinement of the stage: by applause.

Much of Act I, scene ii is occupied by the careful introductions of first Ariel and then Caliban. Shakespeare, in almost mannered fashion, contrives that we think of them in opposition to each other. When Prospero demands Caliban's entrance and his grumble has been heard offstage (ll. 315–17), suddenly Ariel reappears ('*like a water-nymph*') and is promptly despatched before Caliban's actual (and smouldering) first appearance. The sequence demands exact timing (the entrances are upstage left and right) and the stage business is complicated by the fact that Miranda, reluctantly awaiting Caliban, does not see Ariel (who is 'invisible') or catch her father's aside. The whole episode runs thus:

PROS   What, ho! slave! Caliban!
      Thou earth, thou! speak.
CAL *within*   There's wood enough within.
PROS   Come forth, I say! there's other business for thee;
      Come, thou tortoise! when?
       [Re-] enter ARIEL like a water-nymph
      Fine apparition! My quaint Ariel,
      Hark in thine ear.
ARI   My lord, it shall be done. *Exit*
PROS   Thou poisonous slave, got by the devil himself
      Upon thy wicked dam, come forth!
      Enter CALIBAN.

So, much of the play proceeds by pairing opposites and the stagecraft here emphasises that.

The stage appearances of Ariel and Caliban are vital and a Jacobean record would be invaluable. In many ways they are a precise pairing – servants to Prospero, but opposite in their temperaments and physiques. They have complementary, elemental allegiances, to air and fire the one, to earth and water the other. Ariel is a thing of spirit and without human sentience; Caliban a thing of matter, bestial and sensual. In an allegorical reading of the play, they act as linked cyphers. An audience aware of the conventions of the court masque, as a Blackfriars audience would be, would see them as hieroglyphs.

Ariel, who probably owes his origins to Shakespeare's reading in Agrippa and other hermetic writings, is a type of Mercury, the winged god associated by Renaissance emblem writers with the notion, so germane to the play, that 'Art is a help to nature'. (In this role, Mercury is pictured mending a lute.) Ariel is the arch shape-changer in a play of metamorphosis. He shifts costumes readily to act out roles assigned by Prospero, a kind of Face to Prospero's Subtle, and in his own person he is seen only by his master. It was suggested earlier that he was played by a boy and we should expect a boy to express the character's sexlessness well (Caliban is all male libido). One idea for his appearance comes from Jonson's Jophiel, in the masque *The Fortunate Isles* (1625). Jonson may be making, in fact, a deliberate allusion to Shakespeare's character. Jophiel is part of a sustained Rosicrucian satire but is also 'the intelligencer of Jupiter's sphere'. (Dee's presiding spirit, Uriel, a variant of Ariel, was also connected with Jupiter.) In fact, Jonson's description of Jophiel in the text does not square with Inigo Jones's design (see Plate 9). But Ernest Law neatly conflates description and design to give Ariel

a close-fitting tunic of silk in rainbow colours, wings tinctured in harmony with it, a scarf over his shoulders, buskins or blue stockings, and on his head a chaplet of flowers.[12]

If the whole effect strikes us as too pretty for Shakespeare's moody sprite, we should remember again that a boy actor would not bring to the part the naive charm (in its modern sense) characteristically expressed by child performers of today.

There is no certain indication in the text that Ariel was flown, though that became his customary form of locomotion at the Restoration. The Folio text marks his entrance and exits in conventional manner except for '*Vanishes*' at the end of the Harpy episode. In any case, for much of the play he is habited like a sea-nymph and flying would be indecorous. Jophiel 'entereth in running' and we can assume that for the actor of Ariel, a shimmering costume, light and speedy stage movements and the verbal imagery of rapid motion which he employs would do the trick.

His first costume change into sea-nymph requires attention. It is often taken to be a whimsy on Shakespeare's part or a mere excuse to get

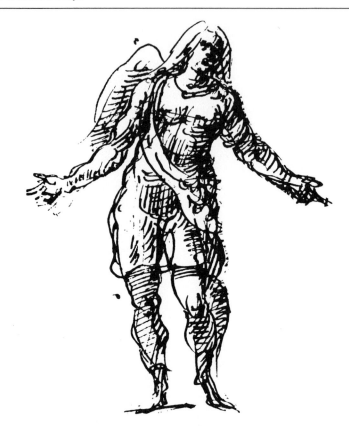

9   Inigo Jones's costume design for Jophiel in *The Fortunate Isles*, 1625

him off stage. But Prospero's purpose is clear enough: the sea-nymph appearance will guarantee invisibility in the presence of all mortals in the play bar Prospero himself. The relevant lines run:

> Go make thyself like a nymph o' th' sea:
> Be subject to no sight but mine; invisible
> To every eyeball else. Go take this shape,
> And hither come in 't. Go; hence.

ARI   With diligence. *Exit*

(I, ii, 301–6)[13]

When Ariel returns, he earns the praise quoted at the start of this chapter: 'Fine apparition! My quaint Ariel'. He is then promptly despatched so that he might invisibly (but audibly) draw Ferdinand to the meeting with Miranda.

The sea-nymph costume that confers invisibility (and Ariel is 'invisible' in stage directions twice – a little later in this same scene, after 1.375, and in III, ii, after l.39) is evidently not the conventional costume in the inventory of the Admiral's Men ('robe for to go invisible') often quoted in connection with this. Ariel's costume confers invisibility by making him look like a sea-nymph, as though the costume merged with the surroundings – the marine ambience of the play-in-performance. How so is not clear, unless (mere speculation, this) the tiring-house facade, or part of it, were hung with curtains representing a seascape. Tapestries or painted cloths were used on stage facades (the *Messalina* woodcut (p. 32) shows one) and at least once in the public playhouses we hear of the stage being draped with black for a tragedy (see the Induction to *A Warning for Fair Women*, 1599). Perhaps Ariel, at will, by standing against such a cloth, 'disappears' – exactly the kind of theatre illusion that evokes and parallels the magic of a spirit world. And of course, almost uniquely here, the playhouse architecture of doors and the like is irrelevant narratively to the play. Ariel's other costumes will be discussed with the staging of those episodes in which they appear.

For Caliban, the text tells us much, even too much about his appearance; it is difficult to create a coherent stage image out of seemingly inconsistent references. For the literary critic, ambiguity is exciting, something that is part of Shakespeare's purpose.[14] But for the King's Men, Caliban needed a precise shape and texture and these had to be created by Lowin (probably) with the careful aid of costume and make-up.

The way of playing Caliban has undergone radical transformations over the centuries (as Hamlet's psyche has yielded to the prevailing ethos, so has Caliban's appearance). There are no contemporary references to his Jacobean shape save those in the text. Resuming stage life at the Restoration in the Davenant and Shadwell adaptations, he is remembered as a type of drunkard and an apt comparison for the bucolic Sir Wilful Witwoud in *The Way of the World*: 'When [Sir Wilful] is drunk, he's as loving as the monster in *The Tempest*, and much after the same manner.' Pepys, going backstage, found Caliban's costume 'very droll'. Rymer stressed his humanity: ''Tis not necessary for a man to have a nose on his face, nor to have two legs: he may be a true man though awkward and unsightly, as the Monster in *The Tempest*.' But the Restoration Caliban is Trinculo and Stephano's. Only they call him monster.

The First Folio *dramatis personae* gives us three separate ideas in 'a salvage and deformed slave'. 'Slave' refers both to a political status and a moral character, for Caliban became slave only after the attempted rape of Miranda. (It was current doctrine that those incapable of being good Christians should be made slaves.) 'Deformed' has both a physical and an ethical colouring, in a play suffused with neo-platonic ideas. 'Salvage', as spelt here, retains an archaic form that refers us back to the word's etymological connection with Latin *silva*, a wood. In part, Caliban is that medieval, mythic creature, the wild man of the forests, hairy and primitive, capable of rudimentary social habits but one 'on whose nature Nurture can never stick'. And his name is probably an anagram of 'cannibal' which itself derives from Carib (a native of the southern West Indies).

Of physical details in the text, fish references begin early (II, ii, 24–39) and return late (V, i, 265–6). But elsewhere Caliban has hands with fingers and nails (IV, i, 245; IV, i, 220; II, ii, 168), bare feet (II, i, 11), is not ape-like with low forehead (IV, i, 246–8) and can be pinched from toe to crown (IV, i, 233). Prospero calls him a tortoise (though probably because of his inertia) and to Trinculo he is 'puppy-headed' (which may only mean stupid). Prospero implies he has a human shape (I, ii, 281–4) and Miranda first regards him as a man (I, ii, 447–8), then later appears not to do so (III, i, 50–2). Prospero calls him 'slave' (five times), 'hag-seed', 'beast' and 'demi-devil'. To Trinculo and Stephano he is 'moon-calf' (four times), 'monster' (thirty-three times) and various 'monster' combinations – 'man-monster', 'half fish half monster', 'servant-monster' and 'bully-monster'. He might be dark coloured ('this thing of darkness') though born freckled. And he wears a gaberdine in II, ii, a cloak large enough for Trinculo to crawl under and play the monster with four legs. There is a description of a sea monster encountered in a voyage of 1597 and not published till 1625 which picks up many of the physical details referred to here. Perhaps Shakespeare read something like this in manu-script. In any case, it seems we can arrive no nearer to how the King's Men's actor got himself up to play the role:

> He was ash-coloured on the back, and white on the belly, hairy like an oxe but rougher. . . . He was ten spans long, thicker than a man; his tail thick, a span long, ears of a dog, arms like a man without hair, and at the elbows great fins like a fish . . . [the natives] thought him (they said) the son of the Devil.[15]

What Shakespeare created was not some version of the noble savage (although Caliban frequently and fashionably appears like that on today's stage) but a genuine grotesque, half man half beast, something outside nature. Jonson scorned Caliban's unrealism in the prologue to *Bartholomew Fair:* 'If there be never a servant monster in the fair, who can help it?' His own moon-calf, Ursula's tapster, is a 'natural' in the Jacobean sense of congenital idiot. When Trinculo calls Caliban a 'natural' (III, ii, 31) he alerts us to Shakespeare's confidence in what he is about as a creative artist (it is of the playwright's invention of this character that Dryden first used 'create' in the literary sense). As a show and taken to Europe, as Trinculo would have him, Caliban, a thing of nature, is the opposite of 'a quaint device'. As Shakespeare's invention, he is exactly that. Finally, it is worth stressing that in the comic, underplot scenes

Caliban shares with Trinculo and Stephano (II, ii, III, ii and IV, i), he is consistently presented as a comic butt and the excuse for a series of *lazzi*. He is the Indian drunk on fire-water who crassly judges Stephano to be god-like and would exchange him as master for Prospero. He leaves the stage at the end of the play chastened and seeking grace. Though his significance as victim of 'plantation' was far from lost on Shakespeare, inevitably, on the modern stage we create a sentimentalised version far from the original. Prospero and Shakespeare knew Caliban was 'A devil, a born devil on whose nature Nurture can never stick'. We no longer have the confidence of a Blackfriars audience in the value of nurture, but Shakespeare's play, in its 'quaintness', is about that very issue.

Caliban's grumbling exit in I, ii is followed immediately by the second of the five major shows that Prospero contrives as part of his moral experiment: the meeting of Ferdinand and Miranda. As Caliban exits through one stage door, Ariel leads in Ferdinand by the other. Prospero and Miranda are downstage, and Miranda remains unaware of the entrance, and of the music which accompanies it, for several minutes. Probably Prospero indicates to the audience that he shields her from it. Ariel, invisible through the sea-nymph costume and accompanying himself perhaps on the lute, sings 'Come unto these yellow sands', which re-enacts the stilling of the sea-tempest, and then 'Full fathom five'. He has a chorus of offstage spirits and the music from above appears to be handled quadraphonically, so that Ferdinand cannot place its origin. Here, especially in rehearsal and conducting, Robert Johnson's skills were essential. The second song acts as a dirge for the dead father. It expresses lyrically the idea of nature renewed by art into beauty, and in the music that remains of Johnson it is surprisingly cheerful, almost gay. The intention is clear. Music that mourns Alonso's assumed death is also therapy that permits Ferdinand to go on living; he grows through the experience from funeral to marriage without appearing heartless. The knell of 'Ding dong bell' is thus also the signal for the magic meeting, and Ferdinand becomes a piece of theatre presented by Prospero to Miranda:

PROS The fringed curtains of thine eye advance,
    And say what thou seest yond.
MIR What is 't? a spirit?

(I, ii, 411–12)

Now the climax of the episode is reached as the couple 'change eyes'. Prospero's commentary and assumed brusqueness have a deflationary force and the whole love-match will proceed only with his hidden connivance. So Ferdinand is humiliated and overpowered. A gesture of the magic staff defeats his attempt at self-assertion: '*He draws, and is charmed from moving.*'

The scene then ends twice over. In the outer play mounted by Prospero, Ferdinand the traitor is harshly imprisoned, but succoured by the affectionate concern of Miranda. In the inner play, Ferdinand's courage and constancy are tested in a rite of passage. And meanwhile, Ariel is organised to oversee the next part of the project.

In III, iii, Prospero's testing of the court party has a profoundly different flavour. The episode is elaborate and full of high design and the stage business is described in three detailed stage directions nominated here (a), (b) and (c).

Alonso and the others enter exhausted and demoralised. There are six maned characters onstage and others in attendance (the entry ends with '*&c.*'). Several sit down while Sebastian and Antonio move to one side to reaffirm their decision to kill the king at 'the next advantage'. Then

(a)   Solemn and strange music; and PROSPER *on the top (invisible).* *Enter several strange Shapes, bringing in a banquet; and dance about it with gentle actions of salutations; and inviting the King, & c., to eat, they depart.* (after l. 17)

After some discussion, the courtiers approach the banquet to eat.

(b)   Thunder and lightning. Enter ARIEL *like a Harpy, claps his wings upon the table, and with a quaint device, the banquet vanishes.* (after l. 52)

Ariel as Harpy charms the courtiers, reproves Alonso, Antonio and Sebastian as 'three men of sin', and demands 'heart sorrow And a clear life ensuing'.

(c)   *He vanishes in thunder; then, to soft music, enter the Shapes again, and dance, with mocks and mows, and carrying out the table.* (after l. 82)

Sound effects, mime, props and costume all combine here to create a piece of theatre that is (characteristically in this play) both emblematic and dream-like. The Shapes carry in the table from behind the curtain across the discovery-space opening and position it well upstage. There are at least four of them but possibly more and they are both stage-hands and grotesques in Prospero's 'happening'. We can only guess at their appearance (they are called '*fantastics*' in the Restoration adaptation), but the courtiers are struck by the contrast between their uncouth appearance and the civilised gentleness of their gestures. Caliban at his most primitive had no (verbal) language with which to express his ideas, even to think

(I,ii,357–60); but Alonso sees in the Shapes' actions a species of communication through art that transcends normal discourse:

> I cannot too much muse
> Such shapes, such gestures, and such sound, expressing –
> Although they want the use of tongue – a kind
> Of excellent dumb discourse.
>
> (III, iii, 36–9)

In effect, a kind of non-verbal theatre, which this play at its most profound moments consistently is.

At the centre of the episode is another grotesque, a classical hybrid, the Harpy, half woman and half bird, but played here, it is important for the audience to register, by Ariel in a costume. He is winged and perhaps wears a bird mask and claws and his meaning (another hieroglyph) is instantly clear as he arrives as a Jovian judgment in thunder and lightning. But like the courtiers, the audience is unprepared for this thrilling moment (typically there is no forewarning except of a most general kind) and the effect should startle.

However, within their visual frame throughout the episode, the audience has Prospero '*on the top, invisible*' (a). 'Invisible' may mean only unseen, but perhaps he (like Ariel elsewhere) is costumed to make him 'invisible' to the other characters. '*On the top*' is an unusual expression. To oversee the action, the actor need only to have been 'above' – on the gallery, 10 feet or so above the Blackfriars stage. The actual expression appears once elsewhere in Shakespeare, in *1 Henry VI*, III, ii: '*Enter Pucell, on the top . . .* '. This was a play written for the Theatre, and in the scene Pucell, having tricked her way into Rouen, signals to her forces with a torch from a tower (called so in the dialogue and also 'turret'). Later in the same scene she appears 'on the walls' while her enemies appear below. Clearly, a position higher than the gallery was necessary for the first appearance. In Fletcher's play for Blackfriars, *The Double Marriage*, there is a '*boy atop*' referring to the main-top of a ship. Action is played below the boy but on the gallery. In the masque *Hymenaei*, on a scenic stage, a statue of Jupiter overviewing the action is described as '*in the top, figuring the heaven*'. Prospero, '*on the top*', is evidently in a position above the gallery, perhaps twenty feet above the stage. He occupies a god-like position, observing the action like God in the mystery play. Why he is not merely on the gallery we must answer shortly.

Sixty years later, in the Dryden adaptation on the Restoration stage, the banquet episode had become two separate but parallel events, at III, iii and IV, ii. In the first, a table was carried on stage by two spirits: '*after the Dance, a Table furnish'd with Meats and Fruits is brought in by two Spirits*'. Alonso and the others prepare to eat but '*Two spirits descend, and fly away with the Table.'* In the second event, as Caliban and his crew get drunk,

> *A Table rises, and four Spirits with Wine and Meat enter, placing it, as they dance, on the Table. The Dance ended, the Bottles vanish and the table sinks again.*

At the Blackfriars, the table was evidently neither flown nor raised on a trap: it was carried in by the Shapes (see (a)) and carried out again (see (c)). The banquet (meat and drink and *alfresco* refreshment) *'vanishes'* when Ariel/Harpy claps his/her wings over it. What seems to happen is that the actor thus provides a temporary masking so that the top of the table (a trick table) may be flipped over by a stage assistant hiding behind (that is upstage) of it. But the best vantage point for the boy actor playing Ariel would be on top of the table itself. There, he not only acts like a Harpy, spoiling the food by touching it, but he is in a strong position to read over the moral disablement to the wicked threesome beneath him.

Now we can assemble the whole sequence. After Antonio and Sebastian's *sotto voce* plotting, *'solemn and strange music'* is played in the music house and Prospero appears above the gallery. The Shapes enter from the discovery space and bring on the trick table carrying an apparent banquet. They dance a dance of welcome to the court party and exit. The table has been placed upstage, close to the tiring-house facade. As the court party approaches it there is thunder and lightning, appearing almost to have been hurled from above by Prospero, and in the distraction so caused Ariel is flown from the gallery on to the table. In the clapping of his wings over the table a stage-hand from the discovery-space spins the table or rather that part (the inner section) carrying the banquet. Ariel/Harpy then speaks to the court party downstage of him, mocks at them as they draw their swords and are charmed, and, as thunder again echoes round the auditorium, is flown out *via* the gallery. (He *'vanishes'* according to (c), so a simple door exit is unlikely. He could slip out through the tiring-house curtains, but flying would best complete an exciting but morally eloquent episode.)

During this, Prospero surveys the whole action and comments on it from a position where he sees all and never masks it: very much the puppet master pulling strings, though not quite, because Ariel as performer is able to fail and so is praised in succeeding:

> Of my instruction hast thou nothing bated
> In what thou hadst to say.
>
> (III, ii, 85–6)

Not the puppeteer – but the magician that joins hands with the playwright and the director and is proud of his own work, a work of 'quaint' illusion. And an episode like this insistently cries out for exact direction.

Pride marks Prospero's next show, the masque of IV, i – but a pride overtaken by anguish at the inevitable ephemerality of the theatrical moment, 'this insubstantial pageant', which brings in turn a painful awareness of the fragility of life itself and of human values. The masque is a donation in the form of an art-work. It enacts a divine visitation which confers blessings and guarantees fertility. Unlike the pantomime of the banquet, the audience inside the play, Ferdinand and Miranda, know that it is a show. The reality for them lies not in the 'majestic vision' *per se* but in its demonstration of Prospero's high art and its promise. For him it is 'such another trick' (IV, i, 37) as the banquet.[16]

What he gives them is a pastoral. The entertainment enacts through its ornate style the sense of civilised values within which, Prospero twice insists, the Ferdinand-Miranda relationship should be conducted. Venus (physical love) and Cupid (erotic anarchy) are banished, so that 'ceremony' (a key Renaissance value) may have pride of place. Ariel, as we later hear, is to play Ceres and so he is despatched to get into yet another costume. Practically speaking, the actor has only a few minutes offstage, during which there is a short discussion of chastity, '*soft music*', Iris's entrance and then her first fourteen lines of verse. Just as Prospero directs Miranda first to see Ferdinand, now with a fine sense of theatre, he directs the couple to see this 'vanity' of his art: 'No tongue! all eyes! be silent!' And they sit stage left and right, Ferdinand and Miranda one side and Prospero the other in front of the stage-sitters, to enjoy the spectacle of the wedding masque.

Iris and Ceres' verse dialogue is spoken, perhaps in a kind of recitative, against the soft music. The language has a leisurely, pageant-like quality and the couplets, quite properly, sound like nothing else in the play. During the exchange '*Juno descends*'. We might expect here a throne descent, winched down from above with the Juno actor on board. The stage direction comes early (opposite l. 72) to allow time for the operation and for a decorous leaving of the throne. Thirty lines later, Juno is ready to step forward and join the downstage Iris and Ceres: 'Great Juno comes; I know her by her gait' (l. 102).

After the song of blessing sung by Juno and Ceres (three verses, perhaps the first by Juno, the second by Ceres, and the third by the two in unison), comes the revels of the Naiads and Reapers. This is pastoral choreography in its most civilised accoutrements. Iris, Ceres and Juno have retreated upstage where Juno sits in the throne, the other two either side of her and the four or six pairs of dancers weave elegant patterns over the stage: the nymphs are 'temperate' (l. 132), the Reapers are '*properly habited*' (stage direction) and the dance itself, '*graceful*' (stage direction). There is a strict formality in the stage picture and the effect is quite different from that of the dance at the equivalent moment in *The Winter's Tale*. There, in a different kind of pastoral, 'a gallimaufrey of gambols' is performed by 'Twelve rustics habited like satyrs', and the celebration, properly in its context, is a folk festival. Here, we have an aristocratic revel in a play in which the satyr figure is the rapist, Caliban.

However, the revel of course is not played out to an aesthetically satisfying conclusion. Prospero's 'present fancies' are abruptly dismissed precisely because the satyr intrudes into Prospero's mind:

> PROSPERO *starts suddenly, and speaks; after which, to a strange, hollow and confused noise, they heavily vanish.*
>
> PROS I had forgot that foul conspiracy
> Of the beast Caliban and his confederates
> Against my life; the minute of their plot
> Is almost come. – Well done! avoid; no more!
>
> (IV, i, 139–42)

We can imagine him rising from his stage-side place and speaking, moving stage-centre on his last line. *'Vanish'* in the stage direction, the third time in the play, again cannot signify a conventional, tiring-house door exit for the six or eight dancers and three masque characters. Its modifier, 'heavily', must mean 'dejectedly' (for 'sluggishly' clearly will not do). As the spirits, their roles snatched from them by Prospero's command, leave the stage informally, perhaps through the discovery-space curtain, what vanishes, in effect, is the formal construct of the masque itself. So the music breaks off in disharmony, the throne, empty, is winched back up, and *'a strange, hollow and confused noise'* enacts the return to the real world of violence, power and, especially, death. And Prospero, marvellously distempered, fills the uneasy moments while the Ariel actor returns to his sea-nymph costume with the profoundly mannerist imagery of the play's best known lines, 'Our revels now are ended . . .' (ll. 418–58).

A court masque of 1604, Daniel's *The Vision of Twelve Goddesses* helps us imagine the main characters of Prospero's show. There, Iris, as here, presents the goddesses and they descend from a mountain:

> First here imperial Juno in her chair
> With sceptre of command for kingdoms large,
> Descends all clad in colours of the air,
> Crown'd with bright stars.

Penultimate comes Ceres:

> Next plenteous Ceres in her harvest weed
> Crown'd with th' increase of what she gave to keep
> To gratitude and faith.

Jacobean companies were always prepared to spend lavishly on costumes. And Shakespeare could not lose here, for if the effect were somewhat poverty-stricken compared with the no-expense-spared practice of the court masque, that in effect is what Prospero alludes to in the disillusioned tenor of his distempered speech. But probably the costumes were splendid.

Prospero's last show, perforce, is contrived of homelier materials, for by then he has joined the workaday world and abjured his 'rough magic'. Nevertheless, with characteristic confidence, he promises to those assembled at the end of the play 'a wonder, to content ye as much as my dukedom'. Probably he draws the curtains of the discovery-space to reveal the inside of his cell: '*Here* PROSPERO *discovers* FERDINAND *and* MIRANDA *playing at chess*' (V, i, after l. 171). The moment has an almost sacramental quality for the onlookers onstage. To Alonso it suggests 'a vision of the island' and to Sebastian 'a most high miracle' (ll. 175,6). As with the incident of Hermione's statue which comes to life and gives back to Leontes a dead wife, so Ferdinand is restored to a grieving father as restitution beyond his deserving. Never are Prospero's god-like powers more palpable than at this moment when he has given them up. Indeed, he has no music to set off the event, for the 'rough magic' is past. Instead, a pair of lovers sit opposite each other across a small table and engage in love-talk about a homely game of chess. It is as affecting as it is simple. And perhaps it is not all that simple, either. For the chess game, which is the excuse for holding the effect for a couple of minutes until those inside the discovery-space see those outside and join them, carries overtones of the power game of Antonio, Alonso and Prospero which starts up the story, but rendered in the lovers' affectionate teasing into the commerce of love and a kind of communication: love's kingdom is already lost and won; its battles are bloodless.

Alonso sees a miracle and identifies Miranda as the goddess responsible, and Ferdinand must assure him that she is mortal (l. 188). The remainder of the play will be suitably downbeat. There is no wedding celebration, which would normally end a play of this kind. Prospero's response (it may be an aside) to Miranda's excitement in the 'brave new world' she now meets is devastating – 'Tis new to thee'. There is his anticipation that in retirement to Milan 'Every third thought shall be my grave', and intimations of mortality will not be dismissed. In a heart-rending moment, Ariel's promised freedom is granted; and then as Prospero-Burbage is left alone on stage, an isolated figure down-centre, the indulgence of the audience is begged in the most poignant Epilogue in all the drama. For that, from the Blackfriars audience, will alone release the theatre-artist which Prospero-Shakespeare has consistently been in the play:

> As you from crimes would pardon'd be,
> Let your indulgence set me free.

For 150 years it has been fashionable to identify Prospero and Shakespeare to the extent of seeing in the magician's abjuration of his Art the play-wright's retirement from the stage. In fact, Shakespeare was still to write *Henry VIII* and collaborate (probably) on *The Two Noble Kinsmen* (both 1613). But is is difficult not to read into *The Tempest* a sustained analogy between Prospero and the theatre-artist, capable always of creating 'far other worlds and other seas' but drawn back always to the reality of the human condition in an imperfect world.

The Tempest is insistently an art-object. It does not imitate in vigorous action the hurly-burly dynamic of human experience but reduces the story to the unified and elegant shape of Keats's urn. It does this by turning narrative into anecdote, creating out of the world of Italianate revenge drama a dream-play complete with the abrupt transitions, the lack of compelling logic and the procession of profoundly engaging symbols that we associate with the world of dream. And as with dream, the play has a remote and inaccessible air. Its delicate strategies and carefully mounted shows would have been blown away in the open air at the Globe. A precise control of pace, of aural effects and of the staging of individual episodes is more necessary than perhaps anywhere else in Shakespeare's plays. It is difficult to imagine this produced without careful direction (though the director is unindentifiable on the Jacobean stage). If we cannot play the play well now it is because it is a 'quaint device' that defeats our clumsy handling. We would turn it into our own – as 'cruel' theatre, or psychological theatre, or political theatre. Shakespeare tells us what it is – 'an insubstantial pageant', given significance by an indulgent audience. If that is a disappointingly reductive valuation, it is also bracingly true.

6 · 'A Perspective that Shows us Hell': *The Duchess of Malfi* at the Blackfriars

At the end of Act IV of *The Duchess of Malfi*, with the Duchess dead at his feet, Bosola recognises his bad conscience as 'a perspective that shows us hell' (IV, ii, 358–9).[1] The play is full of references to optical instruments. By 'perspective' here the audience might understand a telescope, a topographer's tool for drawing townscapes accurately or a kind of image-distorting device; and it also referred to a picture so drawn that what appears distorted or jumbled from the normal viewing angle is correct from some other angle. Perspective in its modern sense was a Renaissance invention and Webster's whole dramaturgy is one of perspectives.[2] At the end of the play 'the deep pit of darkness' that Bosola sees has engulfed the entire human condition. He himself is Galilean man, adrift from the old certainties. Amongst his various backgrounds has been a spell at Galileo's university of Padua (Flamineo is another alumnus) where, as a 'fantastical scholar' (III, iii 41) he has pursued his studies to gain the name of 'a speculative man', someone who plumbs the mysteries of things. His name, 'Bozola' in the source-story, is spelled by Webster to pick up 'Bossola', a mariner's compass;[3] but his final journey is directionless, away from justice. The Cardinal would borrow Galileo's telescope and turn it to the moon to find a constant woman (II, iv, 16–19); but in a play about the Duchess's spirit of greatness, at the end, mankind in its pit of darkness is 'womanish and fearful', which seems to mean 'womanish because fearful'.

Webster's much disputed status as a major Jacobean playwright rests largely on the two tragedies, *The White Devil* and *The Duchess of Malfi*, and, to a lesser extent, on the tragicomedy, *The Devil's Law-Case*. Elsewhere, he collaborated with Dekker on *Westward Ho!* and *Northward Ho!* and with Dekker and others on the notorious, now lost, *The Late Murder of the Son Upon the Mother;* and he provided the Induction for Marston's *The Malcontent* and probably added thirty-two items for the 1615 edition of Overbury's *Characters* (including a covert praise of Burbage as 'An

Excellent Actor' and an anatomy of 'The Virtuous Widow'). But the *oeuvre* is tiny and the playwright's own slowness of composition was legendary as well as self-acknowledged. We know a little of his biography,[4] but the source of his bizarre imagination and fierce passionateness as they appear in the two major plays remains enigmatic.

Most revealing of his aims as a playwright is the Epistle he provided for *The White Devil*, published 1612, a short but characteristically pugnacious manifesto of his art. That play had been performed by Queen Anne's Men at the Red Bull playhouse, and it had failed but, Webster maintained,

> it was acted in so dull a time of winter, presented in so open and black a theatre, that it wanted (that which is the only grace and setting out of a tragedy) a full and understanding auditory . . . most of the people that come to that playhouse, resemble those ignorant asses who visiting stationers' shops their use is not to inquire for good books, but new books.

This all has to do with the disadvantages of popular against private – winter weather in 'an open and black' house, the scattered and unsophisticated spectators ignorant of quality.

The Epistle then goes on to excuse the writer's deliberate forsaking of the proper grammar of the 'true dramatic poem', constructed according to the rules of the ancients (so far he had compromised), and to rebuff the criticism of laboured composition. Finally, he pays tribute to 'the worthy labours' of fellow toilers in the field, commending

> that full and heighten'd style of Master Chapman, the labour'd and understanding works of Master Jonson: the no less worthy composures of the both worthily excellent Master Beaumont and Master Fletcher: and lastly (without wrong last to be named) the right happy and copious industry of M. Shakespeare, M. Dekker and M. Heywood. . . .

The praise here is carefully delivered and it too concerns private v. public. For Chapman and Jonson lead, with their high style and their learning (the Epistle to *Sejanus* is the model for Webster's own); Beaumont and Fletcher occupy a characteristic (even slightly grudging) middle ground; and at the rear come the journeymen playwrights of the popular stage whose distinction is copiousness, a 'happy' facility already discredited by the writer. Inevitably, it would seem, Webster's eye would turn to the Blackfriars and in 1620 Fitzgeoffrey (see pp. 11–12) regarded him as a typical Blackfriars *habitué*. So *The Duchess of Malfi*, *The White Devil*'s companion piece, was sold to the King's Men, probably opened at the Blackfriars in the winter of 1613–14 (its title page of 1623 says it was played there and at the Globe) and was evidently a great success in that intimate, 'art' theatre. Certainly, it enjoyed a number of revivals: in 1617–18 and again between 1619 and 1623; and the play was still in the repertory in 1630 when there was a production at court.

Webster's pleasure in the King's Men's performances is registered by his inclusion with the 1623 text of the play of 'The Actors' Names', a cast list. This was a practice unknown at the time, although he had added to the text of *The White Devil* a commendation of the Queen Anne's players, singling out for special praise Richard Perkins who had evidently acted Flamineo. Bosola, who is spiritually Flamineo's heir, heads the cast list, breaking the convention of ranking characters first and marking Webster's own awareness of that character's special place in the play's design. As a 'perspective that shows us hell', *The Duchess of Malfi* is no popular theatre piece. But it is part of Webster's own radical cast that a servant-turned-spy and a woman stand at the front of his play.

'The Actors' Names' tells us a good deal about the Blackfriars performances and is worth reproducing:

BOSOLA,   J. Lowin.
FERDINAND,   1. R. Burbage.   2. J. Taylor.
CARDINAL,   1. H. Condell.   2. R. Robinson.
ANTONIO,   1. W. Ostler.   2. R. Benfield.
DELIO,   J. Underwood.
MALATESTE,   N. Tooley.
The Marquis of PESCARA,   J. Rice.
SILVIO,   T. Pollard.
The SEVERAL MADMEN,   N. Tooley, J. Underwood, etc.
The DUCHESS, R. Sharpe.
The CARDINAL'S MISTRESS,   J. Thompson.
The DOCTOR,
CARIOLA,   } R. Pallant.

Court Officers, three young children and two Pilgrims are also included but without actors' names, and there is also the ghost character, Forobosco.[5] Presumably, Webster himself created the list in 1623, scribbling in names against a *dramatis personae*, and it raises a number of problems mostly concerning the boy actresses. Evidently, the second names opposite Ferdinand, the Cardinal and Antonio show us new actors replacing departed ones. Pallant's bracketed roles might indicate doubling (possible but unlikely) or the fact that the actor played Cariola in 1613 (when he was nine years old) and subsequently took over the part of the Doctor at a revival. Rice cannot have played in the first production. Originally an apprentice in the company in 1610, he joined the Lady Elizabeth's Men the next year but had replaced Field in the King's Men by 1619. So perhaps Field first played Pescara. Sharpe might possibly have originated the role of the Duchess but was probably too young in 1613. He first appears in cast lists with the King's Men in 1616 and he may have been about ten in 1613. By 1623 he was probably too old. Perhaps Webster remembers him as the best, or longest serving Duchess.[6] Thompson, on the other hand, certainly belongs not to the original production but to the revivals, for he was playing female roles between 1621 and 1631.

With the leading adult actors we are on firmer ground. Lowin, whose part is the longest in the play, was in his late thirties in 1613 and was a highly experienced actor. He had already played the Jonsonian parts Morose, Volpone and Mammon, and in Shakespeare Falstaff and (very recently) Henry VIII. These last two roles made capital of his weighty presence and large physique (his Henry must have looked Holbein-like). In Falstaff and Volpone he had already played leading roles which are so constructed as to engage an audience in uneasy collusion: aesthetes both, they act out with exuberant vitality a life-style which conventional morality is obliged to reject. There is a persuasive argument, too, that he played Iago.[7] If true, this part would have offered experience of a villain character who, Vice-like, is able to implicate the audience in his villainy by sharing with it, through soliloquy, his plotting and point of view. Like Iago, Bosola cloaks his duplicity with a truculent display of honesty ('Let me be simply honest' – II, i, 81; 'Give me leave to be honest in any phrase' – II, i, 87); his ambivalent praise of Antonio (III, ii) invites from the Duchess the trusting response Iago inveigles from Othello; and like Iago, he is an old soldier embittered by not receiving his just reward for service rendered. The fashionable image of the Italianate villain, an oleaginous, wiry figure with high cheek bones and hooded and louring eyes is not at all to the point as Lowin's portrait shows (see Plate 10). The Jacobean idea of stage villainy is subtler than that and likely to be more unsettling for the audience (then and now). In any case, Bosola has a conscience; and we shall see how he 'mediates' the play, providing its most consistent point of view.

Second in the list comes Burbage, normally lead actor and playing here the first Ferdinand. He was in his mid-forties in 1613, a veteran with at least one (Tooley) if not a second (Robinson) former apprentice on stage with him. Realistic casting would rate him much too old for the part, for Ferdinand is evidently the Duchess's twin (IV, ii, 267) and she is 'a young widow' at the beginning of the play and actually nineteen in the historical sources. But Jacobean casting was conventional. Ferdinand's role is a major one (third in length after Bosola and the Duchess) and it calls for an aristocratic manner: the Aragonian blood is an important element of the play's meaning as well as characterisation. Also, Burbage possessed the ability to personate the range and weight of passionate

10 Portrait of Robert Lowin in the Ashmolean Museum, Oxford
(anonymous)

display the part calls for, rising to frenzied lunacy. Othello's turbulence,
and perhaps something of his jealousy, is relevant here (and if Lowin had
played Iago aspects of that earlier relationship were available to the two
actors), and something of Hamlet's complexity. It might well have been
Burbage's well-proven tragic intensity that encouraged the playwright to
give the Ferdinand role great prominence over the Cardinal's and
construct it in quite a different way. In the source story, the narrator
seldom differentiates the brothers, fails to develop them and, normally,
allows the Cardinal, who is the angrier of the two, to take the lead. For

Burbage, Webster wrote a part of complexity and power, a choleric man with enigmatic obsessions he never himself identifies. (We shall return to this later.)

At Burbage's death in 1619, Taylor, 'The Actors' Names' makes clear, took over the Ferdinand role as he did other Burbage parts. At that date he was in his mid-thirties. Like Burbage he would be a successful Hamlet (although he did not play Othello) and could act an aristocrat to the life, for his gentlemanly bearing enabled him to move easily in court society.

Condell, the original Cardinal, also brought long experience to his part but, though a stalwart of the company, was evidently not a great or magnetic actor. No doubt he coped easily with the laconic style of the rational churchman. His was half the size of Burbage's part, but the Cardinal's passionless pursuit of glory and sex is played off carefully against the fiery temperament of his brother. More than a personated authority is needed at the end of the play. The Cardinal is absent entirely from Act IV, but as the world of the play crumbles in Act V, so the actor of the Cardinal becomes a key means of holding the performance of the finale together. While his character disintegrates, it is important that he remain in charge of the staccato rhythms of the final scenes.

In 1619 or soon after, Condell retired from acting and his part in the play was taken over by Richard Robinson. Robinson was never so successful as an adult as he had been as a boy actress. In 1616 his ability as a female impersonator was legendary, as *The Devil is an Ass* tells us. Ironically, in connection with a play about a widow remarrying, the adult actor married Burbage's widow. In his playing of the Cardinal, perhaps elements of the refined fastidiousness and epicene beauty of the boy actress remained to give his presentation of the role an apt, sphinx-like appearance and a cool, aesthetic tone. As with Condell, something self-effacing and underplayed was expected of him, so that with both, that brief flash of a haunted conscience and the image of the rake (V, v, 5–7) would burn the brighter for its unexpectedness.

A last speculation about Robinson concerns his playing the Duchess in the original production if Sharpe was indeed too young then. We might expect Webster to identify the first Duchess (though he did not identify the first Julia), but if he had already nominated Robinson for the Cardinal that might have stayed his hand. Robinson was a leading boy actress with the King's Men in 1613, although an older apprentice, James Sands who was seventeen, might have been entrusted first with the tragic, contralto tones we might associate with the world-weary Duchess of Act IV; but this is to foist on to the problem our own prejudices of dramatic propriety not relevant to an all-male acting company.

Lowin, Burbage and Condell, playing the 'heavy' parts, represent an Elizabethan generation of actors. Webster had already written dialogue for them in their own persons in the Induction he devised for *The Malcontent* ten years earlier. Ostler and Underwood, playing Antonio and Delio respectively, represent the next generation and were 'private' actors by training. They had been fellow performers in the Children of the Chapel before 1608 and so were accustomed to the Blackfriars playing conditions and would have been well-known to the Blackfriars audience (though such distinctions would no longer be clear by 1613). Used to working together over many years, they make a natural partnership for the kind of double act Webster has contrived at various points in the play (I, i; II, i; III, i; V, i). Delio's role has little more than an expository function, providing Antonio with the excuse to externalise his problems, and Ostler, evidently the abler actor, was given the larger and more demanding role. Two years previously he had been extravagantly called 'sole king of actors',[8] but he was evidently steady and reliable rather than conspicuous, regularly taking third– or fourth– length parts (here the fourth). This gives us a clue to the acting of Antonio, for though the role is important, it should not elicit a bravura performance. The character's ordinariness is deliberately counterpointed with the Aragonian siblings' egregiousness and he is, technically speaking, a comedian caught up in a tragic world he never understands. He dies not bravely nor well but in the dark and in a muddle of mistaken identities. For the actor, the problem is to be at once unheroic and a proper soul-mate for the Duchess. In fact, Ostler struggled with the problem only a short while for he died in December 1614 (which gives us a last date for the first production) and the role was taken over by Benfield who was to develop into a major tragic actor. Benfield, in fact, may well have readjusted the subtle, internal tensions of the play merely by his taking part. The stronger Antonio is played, the greater sympathy the Duchess in turn generates. But, as we shall argue, sympathy was not Webster's first aim.

Our attempts to square Webster's aims and the King's Men's interpretation is complicated by the 1623 title page advertisement that the published version represents 'the perfect and exact copy, with diverse things printed, that the length of the play would not bear in the presentment'. *The Duchess of Malfi* is the longest of Webster's three plays and is a good deal longer, by about a fifth again, than the average Globe play and longer almost by the same amount again than the average Blackfriars play.[9] Assuming that the play was designed for 'private' presentation (the act divisions suggest this) we must conclude that Webster, in the composition, must have been aware that the cutting would be necessary. Only a playwright with a pressing need to express ideas on his own account (as opposed to a more 'professional' writer with a steady awareness of the theatre's needs) would have written in this way. Whether

Webster himself was responsible for the cutting we cannot tell. The publisher of the Beaumont and Fletcher First Folio tells us 'when these Comedies and Tragedies were presented on the stage, the actors omitted some scenes and passages (with the author's consent) as occasion led them'. Probably something similar operated here.

What was left out is difficult to determine. In a modern adaptation, shortening is easily effected by the removal of the Cardinal/Julia subplot (II, iv; V, i; V, ii) but a contemporary account, together with our own awareness of the echoic effect of Jacobean dramaturgy, tells us that this did not happen at the Blackfriars. Other episodes stand trimming with small loss to narrative coherence – the instalment of the Cardinal, Delio's temptation of Julia (II, iv), the Officers and Switzer plot (III, ii), the anatomising of Malateste (III, iii), the Doctor's scene (V, ii) and the Echo scene (V, iii). At places, one can argue an overelaboration of effect – the discussion of the French Court (I, i, 1–22) which was almost certainly added after 1617, the fable of the Salmon and the Dogfish (III, v, 123–44), Bosola with the Old Lady (II, i, 1–62), perhaps the episode of Pescara and Antonio's land (V, i, 15–56). But most, if not all, of these passages are characteristically Websterian and are justifiably part of the design. If piecemeal cutting is the proper approach (though very difficult in the playhouse), then that would have shortened in particular Bosola's part which shows some of the obsessive verbosity of Flamineo. But we know from 'The Actors' Names' that this is a key role and a radical shortening there would seriously affect not only the balance of the play but its very point of view. All our attempts to devise a shortening fail to satisfy and this serves to highlight the special sense of design, based only partly on narrative and character, which is the hallmark of the play's action.

In this action, the five-act structure acts like an armature. Its firmness is quite different from Webster's practice in *The White Devil*, a popular theatre play, and shows the playwright responding to the private theatre convention of providing instrumental music between the acts, possibly to supply an opportunity for mending the artificial lighting. Webster divides his story into five sequences of continuous time bounded by time-lags, and through this means successfully articulates a plot in which child-bearing is a crucial motif. So II follows I after a gap of at least nine months, and III follows II after an interval of about two years during which the Duchess bears two more children. The pace quickens in the second half. After III, there is a gap of perhaps some weeks while the Duchess suffers the privation of a different kind of confinement ('How doth our sister duchess bear herself in her imprisonment?' – IV, i, 1–2), and between IV and V, we learn from the Cardinal (V, ii, 268–70), that four days elapse.

Normally in plays, narrative time is telescoped and chronic gaps camouflaged in the interest of stage-convincingness. Here, Webster actually mocks at the convention (III, i, 4–11) after the longest time-lag in the play and employs the practical, performance rhythms of the Blackfriars to cunning effect. He does not attempt to dramatise time passing but uses the inter-act music to mark time passed. (And we may speculate that the music itself may have prepared the audience, through tonal changes, for the deepening tragedy after Loretto.) The play is much concerned with death but little with ageing; death is a fact of 'the pit of darkness', but mortality is a condition, not a process, except briefly in the Duchess's awareness of grey hairs (III, ii, 58–60) and in Bosola's medieval homily (IV, ii, 135–7). Elsewhere, experience, like the audience's perception of time, jumps from frame to frame of a time-lapse camera.

Disjunction, not continuity, is at the centre of both Webster's spiritual vision ('the perspective that shows us hell') and his practical stagecraft. The camera – a modern viewing device – gives us an apt analogy in 'cinematic' for characteristic, Websterian staging devices. There is, inevitably, the effect of collage and rapid transition typical of Shakespeare and his contemporaries. More interesting because a personal idiom is Webster's fluent use, in overwatching scenes, of alternating voices and viewpoints, shifts, as it were, of camera angles (and microphones) or a constant use of zoom lens. The effect, curiously, is emphasised for the reader in the 1623 printed script because there the playwright, apeing classical models (and Jonson), eschewed character entrances (and most exits) mid-scene, only listing all the characters in the scene in a mass entry at the beginning. So, for the reader, figures loom up unexpectedly, or suddenly one eavesdrops on a different grouping which is brought into a new, sharp focus.

III, iii is a simple example of this complicated technique (complicated in the writing and in the performing) and shows what fluent stage-work Webster demanded of the acting company. It is a brief scene, seventy-six lines of dialogue and a mere four minutes in the playing. However, it is a narratively important scene. In the first half, it tells of the military preparations which prompt the Cardinal's investiture; in the second, we might think more importantly, it brings Bosola to the brothers with the identity of the Duchess's secret husband and the news that the guilty pair use a pilgrimage to cover their flight from Malfi. Webster's dramaturgy here is extraordinary. On the page he seems almost to miss the climactic moment of the second half. On stage, Ferdinand's learning about Antonio is a kind of dumb-show or a short piece of silent cinema.

At the beginning of the scene, and entering on the heels of Bosola's sententious couplet of the scene before, come six actors who form two discrete groups. One remains upstage (those playing Ferdinand, Delio,

Silvio and Pescara) and meanwhile the Cardinal leads Malateste down for
eight lines about the Cardinal's calling. As they move to the side of the
stage still talking, the other group comes down and we hear from them
a twenty-five line commentary on Malateste's cardboard qualities as a
soldier. At some point in this, Ferdinand sees Bosola arrive onstage and
he crosses to the Cardinal where Bosola joins them. Now the commentary
of the Delio group plays on Bosola, Ferdinand and the Cardinal and we
are directed to watch how the brothers receive Bosola's news. Part of the
fineness of this lies in the fact that, unlike the audience, the commentators
do not understand what is happening – they merely observe the outward
manifestations: for the Cardinal, according to Silvio,

> lifts up's nose, like a foul porpoise before a storm.
> PES The Lord Ferdinand laughs.
> DELIO   Like a deadly cannon
> That lightens ere it smokes.
> PES These are your true pangs of death,
> The pangs of life that struggle with great statesmen –
> DELIO In such a deformed silence, witches whisper
> Their charms.
>
>   (III, iii, 52–9)

The episode played on a small stage cannot be acted realistically. In
Delio's last lines, the whole mime seems to freeze, the two brothers and
Bosola are caught in a tableau of infinite menace, though its purport is
available only to the audience.

Suddenly, the freeze over, what was in longshot becomes close-up,
almost literally as Delio's group moves upstage and the Cardinal's takes
centre stage. Here, they may whisper their hatred of the base marriage
and plan their response. Then after l. 68,[10] the Cardinal takes his leave,
with Malateste (displaced after Bosola's entrance) and the others in tow,
and Ferdinand and Bosola briefly hold the stage for the Duke's dismissal
of Antonio 'that only smell'd of ink and counters' and his ordering of the
band of soldiers to capture the errant pair. And then the stage is clear
and another sequence may begin. The whole episode calls for instinctive
movement from the actors – forming groups, redeploying, finding their
best positions – and accurate timing so that the bursts of dialogue inter-
leave exactly and, in intimate circumstances, the convention of not overhearing is understood by the audience. In a screenplay, the camera
replaces both the cunning writing and the technically proficient acting
needed to work it.

What III, ii does in short, Act I, which is all one scene, does at length,
thus establishing at the outset the play's characteristic idiom. Webster
manages his opening exposition, the introduction of his characters and
the rapid onset of the action with a fluid stagecraft involving a constant

regrouping of the characters as they jostle about the Malfi court. Some-times, the rapid deployment of personnel onstage appears to take the characters themselves by surprise – 'Are you gone?' says Bosola (I, i, 44–5) after the Cardinal has slipped away unseen. But the total effect is of a populous court society straining to preserve its decorous public face while exercising its vicious private wishes; and in that public/private opposition resides much of the Duchess's special predicament and the energy which sparks the Websterian world. Society would have her a Duchess, but nature (her own) casts her as lover and mother. 'The misery of us that are born great', she complains, but the full force of the problem is only clarified much later.

The scene (and play) opens in conventional fashion as two courtiers discuss their betters – an expository device of long-standing, used here in a stylised fashion, but innovative in that one of the interlocutors is destined to be a protagonist in the ensuing story. But that is developed only gradually. Firstly we get a series of 'characters', a parade of the main figures, as Antonio and Delio anatomise the visitors to the Malfi court. But Webster mixes in the development of the intriguing of Bosola and the two brothers, and so the camera moves back and forth: sometimes we see via Antonio's commentary, sometimes we are given close-ups of pieces of business Antonio remains detached from.

As 'the presence 'gins to fill' we are reminded that this, for the moment, is the court's public face. Perhaps an upstage throne makes the scene. Ferdinand and the other courtiers enter and an extended exchange presents the banter, small talk and jostling for position of courtiers around a great Duke; and at the same time we learn the occasion of the gathering – a tilt. Curiously, Webster does not stress the narrative meaning of this, though its implications are forcibly present, we quickly learn, in the minds of Ferdinand and the Cardinal. For the tilt marks the end of the mourning period of the Duchess for the death of her husband. It is a *giostra*, a significant event in the great Renaissance household and, like a rite of passage, it will return the Duchess to the everyday currency of the social world and thus make her available once more for courtship and marriage.[11] So this is a festivity, marked also by masques and masked balls, and some such consideration lies behind Ferdinand's

> I would have you give o'er these chargeable revels;
> A visor and a mask are whispering rooms.
>
> (ll. 33–5)

Later, Ferdinand himself will provide a special marriage masque for his sister. For the moment, and with a significance he himself cannot yet know, he presents the tilting prize of a jewel to Antonio. Perhaps music and hand-held masks were used in these exchanges to mark the court ritual. The Duchess is at a crossroads; in a little while she will reward with the wedding ring from her finger this man 'who took the ring oftenest'.

First, the Duchess enters this public place with her guests for their leave-taking and Antonio characterises Ferdinand and the Duchess while the court party remain onstage, 'frozen' or in quiet, realistic business. This passage ends with Cariola's conveyance to Antonio in an aside of the message from the Duchess. So the private story develops amidst the public. Now the focus changes abruptly once more and Ferdinand, public voice and private intent, commends Bosola into a job in the Duchess's household. The stage momentarily clears and we overhear Ferdinand's purchase of Bosola's service as a spy – a strain on his loyalty, to serve two masters. The key property is a bag of gold, offered, punned about, and reluctantly taken, that will bind Bosola to a course of action he will reject but never escape from.

At the return of the Duchess, the stage is the place of a fierce family colloquy. A formal patterning which the Duchess ironically recognises – 'I think this speech between you both was studied, It came so roundly off' (ll. 328–9) – calls for parallel blocking: the Duchess centre stage, the brothers on either side, moral spokesmen reading over their litany. The dialogue is patently artificial but theatrically compelling, and behind the ethical platitudes is the ambiguously erotic threat of the poniard produced by Ferdinand and of his final obscenities.

Finally the Duchess is alone and the scene is now the gallery to which Antonio was earlier summoned. The throne has been unostentatiously struck and there is nothing else needed for the scene change: the privacy is projected by the actors. But the exchange between the Duchess and Antonio is both private and public. For Cariola is concealed behind the arras to witness and then officiate in the betrothal. What follows is a ritual of the Duchess's making, in effect a wedding: 'What can the church force more?' (l. 448); and the pair leave the stage to go to the extreme privacy of their marriage bed.

So the scene ends, but not happily, for the final moment is Cariola's prescient three-line summary of what we have witnessed. Characteristically there is an ambiguity there – the Duchess is ruled by the spirit of woman or greatness – and the whole scene, lasting thirty minutes, is a restless, fluid alternation of commentary and action, public ceremony and private exchange, formal tableau and intimate grouping. If the music and masks of the masque are part of the stage imagery, the whole movement has the variety and choreographic shaping of a court revel and lends itself to playing with the formality of a masked ball. The camera is never still and the whole nervous and dangerous culture of a Renaissance court is acted out through an imaginative, daring dramaturgy.

As the play progresses its special tone is developed through the deployment of commentary devices and the accompanying shifts of perspective these create. If Act I shows a constant and fluid movement of point of view, Act II immediately finds the play's most insistent voice, that of Bosola, whose mixture of reductive satire and moral indignation plays round all the ensuing episodes, mediating them for the audience. In the last four acts, he opens four of the scenes, once solo; and more importantly he ends five scenes, each time solo. Progressively, he develops an intimate relationship with the audience, even generating sympathy for himself, and in doing so he obstructs a simple sympathy for the Duchess, constantly forcing the audience to adjust its point of view.

II,i is a model of his activities. The opening is all rough satire, the biting malcontent with hapless victims in the ambitious courtier and the vain old lady. The influence is Marston's, and like in Marston, the tone of knockabout aggression can deepen, at ll. 45–60, to the richer and more sombre tones of Hamlet. But this is all preparation. In sweeps the Duchess and her court to face, unknowingly, Bosola's 'private-eye' trick with the apricots. Again, this is a public occasion with, the audience knows, complicated, private undercurrents. The Duchess, whose private life belongs to Antonio, parades it wilfully in innuendo and pun as she rallies with her steward about hats and grafting. In this context, Bosola's asides to the audience work superbly. If we are inclined to view the love affair warmly, Bosola, who ironically knows less than we, directs us to view the relationship from the outside. The Duchess, her women fluttering about her, Antonio nervously in attendance, gobbles the apricots and indulges her secret flirting. But as the scene develops, we are repeatedly drawn to the figure of Bosola, downstage left or right, physically detached, whose coarse, obscene ironies give us an uncomfortable pleasure:

> DUCH   I am
> So troubled with the mother.
> BOS   *(Aside)*   I fear too much . . .
> DUCH   This green fruit and my stomach are not friends –
> How they swell me!
> BOS   *(Aside)*   Nay, you are too much swell'd already.
>   (II,i,116–17; 154–5)

The jokes are obvious, but they work not because they are witty and unexpected (which they are not) but because we ourselves are inclined to make them. Bosola's commentary thus confirms as much as directs, and the intimate relation of Lowin to the stage-sitters made that the more feasible. As will be shown later, the play is in part a tragedy of scandal.

Act III, scene iv is all commentary and detachment. It is a ritual episode, the investiture of the Cardinal, played formally and with considerable elaboration in dumb-show. The two pilgrims provide the commentary, explaining what they (and the audience) see in the banishment that follows, and provide a moral gloss. The device provides for Webster a kind of narrative foreshortening, but it invests the proceedings too with an outrageously ceremonial quality which alienates the audience.[12] There are about eighteen characters in all on stage and perhaps the pilgrims were placed on the gallery over the stage to ensure that they could properly be seen by all the audience. (Again, the effect of moving from close-up on detail to long-shot of the whole action is cinematic.) On the main stage, the business in its two parts would require careful blocking and accurate playing.

A contemporary account of the scene gives us confidence to determine what Webster intends here. The writer was Orazio Busino, who came to England in 1617 as chaplain in the small train accompanying ambassador Piero Contarino. We learn (what will be important to note) from letters and notes of his stay that he was old and half-blind. But he visited the theatre and also a court masque, and he wrote about these things in a lively fashion. His report of *The Duchess of Malfi* is part of a general complaint that the Catholic church is presented in a poor light on the London stage:

> On another occasion they [the English actors] showed a Cardinal in all his grandeur, in the formal robes appropriate to his station, splendid and rich, with his train in attendance, having an altar erected on the stage, where he pretended to make a prayer, organizing a procession; and then they produced him in public with a harlot on his knee. They showed him giving poison to one of his sisters, in a question of honour. Moreover he goes to war, first laying down his Cardinal's habit on the altar, with the help of his chaplains, with great ceremoniousness; finally, he has his sword bound on and dons the soldier's sash with so much panache you could not imagine it better done. And all this was acted in condemnation of the grandeur of the Church, which they despise and which in this Kingdom they hate to the death.[13]

Obviously, the account merges details of the murders of Julia and the Duchess, and perhaps Busino himself did not attend the play, but such misremembering is not inconsistent with seeing a play (with difficulty) and being unable to follow the dialogue. Even if he is obliged to another witness (perhaps the more so), his response to the spirit of the play is valuable. He concentrates, naturally, on the Cardinal's most distinctive moments save his death scene. The first, in 'They produced him in public with a harlot on his knee', evidently refers to II,iv and directs us to see a brilliant piece of stage business behind the first word 'Sit' – for Julia sits on his knee, and the ensuing dialogue, full of spite and distrust, is played in that manner. The second is his management of Julia's death (V,ii) but merged here with the killing of the Duchess. And at greatest length, in a separate part of the report, the Loretto scene.

Busino's description of the investiture matches the play text in its emphasis on ritual solemnity. The Cardinal is shown 'in all his grandeur', his habit is placed on the altar with 'great ceremoniousness', and his adoption of the military insignia is done 'with so much panache you could not imagine it done better'. In the text, the pilgrims expect 'a noble ceremony', and 'ceremony' occurs twice in the elaborate stage direction provided by Webster:

> *Here the ceremony of the* Cardinal's *instalment in the habit of a soldier,*
> *performed in delivering up his cross, hat, robes and ring at the shrine,*
> *and investing him with sword, helmet, shield and spurs; then* ANTONIO,
> *the Duchess and their Children, having presented themselves at the shrine,*
> *are (by a form of banishment in dumb-show expressed towards them by*
> *the cardinal and the State of Ancona) banished: during all which*
> *ceremony, this ditty is sung, to very solemn music, by divers Churchmen;*
> *and then exeunt.*

(III,iv, after l.7)

The ritual handling of the insignia is stressed – Busino adds a sash, and perhaps this was used instead of the shield – and they are vital stage properties. The business is organised around the altar/shrine which, Busino shows, was erected on stage at the beginning of the scene, not revealed, as we might expect, in the discovery-space. And all is accompanied by the solemn music and ditty (which the first printing of the text called a hymn).

Behind such elaboration, Busino or his reporter understood 'a condemnation of the grandeur of the church'. The solemnity created an effect that was satirical or critical but non-comic. What Webster aimed at, as Busino knew, was demystification. Contemporary English commentators regularly condemned in the Catholic church its idolatory, feigned holiness and crass materialism, and this episode was designed to echo these criticisms, operating as a theatrical demystification of the kind Jan Kott defines. A religious ceremony, he says, is not ritual proper

> but a profanation of the ritual. . . . The *theatrical* mime of a sacred
> mime played on the stage is shocking – it is a demystification of
> ritual. . . . To mime love is to demystify love, to mime power
> [Webster's dumb-show goes on to do this] is to demystify power, to
> mime ritual is to demystify ritual. . . .

(He then relates the presentation of ritual to Artaud and the Theatre of Cruelty and this will be relevant later.)[14]

Busino saw this clearly in the Loretto episode, and in fact demystification is a general impulse of the play. Much of its dramaturgy – the mobile viewpoint, commentary devices, a certain narrative naivety (in, for example, its use of time-lags), and the reductive humour centred on Bosola – is intended to demystify. There are dark forces at the centre of Webster's universe and in the heart of man; but the audience is constantly invited to view, with judicious detachment, attempts by characters to dress up, glamorise or misrepresent the meaning of their actions, as does the Cardinal here. So two valuations are present simultaneously:

> IST PIL Here's a strange turn of state! Who would have thought
> So great a lady would have match'd herself
> Unto so mean a person? yet the cardinal
> Bears himself much too cruel.

(III,iv, 24–7)

Elsewhere, this ambivalent effect achieves more obviously grotesque results, and the middle of the play is all grotesque. The waxworks episode of IV, i is a notorious example, notorious because of the charges of melodrama and implausibility that conventionally attach to it. But both charges disappear when we examine its theatrical impact and point. If the whole thing is faintly ludicrous it is intended to be so because it is a theatrical demonstration of the action of deceit: the audience goes through something of the experience of the Duchess, recognising only after the event that the bodies of husband and child are in fact waxworks. For the reader, the information comes at the beginning, in the stage direction: '*Here is discovered, behind a traverse, the artificial figures of Antonio and his children appearing as if they were dead*' (after l. 55). Evidently, when adding the stage-direction for publication, Webster had forgotten that logically only one child should be represented, the elder son. But we can be sure that the King's Men would not have gone to the trouble and expense of providing waxworks dummies, intended in the narrative to be entirely life-like, when the actors themselves might act them at no cost and very well. The Blackfriars audience would have been deceived as utterly as the Duchess, and Ferdinand does not disclose the true state of affairs for another fifty-five lines and after the Duchess's painful grief and her exit. That Webster intended this deceit on the audience – a mannerist *trompe-l'œil* – is shown by his literary inspiration here, the torture of Pamela and Philoclea by Cecropia in *Arcadia* III. Each of the sisters of Sidney's romance sees the other apparently dead and the reader is as assuredly hoodwinked as the characters themselves.[15]

So Ferdinand's apparently laboured boasting about his clever illusion, including the otherwise gratuitous detail of the artist's name who fashioned the dummies, is apposite. If the audience already knows the figures are wax, Webster works too hard; but if not, the theatrical effect is well judged: the audience is undeceived, but in the manner of a *coup*. The over-theatricality is Ferdinand's, and both his and Webster's art have mocked at truth.

We can go further about the staging. William Archer, who deplored the episode (and most of the play), found it implausible that the Duchess apparently makes no attempt to approach the 'corpses' (when she might discover the deception): 'A grief stricken woman might be expected to kiss her dead children, and so discover the fraud.'[16] If the wax figures were displayed in the discovery-space, a first idea made tempting by the reference to 'traverse', Bosola might physically prevent her approach. But if the 'traverse' (used only here in a stage direction for a Blackfriars play[17]) were drawn on the upper level, the bodies would in any case be out of the Duchess's reach. In Jones's Cockpit-in-Court, where this play was performed in 1630, the practical window in the stage facade (see Plate 5) would have served admirably. Probably some arrangement of pillars and arch similar to that at the Phoenix (see Plate 6) was available at the Blackfriars. Webster may well be remembering a spectacular scene in a private playhouse play of a decade earlier, Marston's *Antonio's Revenge*. This is full of anticipations, in mood and imagery, of Webster's play and contains the character name, Forobosco, that occurs in Webster's 'The Actors' Names' and in the dialogue (at II,ii, 31–2). The beginning of Marston's second scene opens: '*the curtains drawn, and the body of Feliche, stabbed thick with wounds, appears hung up*'. This is a display at an upper window and those on stage can only look up in horror.

So the Duchess, referring to the traditional punishment for adultery, asks for her body to be bound to Antonio's which is on display in the window, and her distance from the dummy allows the boy actress the freedom and (literally) the space to play out the verbal histrionics Webster has written for him. The whole episode is not at all clumsy but an ingenious piece of theatre, unsettling the audience but, finally, making a precise moral point. The theatrical joke starts out as Ferdinand's at the expense of the Duchess (a cruel trick) but ends up as Webster's at the expense of the audience (cruel but good theatre). The audience looks into a distorting mirror in which reality, or its own hold on it, is challenged, and this is always the effect of grotesque art.

Webster's grotesque theatre rises to a series of bizarre climaxes in IV and V, but even in a more restrained scene, the mixing of comic and tragic and the alternation in fluid and unstable mix of realism and convention achieves vivid results. In III,ii, the bedchamber scene, the playwright's 'impure art'[18] is seen at its most dazzling.

It opens in an apparently realistic way and in an atmosphere of relaxed domesticity as the Duchess prepares for bed. But the playful tone contrives to hint at both the joyful and dangerously secretive faces of the relationship as though the one is sauce to the other. Antonio, from his fearful beginning in I,i, is now secure (in its seventeenth-century sense). The jokes are warm, but to the husband's 'I must not live with you', the Duchess's 'Must? you are a lord of misrule' (l. 7) confirms the audience's misgivings about the Duchess's impropriety in the match and about Antonio's presumption.

However, in its staging, the scene's iconography is yet more complex. The properties called for in the script are a jewel casket and a hand mirror as the Duchess begins her undressing, and she sits on a chair or stool. Later, she evidently uses brush or comb. It is a scene of *déshabillé* (like that between Desdemona and Emilia in V,iii of *Othello*) and it would be tempting in production (then as now) to put a bed onstage to make the place and occasion clear and add point to the dialogue:

DUCH   You get no lodging here tonight, my lord. . . .
ANT   I must lie here.

(ll. 2,7)

What the audience sees is a picture like the late Elizabethan portrait of Elizabeth Vernon, Countess of Southampton (Plate 11). With jewel casket and comb, her hair down and formal day attire set to one side, she is caught as a private person in an off-guard moment, interrupted in her boudoir but looking out from the picture unconcernedly as though at someone known to her.

After the elaborate pleasantries of Antonio's praise of the married life, in which the tension of the moment stretches for a while (for we know Ferdinand approaches with the key), Antonio and Cariola 'steal forth the room' with that besetting levity that surrounds the Duchess. The actors, we presume, exit into the discovery-space (they will see and hear what happens) and Ferdinand enters from an upstage door. He may already have been seen by the audience, approaching by way of the upstage balcony ('That gallery gave him entrance'), for in a play of overwatching he has already spied someone with the Duchess in the bedchamber. As he quietly comes downstage, the Duchess sits and prattles on, brushing her hair, and she perhaps sees him for the first time, poniard in hand, in her mirror.[19] Now a Renaissance moral emblem of shattering power is achieved: the vain woman, her vanity symbolised by the mirror, visited by Death as a retribution for a moral laxity of which the play never acquits her. There are striking illustrations of this motif in Dürer and Baldung Grien amongst others: the woman attends her hair in the mirror, Death holds out to her an hour-glass, the reflection of which she can see, and nearby lurks the Devil. Ferdinand constantly associates his sister with devilish imagery and with his poniard he plays Death. In other moral pictures, Death seizes adulterous lovers *in flagrante delicto:* the man

11 Portrait of Elizabeth Vernon, Countess of Southampton

attempts to fight Death but is overthrown. Here that death is merely delayed.

So at the Blackfriars, sympathy for the Duchess was not the only or even the major note: alternative perspectives from the moral world would come thrusting in and lead, naturally enough, to Ferdinand's elaborate allegory of Reputation, Love and Death. The whole thing reminds one of the closet scene in Hamlet and if the bed is, in that case, an invention of twentieth-century productions, the sexual tension in Webster's scene is palpable and a product of the careful staging he has demanded.

The sequence ends with the re-entry of Antonio and Cariola, the futile gesture with the pistol and then the descent of the pair of lovers further into intrigue and deception issuing in the bungled plotting of the second half of the scene. The Duchess's confession to Bosola, like Antonio's catastrophic carelessness with the nativity in II,iii, is a Freudian parapraxis. And the whole scene has mixed elements of 'realism' and emblematic action, set speeches and allegory, to give a complex series of views of the play's protagonists which demanded an intelligent and sophisticated attention from the audience to construe its meaning. Webster must have been grateful this play was not premiered at the Red Bull.

The Duchess of Malfi reaches its major climax in IV,ii with the murder of the Duchess, and this has brought down on the play the charge that its last act is inevitably disappointing and the shape of the play artistically unsatisfying. Certainly, in the way of mannerist art, there seems a displacement here of the central motif, but Webster has a design and we must respond to it.

Kott's notion of demystification, quoted earlier, attaches to the work of Artaud, and an awareness of the aesthetics of the Theatre of Cruelty illuminates Webster's play in general and this scene in particular. Artaud was himself much drawn to Jacobean drama and, as Webster achieves in this play, he set himself 'to create a show around various famous personalities, horrible crimes and super-human self-sacrifices'. His 'cruelty' is not merely the barbarism practised on one man by another 'but the far more terrible, essential cruelty objects can practise on us'. He continues the idea in the spirit of Bosola's agnosticism: 'We are not free and the sky can still fall on our heads.' Artaud recommended a kind of total theatre which is capable of having an immediate and physical impact on the audience and his summary of stage effects to be deployed reads like a prompter's list of props and effects for Webster's play: 'Cries, groans, apparitions, surprises, all kinds of *coups de théâtre* . . . beautiful incantations . . . rare mixed sounds, masks, outsize puppets'.[20]

IV,ii is fifteen minutes of the most compelling Theatre of Cruelty in Jacobean drama. In narrative terms, little enough happens. In the source story, the Duchess is warned of her impending death, prays in conventional manner for God's mercy, makes provision for her children and then, as the account briskly concludes, 'the two ruffians did put a cord about her neck and strangled her'.[21] No Ferdinand lurks nearby, his sanity cracking, there are no madmen, no coffin and bell, and Bosola has yet to enter the story. So most of IV,ii comes from Webster's bizarre imagination. The scene is in two halves and the second concerns the bad bond between servant and master and Ferdinand's initial descent into an almost literal bestiality. We shall concentrate on the first half up to the death of the Duchess.

It follows the structure of a court masque[22] and so echoes the opening of the play in 'chargeable revels'. The madmen sent to torment the Duchess provide the antimasque with appropriate song and dance and the disguised Bosola brings in the main masque of gifts for the Duchess (coffin, cords and bell) and an invitation to her to join the (parodic) festivity. It is a kind of marriage masque donated by Ferdinand but its intention is desecration, not celebration. However, paradoxically, the inverted rituals fortify the Duchess, allowing her to die not in the lunatic nightmare Ferdinand would impose (that fate is reserved for him) but in the odour of sanctity. The energies of the scene pull first towards demystification and then back towards consecration, and the perspective shows, for a short while, a kind of heaven.

The action proceeds from complexity to simplicity and from noise to quiet. At the beginning, anticipated in their offstage cacophony, the madmen bring disorder in order. They are presented with mock formality by a servant as master of ceremonies and they process on to take their positions in front of (downstage of) the seated Duchess and Cariola. Their song, sung '*to a dismal kind of music*', was scored for the Blackfriars production by a company regular, Robert Johnson.[23] The music imitates the ominous animal sounds the song speaks of and the singing is accompanied by the lute and perhaps other instruments from the music house. The piece is harsh and unharmonious but ends mockingly in a harmonious resolution – 'And die in love and rest', the opposite of the fate intended for the Duchess.

In the lunatic and fragmentary dialogue that follows, the madmen rehearse important themes with which the play is much concerned – death, hypocrisy, illicit sex and the pursuit of knowledge. But the crazed worlds of the madmen are isolated each from the other and the general effect, more telling than the individual speech, is of Babel. The clearest statement is the first: 'Doomsday not come yet? I'll draw it nearer by a perspective.' There follows a strange, grotesque dance, '*with music answerable thereto*', in which the Renaissance ideal of choreographic harmony is parodied in angular movements and obscene gestures behind which the court revels are still discernible. This irregular ballet ended, probably in mocking obeisance to the Duchess and with giggles and cat-calls, the madmen make a disorderly exit. They are replaced by Bosola who brings in the main masque.

Now order and a kind of decorous propriety take the stage. After the cacophony, the stage events are defined and precise. Bosola who has promised never to visit the Duchess again in his own shape now personates, successively, Old Man, Tomb-maker and Bellman. We have no indication of his actual appearance, but he surely wears black robes and a grotesque 'old Man' vizard. If the Duchess recognizes him she pretends not to, because she willingly enters the pantomime he initiates and her role-playing will save her from the despair Ferdinand intends. She confronts the macabre properties shown to her, '*a coffin, cords and bell*', with devastating equanimity. The coffin is carried in by Executioners, also in black and hooded, and laid before her. It is her 'last presence-chamber' and represents an ironic reversion of the privacy she has claimed from the opening of the play.

Progressing through her apt questions, 'Dost thou perceive me sick . . . dost know me? . . . Who am I? . . . Am I not thy Duchess?' to her ringing claim of integrity, 'I am the Duchess of Malfi still', the Duchess is invited to participate in and finally organise her last ritual. It begins with incantation – 'Hark now everything is still . . .' – and the rhythmic tolling of the bell and in all probability the actions the verses speak of are precisely carried out: the Duchess's hair is strewn with powder, she is dressed in a white gown, her feet are bathed, and a crucifix is placed at her neck. She willingly partakes as a bride and celebrant and the poem serves her for an epithalamium and a requiem. So her improvised wedding of I,i is completed and she will, in fact, 'die in love and rest'.

Cariola, who as in the earlier ritual is a witness, is now tactfully removed and a tableau of utmost simplicity arranged. The Duchess, stage managing these last rites to wrest Christian solace from a black mass, kneels, the coffin serving for an altar before her, the Executioners on either side holding the rope that will throttle her. On the intimate but open Black-friars stage it is a scene of shattering power, pitiful but also sublime. Out of the source story's laconic statement, Webster has created a piece of stylised theatre that is heart-rending and beautiful:

> Come violent death,
> Serve for mandragora to make me sleep!
> Go tell my brothers, when I am laid out,
> Then they may feed in quiet.   *They strangle her.*
> (IV,ii,234–7)

This is a stage moment of unity amidst the fragmentary imagery of an absurd universe, a baroque statement of martyrdom and heroism in a mannerist play. Webster has the courage not to end there (as a popular playwright would): almost immediately Cariola will be brought on stage to bite, scream and prevaricate to save her life, Ferdinand will 'go hunt the badger, by owl-light', and the absurd universe comes crowding back for a whole last act. As the Duchess dies, a thorough-going naturalism would demand choking noises, hands tearing involuntarily at the rope, a thrashing of limbs, the face contorted. But as Ferdinand later says, with a strong memory of what happens here, 'Strangling is a very quiet death.' The brutality of the event is insulated by its ritual formality.

Act V is a controlled, almost perverse, exercise in anti-climax. It rattles by at great speed after the leisurely narrative movement of IV, and the King's Men's staging would contrive a steady acceleration in the action. Free of his source story, Webster now creates, by way of Bosola's con-science-torn viewpoint, a meaningless topography which is man's hellish life on earth. The machinery is hectic farce and the dialogue is studded with one-line jokes and more extended passages of ferocious humour, including the *Commedia*-like episode of the incompetent doctor (V, ii).[24]

Peripeteia is the key; everything the characters do rebounds upon them. The Cardinal recruits in Bosola a man intent on killing him and then, to conceal his crime, diverts all hope of his own rescue; the doctor is beaten for his pains; Antonio is killed in a 'direful misprison' by one intending him succour; Ferdinand kills his brother believing him to be the devil. As the ironies beget ironies, two scenes stand out in tone, V,i in which Pescara's moral strictures are delivered straight-facedly, and the echo scene of V,iii, with its plangent tone and affecting development of the theme of mortality (irony operates here too, but not comically). Outside these, the stage action is all comic stage business, with rapid exits and entrances, concealments, bodies being hidden, much stumbling about in (stage) dark, and, in the stock joke of the house guests sworn to non-intervention, the only certain use in the play of the upper level (V,v,19–33). Bosola inevitably points up the sheer theatricality of all this. He declares himself 'an actor in the main of all' and describes Antonio's death as 'Such a mistake as I have often seen in a play' (V,v,85, 95–6). Webster's conscious control is never more evident. The final moments with Antonio's son provide a kind of promise for the future but it is perfunctorily handled. Catharsis seems not the intention; in a way the audience has not deserved it.

Eric Bently has invited us to see all theatre as 'an extension of the range of scandal'.[25] Every play exists in that special place where actor and audience interact, but the interaction of this play is a peculiarly complex one. This is a tragedy of scandal, so well suited to the enclosed and intimate circumstances of the Blackfriars playhouse that it is difficult to imagine it played at the Globe. Amongst the scandalmongers are the audience as they sit around and upon the stage, forming a scenic background of innuendo, moral indignation and prurience in which the Duchess and Antonio, like the fine lady with her gamekeeper, conduct their love affair. In 'so open and black a theatre', as the Red Bull or the Globe, the play's disquieting tensions would be dissipated, as would its potential to embarrass. At the Blackfriars, 'privacy' has a double effect: the audience can be private (voyeurs) and they are invited (as voyeurs) to view private things.

The lovers are aware of the gossip that surrounds them. Antonio tells Delio, 'The common rabble do directly say she is a strumpet' (III,i, 25–6), and the Duchess teases Ferdinand with 'a scandalous report. . . . Touching mine honour' (III,i,47–8). Rumours of this kind are exactly what the Aragonian brothers most fear, for they know that personal misconduct may not be kept private: 'There is a kind of honey-dew that's deadly:' Twill poison your fame' (I, i, 307–8). Ferdinand's allegory about Reputation in III, ii expresses real ideas, the justice of which a private theatre audience would readily acknowledge. About to die, the Duchess, in a memorable phrase, looks forward to being 'out of your whispering' (IV, ii, 223), where the whispers belong firstly to the Executioners but more generally to the world of gossip that surrounds her. (This is the purpose of the wretched Switzer passage of III, ii, for the Duchess has wilfully made herself a prey to bawdy jokes and coarse satire.)

So the Blackfriars audience becomes an extension of the stage action. In Bosola's asides of II,i, addressed directly to the stage sitters who probably responded visibly if not audibly, ironies already available to the audience are articulated and the audience is invited to contemplate its own, Bosola-like attitudes.

A world of innuendo and deceit is a brittle world and, for all the Duchess's heroic death, the play generally is cynical about generous motives and expansive ideals. It presents a picture of discontinuity and estrangement. Despite making subtle use of the Blackfriars playing conditions, the play made no special demands of the King's Men in staging or production. Props and costumes are carefully deployed but easily supplied, and in casting, a conventional use of doubling provides extras for the populous dumb-show of III,iii and the madmen's antimasque of IV,ii. But of the principal actors, this presentation of a world of discontinuity asked a great deal.

Webster's sharp alternations between comic and tragic, realism and pantomime, private and formal demand a special attentiveness from the cast and much trust. In particular, they must eschew the actor's characteristic tendency to seek sympathy for his character (and consequently himself). Even with Antonio and the Duchess, as this commentary has continually stressed, Webster is at pains to deflect an obvious and ready sympathy. To a modern eye, the Duchess is all heart; to a Jacobean 'Private' audience, her behaviour was also (not 'on the other hand') morally culpable.

She is denied in the play the revelations of inner life that come through soliloquy. The soliloquy, by the time of writing, may increasingly have looked old-fashioned, a part of the barn-storming repertoire of the public stage. She is seen in dialogue and often an undercurrent allows her a private communion with Antonio but not with us. We consistently see her from the outside (in her relation to others and in their attitudes to her). She is defined, existentially, by her initial decision to go into the wilderness (the expression is hers, at I,i, 359–61) and then subsequently by the series of roles by which she creates a life-style that enables her to confront death. Significantly, her moment of greatest self-awareness – 'I am Duchess of Malfi still' – presents her in her social role; we never learn her personal name.

The boy actress Sharpe (and perhaps earlier, Robinson) had training and stage experience to draw on but little relevant emotional experience (and no acting theory). He would need to identify, or rather be shown, tone and meaning in each episode and deliver them with force and clarity. Even the individual speech looks like, and has to be performed as, a linked series of discontinuities, staccato in effect, without the cumulative momentum of a Shakesperian paragraph. In the intimate playing conditions of the Blackfriars, Sharpe could concentrate on brief, passionate expressions, not sustained, rhetorical structures. Declamation would make the verse appear jagged and contrived.

Discontinuity marks characterisation and language throughout the play. Webster initially conceived the four main characters according to humours psychology (and the determinism of that is part of the play's cruel logic) – the Cardinal is phlegmatic, Bosola melancholic, Ferdinand choleric, the Duchess sanguine.[26] The actors would have grasped this initial premise. But the playwright's handling of the roles evinces a constant pragmatism and they never achieve the consistency (or descend into the lifeless rigidity) that such a programme promises. However, as we have seen with the Duchess, neither are they given the individuating marks that we often find in Shakespeare. For Burbage, as for us, Ferdinand's motives remain ambiguous. Webster, like a modern novelist, is himself content to be puzzled. The character's concern with family honour is held by modern commentators to be an inadequate 'objective correlative' for the blood-thirsty vindictiveness his actions demonstrate and incest is much discussed. But Burbage, pre-Freudian, would have 'believed' the holding position that his character proposes immediately after his sister's death:

> I had a hope
> Had she continu'd widow, to have gain'd
> An infinite mass of treasure by her death
>   (IV,ii, 283–5)

and been satisfied with the moral generalisation at his character's own death:

> Whether we fall by ambition, blood, or lust,
> Like diamonds, we are cut with our own dust.
>   (V,v, 72–3)

Elsewhere in the play, Burbage had to play a 'discontinuous' character whose inner passions are illuminated powerfully at times, but not with the consistency to reveal the whole man. Then, as now, the actor would perform confidently only if he trusted the play's larger design.

Much the same may be said about the part of Bosola. The play is his tragedy as much as the Duchess's, and something of the special function of Bosola as mediator has already been discussed. Lowin would have found here a conspicuously diverse set of roles to play, like a series of music hall acts – comedian, showman, master of ceremonies. Again, a discontinuous style of playing (which, incidentally, we should connect also with the Theatre of Cruelty) is appropriate as the actor of Bosola shuffles through a pack of identities. If, unlike the others, the character learns something of his own moral nature during the play, he is most appropriately seen as a macabre point of view. For Lowin, Bosola was a great role but not, in the realistic manner the expression suggests, a great character.

To play their parts, the King's Men actors remained outside their roles but passionately engaged with them. They would have played the text, with its surface tensions, paradoxes and contradictions, and not concerned themselves too deeply with a subtext. For this is grotesque theatre and Webster could evidently count on his actors' ability to present in rapid alternation a sequence of different faces and moods. The play's final statement is one of integrity:

> Integrity of life is fame's best friend,
> Which nobly, beyond death, shall crown the end.

But the play is 'a perspective that shows us hell' and such integrity, Webster bravely asserts, is seldom achieved, and then won at colossal expense.

7 · 'Some High-Tuned Poem': *The Broken Heart* at the Blackfriars

In V,iii of Ford's *The Broken Heart*, Orgilus is executed by his own hand in a style that wrings admiration from the bystanders. Bassanes, one of them, declares that

> Some high-tuned poem
> Hereafter shall deliver to posterity
> The writer's glory and his subject's triumph.
> (IV,ii,132–4)[1]

The play itself is this 'high-tuned poem', where 'high-tuned' evidently refers both to a lofty and melodious style and to elevated sentiments ('high-toned' is included).[2] Ford fashions here a tragedy of unusual solemnity, heroic and in the grand manner, yet about the softer sentiments of love and melancholia. It is the playwright's masterpiece and a monument (the word is inevitably attracted to this marmoreal play) to European baroque.

John Ford is the last great tragedian of the pre-Commonwealth stage. During the 1620s he collaborated with established playwrights, principally Dekker, on a number of plays, mostly now lost, for the popular stage. Between 1628 (when *The Lover's Melancholy* was licensed for performance) and 1639 (when *The Lady's Trial* was published) he wrote the seven surviving, solo plays on which his reputation rests. Dates of the first performances and of the order of composition of these plays are uncertain, but all were written for the private theatre and for the companies working in the two major private houses:

THE LOVER'S MELANCHOLY, performed by the King's Men at the Blackfriars (publ. 1629)

LOVE'S SACRIFICE, performed by Queen Henrietta Maria's Company at the Phoenix (publ. 1633)

'TIS PITY SHE'S A WHORE, performed by Queen Henrietta Maria's Company at the Phoenix (publ. 1633)

THE BROKEN HEART, performed by the King's Men at the Blackfriars (publ. 1633)

PERKIN WARBECK, performed by Queen Henrietta Maria's Company at the Phoenix (publ. 1634)

THE FANCIES CHASTE AND NOBLE, performed by Queen Henrietta Maria's Company at the Phoenix (publ. 1638)

THE LADY'S TRIAL, performed by Beeston's Boys at the Phoenix (publ. 1639)

Ford is the quintessential private theatre playwright. Educated at Oxford and the Middle Temple, he evidently had an income other than from his playwriting. He published his plays with a writer's care, supplying epistles and dedications, and in two of these he stressed his amateur status: the dedication of *The Lover's Melancholy* maintains that 'The account of some leisure hours is here summ'd up' in the play; and, in similar vein, *'Tis Pity* is called 'These first fruits of my leisure'. Prologues and epilogues stress the writer's seriousness of intent and make high claims for his style of theatre. The professional is sneered at in the prologue to *The Lover's Melancholy:* 'It is art's scorn that some of late have made the noble use of poetry a trade'; and the prologue to *Perkin Warbeck* despises popular esteem: 'Nor is here Unecessary mirth forc'd, to endear a Multitude'. In the epilogue to *The Broken Heart*, in evident recognition of the fastidiously grave nature of the play, Ford or another develops a lengthy apologia, on the lines of Jonson and addressed to a learned audience, in which, he declares, 'Our writer's aim was in the whole address'd Well to deserve of *all* but please the *best*.'

Ford had learned assiduously from Shakespeare and from the Jacobean dramatics of Fletcher, Middleton and Webster, borrowing sometimes a plot motif, sometimes a style of writing, sometimes a way of analysing his characters. *'Tis Pity* is the most 'Jacobean' of the plays, an Italianate tragedy of revenge, depending narratively on *Women Beware Women* (as well as *Romeo and Juliet*) and remixing the stock ingredients of a decade or two earlier into a sensational and lurid melodrama. But in Ford's *oeuvre* the play has a faintly old-fashioned air. In its major protagonist, Giovanni, mannerist narcissism receives its ultimate form: the incestuous hero whose final entrance *'with a heart upon his dagger'*, his sister's of course, is the supreme, existential gesture. The play generally apes (with considerable success) the neurotic energy, grotesque heightening and agnostic pessimism of the best days of Jacobean tragedy. But elsewhere, even at times in this play, Ford cultivates a more individual voice and theatrical style when he explores a line of heroic martyrdom and aristocratic sufferance.

Perkin Warbeck is exemplary of this more authentic Ford. Superficially, the play is a late version of the Elizabethan chronicle play dramatising another chapter from Tudor history, the story of a counterfeit's outrageous claims to the English throne. But Ford's Perkin, unlike history's, refuses when imprisoned to admit the deception, maintaining to the death the truth of his self-declared identity as England's true sovereign. He dies a political martyr. King of love's affections in his marriage to Katherine and, by his courage and steadfastness, victor over death itself, he accumulates steadily through the play a moral legitimacy denied to his lawful opponents. *Perkin Warbeck* can be read as a psychological study in self-deception, but its theatrical effect is one of baroque illusionism. It achieves a tragic climax which is neither violent nor sensational but which is entirely compelling.

In *'Tis Pity*, Annabella knows, together with a line of Jacobean tragedians, that 'there's but a dining-time 'Twixt us and our confusion'. But Duke Perkin's end has a quite different resonance:

> But let the world, as all to whom I am
> This day a spectacle, to time deliver
> And by tradition fix posterity
> Without another chronicle than truth,
> How constantly my resolution suffer'd
> A martyrdom of majesty.

So he too would have a 'high-tuned poem' and his sentiments project him towards a kind of apotheosis. They record, also, a vein of self-presentation and a theatricalising of experience which are witnessed in the elaborate syntax of the lines. Martyred resolution, theatrical self-presentation and an elaborate style which embellishes experience: these are the hallmarks of Ford's art at its most Fordian and they are baroque qualities. They appear most refined in *The Broken Heart*. The play was published in 1633 and the title page bears the information, 'A Tragedy: Acted by the King's Majesty's Servants at the Private House in the Blackfriars'. There is no mention of the Globe, and one would not expect this play to be an offering in the popular theatre. Neither is the playwright mentioned by name, although he did sign the dedication. Instead, the title page bears Ford's anagrammatic identification, 'Fide Honor', meaning 'honour through fidelity', which itself is an apt commentary on the play.

The date of composition is unknown and we can be no more exact than to suggest the late 1620s to 1633. A witty couplet written not after 1634, besides drawing attention to the playwright's narrowness of range and repetitiveness of subject, seems to imply that the play preceded another of the tragedies published in 1633:

> Thou cheat'st us Ford: mak'st one seem two by art;
> What is *Love's Sacrifice* but *The Broken Heart?*[3]

Although, as we shall see, aspects of the play have the emblematic formality of the masque, the King's Men would have found *The Broken Heart* relatively undemanding in its staging requirements. The play makes no use of trap or upper level and only once, apparently, of the discovery-space (in III,ii); and there are no complicated entrances or exits, except the opening of the last scene. Little of significance is required in stage furnishing and only the altar in the last scene and half a dozen chairs would have busied the stage carpenter. These chairs, however, are significant and their effect on stage blocking and movements is of crucial importance to the theatrical feel of the play.

At the opening of III,iii, Ithocles is '*discovered in a chair*', and Penthea sits by him but at some little distance (his first line is 'Sit nearer, sister, to me; nearer yet'). He is evidently on some kind of day-bed for he has just awakened from sleep and is sick, and Penthea sits on a stool. The subsequent duologue, until the violent entrance of Bassanes, is delivered sitting. Presumably, the whole exchange did not take place in the discovery-space, but if not, we may assume that as Ithocles is revealed extras bring him forward on his chair on to the main stage and Penthea joins him there, also from the discovery-space, carrying her stool. As she sets it down, Ithocles invites her to sit closer. (All the preparations in the audience's mind for this private encounter have been made in the previous scene in which the offstage Ithocles is heard awakening to a gentle song and Prophilus clears the room while Bassanes expresses his unease at the situation.)

In IV,iii, a chair is again associated with a sick and enfeebled character, for at the opening the dying Amyclas is brought in and settled in a chair – '*Enter* LEMOPHIL *and* GRONEAS *leading* AMYCLAS *and placing him in a chair*' – and later he is carried out in it – '*Exeunt carrying the King*'. Three chairs in the next scene determine the staging. The dead Penthea is carried on in a chair by Chrystalla and Philema who place it centre-stage while two servants each set a chair on either side, one for Orgilus, though he will barely sit in it, '*the other with an engine*' which is Orgilus's trick chair to trap Ithocles. All the action of this scene is necessarily managed around these chairs. Finally, in the last scene, the dead Ithocles is carried in '*on a hearse, or in a chair*' and is placed to one side of the altar where he and it will become an important centre of activity for the last moments of the play.

In this way, *The Broken Heart* is a play of chairs. At a practical level they allot stations for the characters and allow them to remain still, even statuesque, during passages of intense dialogue. But they also reflect togetherness and divorce in two of the scenes, and their echoic effect lends fine irony to two of the deaths. The chair is a sick bed, a throne or a trap, and it emphasises those key moments of the play when characters reach their nadirs of physical or mental exhaustion, or death itself. The

King's Men may have had chairs in store to serve most of these occasions, but the trick chair, at least, would need to be constructed with care.

Like the furniture of the play, the props are few in number but
significant in effect, and the King's Men's stage manager would need
little industry but some care to provide them exactly. In order of appearance they are: I,ii – the laurel wreath that Calantha has prepared for
Ithocles (he is a triumphant soldier at the play's opening); I,iii – a book
which Orgilus, turned scholar, may wrangle with to deceive Prophilus
and Euphrania[4]; III,i – a box with a scroll, the communication from the
oracle at Delphos which Armostes delivers to Tecnicus, the contents of
which are displayed and enigmatically explained in IV,iii; III,iii – the
poniard with which Bassanes threatens Ithocles; III,vi – the paper in
which Penthea's conceit of a testament evidently takes literal form ('In
this paper my will was charactered . . .' ll. 45–6); IV,i the ring Calantha
uses to rebuff Nearchus and speak indirectly to Ithocles; IV,iv – Orgilus's
poniard used to kill the trapped Ithocles (and the same weapon does duty
for his self-slaughter of V,ii); V,ii – fillets for Orgilus's arms, two staves,
and probably some contraption for catching the blood; V,iii – crowns
worn by Calantha and the dead Ithocles and another ring with which
Calantha weds her dead lover.

In a play about love, honour, ambition and death, these few properties
act as vital stage imagery. In particular, a group of them imply notions
of contract, oath and prophecy, all binds on the future – the rings, the
will and the Delphic scroll (and notice that Calantha's last speeches form
another 'testament'); while the laurel and the crowns imply victory in life
and in death and an ironic reversal for human desire and ambition. The
circularity and continuity of rings, laurel and crowns, in form and
meaning, are part of the stoical strain of the play at large (see Orgilus at
V,iii, 148–9). This economical use of properties is richly eloquent though
the effect, we might say, is laconic.

'Our scene is Sparta' begins the play's prologue and 'laconic' derives
from Lacedemon, Sparta's other name or that of its surrounding region.
The locale is important to the playwright and the wars between Sparta
and Messenia (743–453 B.C.) form a backdrop to the domestic tragedy
of the play: Ithocles returns from them in the second scene bringing
'Triumphs and peace upon his conquering sword'. Sparta symbolised for
Ford's audience the values of physical courage, constancy, self-discipline
and female chastity. In *The Lover's Melancholy*, the classical world of
Cyprus is only nominally the scene, nothing more than a faraway setting
for a romance story. Here, Spartan values determine the fabric of the
plot, Spartan customs and beliefs colour the language and Spartan ideals
provide keys to the characterisation. Laconicism is a virtue and a vice in
the play.

In visual terms, one should expect the King's Men to render a kind of classicalness in the costumes, and significantly in the dialogue of *The Broken Heart* there are none of the anachronisms in dress references that there are in *The Lover's Melancholy*. The only actual indications of character costume are the veil which Penthea chooses to wear when dead in IV,ii, the scholar's gown or the like, hooded presumably to give sufficient disguise, which Orgilus wears as his 'borrowed shape' (so called by Penthea and Tecnicus at II,iii, 76 and III,i, 4), and the ceremonial costumes of V,iii: the dead Ithocles wears '*a rich robe*', Calantha and the other ladies '*a white robe*', and, already mentioned among the props, Calantha and Ithocles have crowns. Probably the cast wore a mixture of classical and contemporary dress in the manner of Henry Peacham's sketch of *Titus Andronicus* and this would be entirely appropriate. For Ford writes both about historical Sparta and the contemporary world centred on a Caroline court culture; and his characters were understandable to a Blackfriars coterie audience sympathetic to the tone of Henrietta Maria's household. They were recognizable in their manners as sophisticated pagans.

As with furnishings and props, there is not an abundance of music in *The Broken Heart* but what there is is used to maximum effect, underscoring ideas, defining characters and contributing fully to the masque-like, baroque event of the play's last scenes. Besides the standard opportunity for four inter-act sonatas, the play contains four songs and two important passages of instrumental music. Though no arrangements survive, Ford's script clearly calls for expert and tactful musicianship both in the scoring and in the playing and singing. Indeed, in a general sense, music goes to the heart of the play's meaning, and at various moments characters allude to its moral and symbolic force (see II,ii, 8–10; II,iii, 18–20; IV,ii,69–71; V,iii,34–5).

Of the four songs, and catching the general tone of the play, three are sad and elegaic, one cheerful and celebratory. In the first, Ithocles's song in III,ii, Bassanes sees a degenerating effeminacy. '*Soft music*' (stage direction) ushers in the exquisite lyrics of 'Can you paint a thought . . .', sung probably by a single tenor voice and accompanied by the lute. It sets a gentle mood for the scene that follows and speaks volumes for Ithocles's state of mind. The second song is Orgilus's donative for the wedding of Prophilus and Euphrania, the sanguine 'Comforts lasting . . .'. There is no clue as to how this is presented. Perhaps Orgilus performs it himself, but more probably he introduces another singer, accompanied by the band, for the effect should be solemn and hymn-like, if joyous. The third song is sung offstage by a boy soprano and accompanied by a lute (Philema in the next scene tells us she sang the song and Chrystalla played). It is a tragic love song, seen from the woman's point of view, and Ford's fine writing demands a delicate scoring. The keynote is 'sad' (once in the stage direction, twice in the dialogue). The last song is Calantha's, sung on stage by 'the voices Which wait at th' altar' (V,iii, 78–9) which are male tenors and basses singing partly solo, partly in chorus and probably unaccompanied. It provides an aptly melancholy summary for Calantha's story but more importantly it contributes richly to the emotion-charged climax of the action. The first important instrumental passage is the celebratory music of V,ii which accompanies the opening processional entry with *'loud music'* (stage direction) and then, when the couples are set, becomes the dance music for the revels. For this, presumably, the band is in full view on the balcony over the stage where it plays as a broken consort (wind and string instruments mixed) with a heavy, rhythmic beat. The other instrumental passage, very different in kind, is used to create a sacramental atmosphere at the beginning of the last scene where Ford's stage-direction calls for *'Music of recorders'* and marks its cues during the opening sequence.

The Broken Heart is by no means a piece of music theatre. But the musical effects are important in the play, nicely conceived so as to give maximum support to the actors.

We have no indication how the parts were cast amongst the King's Men. Ford gives a list of King's Men actors, though without assigning roles, with the 1629 printed text of *The Lover's Melancholy* (seventeen actors for sixteen named parts); but there is no cast list with the 1633 *The Broken Heart*. There are twenty speaking parts, sixteen male (though Amelus of III,iii and IV,iii and the servant of IV,iv are tiny) and six female parts. The five main parts are Orgilus (553 lines), Ithocles (399), Bassanes (367), Penthea (363) and Calantha (211), and the interplay between them and the conflict within each is the double heart of the play. None is clearly the principal. Their intertwining stories form a unified, larger structure and the various plots are fused into a harmonious design unlike the characteristic multiple plot of Jacobean drama (and of *'Tis Pity*). Ford patently eschews the blandishments of a comic subplot involving Groneas and Lemophil and even determines not to extend the intrigue possibilities of 'Aplotes' as a go-between for Prophilus and Euphrania. The actor of Orgilus might have initially identified his role as the revenging villain-hero (and the play therefore as a revenge tragedy), and the actor of Ithocles may have identified his role as a *de casibus* villain-hero (and the play therefore as a tragedy of ambition). But rapidly the detailed attention Ford gives to Bassanes (who plays an Othello in reverse), the exquisite pathos of Penthea's progress and the great climax centred on Calantha must have led the cast to a sense of the play's novel structure (novel as new and, to us, as in the novel). Often, Penthea has been selected by modern criticism as the focus of the action, which wrongly turns the play into a *pièce à thèse* on the theme of enforced marriage.

There are three related love stories in the action: Penthea and Orgilus; Calantha and Ithocles; and Euphrania and Prophilus; and these are organised like the love relationships of a Restoration comedy into a sequence of right way/wrong way examples, or rather as a series of tragic/tragic/comic. The actors had quickly to grasp that they were not playing an intrigue tragedy but an almost unique kind of tragedy of manners.[5] There is no conventional villain or hero here, and just as Sparta is trapped by the prophecy from Delphos about its future, so these characters are trapped by the past and barely capable of significant action: they react rather than act, and their chief aim is to reconcile the dictates of their heart with the imperatives of a personally defined honour. So the static quality implied by the special use of chairs reflects an inner, psychological stasis, and the play generates a feeling of claustrophobia in its proceeding unlike anything else in the tragic drama of the period.

An exemplary scene, III,v, shows at once Ford's democratic interest in character and his preparation for Calantha's startling end, an end seen by many commentators as merely tacked on. The scene is ostensibly Penthea's. Hers here is the foregrounded story, hers the powerful but restrained emotions on view; she it is who speaks almost all the lines and it is her self-regarding air, even while she superficially concerns herself with the fate of her brother, which most forcefully impresses on an audience. Certainly, the boy actress would have enjoyed the histrionic conceit of the testament and the initiative his character takes throughout the exchange, organising, as it were, the future of the other characters in the play.

On stage, however, the actor of Calantha is no mere support. The character is given, during the middle part of the scene, a series of brief replies easily overlooked or undervalued in the reading:

> Do not doubt me . . .
> What saidest thou?. . . .
> Shall I answer here,
> Or lend my ear too grossly?
> What new change
> Appears in my behaviour, that thou darest
> Tempt my displeasure?. . . .
> You have forgot, Penthea,
> How still I have a father.
>
> (III,v, 71–104)

Played with due weight to an attentive audience, these laconic statements declare Calantha's love for Ithocles and demonstrate her self-possession (a key notion in the play) in not choosing to declare that love. All the tension of the part, here, lies in what is not admitted. A vital inner life has to be played by the actor, but it will be an inner life that Penthea, in her cocooning melancholia, will fail to notice. If the audience fails too, the actor of Calantha has fudged what Ford intended.

Calantha's whole part, until the last scene, is developed through such hints. She has the fewest lines of the major characters but she is major by virtue of, not despite, her not wearing her heart upon her sleeve. (That she has a heart the ending will of course prove forcefully.) So, in IV,i she plays a courtly game with Nearchus that allows her to express obliquely her feelings to Ithocles; and in IV,iii she reconciles public restraint and personal emotion by claiming her lover as a courtly suitor yet withholding from view the actual force of their mutual understanding.[6] When the news of the three deaths arrives in the dance scene, V,ii, her laconic response is thunderous. In this way her characterisation proceeds by way of understatement and the actor would have generated great expressive power through his/her silence. The hint for this kind of characterisation perhaps came from Cordelia; whose own tragedy is generated by her inability to be oratorical; but the development is all Ford's. We understand Calantha's dilemma and her emotional vitality with full clarity only at the moment when we should:

> They are silent griefs which cut the heartstrings.
> Let me die smiling.
>
> (V,iii,75–6)

The rest is music.

Penthea's is the more exotic role of the two (love-lorn heroine trapped in a marriage bed which is rendered adulterous by her own moral austerity), but both female characters demonstrate a characteristically sympathetic understanding on Ford's part and one which has led critics to a general notion that he wrote in anticipation, if only in an ideal world, of the availability of female actors.[7] Support for the idea is adduced from a passage in *Love's Sacrifice* in which a character, Fernando, speaks enthusiastically of women performers he has seen in Brussels, though these are obviously court ladies playing in royal entertainments such as masques. In 1629, French actresses had played at the Blackfriars but incurred great disapproval for their immodesty; and in the year that *The Broken Heart* was published Prynne had tactlessly written of female performers – 'notorious whores' – in such a way that the Queen herself, believing her own court dramatics were being referred to, instigated a savage punishment on him (see p. 57).

Even if the use of female actors was in the air, it seems improbable that Ford would write his female roles with any other than boy actresses in mind. In fact, there is little in the roles of Penthea and Calantha, for all the delicacy and insight with which they are composed, that a trained boy actress would have found especially taxing. Ford's 'feminism' lies in the qualities of constancy and strength with which he endows the two women characters and in his evident admiration of these qualities. It does not lie in the special skills he requires from the performers. The characters' sexuality is presented ambiguously through their chaste behaviour, and the boy actress had always transmitted a kind of sexual ambivalence. Two of the experienced boys at the Blackfriars, perhaps Honeyman and Thompson who had both played in *The Lover's Melancholy* a little before, would no doubt have played Penthea and Calantha expertly, helped to express the striking consistency inside their roles by their adult advisers. So unworried was Ford about the range or expertise of the boy actors that he wrote his last play, *The Lady's Trial*, for Beeston's wholly boy troupe at the Phoenix. If Penthea's last scene seems to us technically and emotionally difficult, it is no more so than Ophelia's last scene on which it is part based.

For the men, we might guess that the excellent, principal actor Taylor played Orgilus, Benfield, already a player of tragic weight, Ithocles, and the old-stager Lowin, Bassanes. The first two might well have chafed at the lack of range in their parts (Orgilus is no Hamlet), but the characters are deliberately hemmed in by Ford's notion of decorum which concerns both manners and psychology. The playwright added a curious list to the playtext (did the actors see this?) called 'The Speakers' Names, fitted to their Qualities', in which the Greek names of the characters are translated to show their aptness. Here, Orgilus is glossed 'Angry', Ithocles 'Honour of loveliness' and Bassanes 'Vexation'. (The second gives the lie to the idea that Ithocles's tragedy is one of ambition: his passion is the fashionable one of neo-platonic love.) The characters are trapped by these tag-names against their will and the names themselves underline a certain fatalism in the play itself. But for the actors, they imply a coherent sense of design in the play at large and individually a key to characterisation. The parts are consistent and the psyches of the characters, though not simple, must be played by the actors continuously and with a clearly defined intent. The result onstage will be an interlocking of the roles and a steady purposefulness in the play's progress. Even if, by modern standards, the King's Men had little rehearsal time to develop their characterisation, they would readily have been able to identify what we may call a 'through-line' for the character, a continuous intention expressible in terms of action, and to play it with conviction. (A Stanislavskian actor of today would respond to this quality in Ford as a rare thing in Jacobean and Caroline characterisation.) For tragic actors experienced in the discontinuities of Websterian drama, there was something new here to master.

Consistency is particularly interesting in the case of Bassanes because his is the role most variously drawn. Consistency in this play is important as a keynote both for the actor to play the role and for the character as a right way of living. Through the latter idea, Ford develops his idea of Spartan stoicism. The highest achievement for the stoic man is consistency itself, which means being true to oneself when that self has been discovered and refined. Consequently, change is the chief stoic evil. Bassanes works hard to learn this lesson from III, iii onwards when he recognises that his intemperate, rash behaviour has shocked everyone and caused him to lose Penthea. Though unstoical by temperament (he cannot simply cease to be 'vexatious'), his very emotionalism is a constant in the play. He cannot change – his character is his fate – but he can work hard to repress the destructive elements in his make-up, which we see him doing in IV and V.

Outside the rash Bassanes, Ford's parts demanded from the Caroline actors a style of understatement not cultivable on the public stage (the title page makes no reference to a Globe performance) and only perhaps developing at the Blackfriars as a house style as the period progressed. We have seen earlier that dialogue at the Globe required a loud delivery and that the King's Men were noted for their restrained and natural action (see pp. 49–52). Nowhere more asiduously than in this play is the intimate ambiance of the Blackfriars exploited.

The three duologues Penthea shares first with Orgilus (II,iii, 10–131), then with Ithocles (III, ii, 1–86), and finally with Calantha (III, vi, 5–106) show to perfection Ford's restrained manner of writing. The first is also restrained in its staging by the use of chairs, and the characters may well be seated in the third too, but Ford does not indicate this. Though the middle dialogue has some passion and movement, all three exchanges are studiedly small scale in effect. In the first and second, Penthea dictates the mood and tempo, and in the last, Penthea and Calantha both play subtle games (different ones) of decorum. In II, iii there is the small (and deliberately perfunctory) kneeling ceremony which is a betrothal in reverse to unmake a vow already in effect broken; and in III, vi the will passes from one hand to another. Otherwise, movement, like emotion, is restricted and the audience is able to concentrate fully on the nuances of language and the parsing of the conversations. In fact, these scenes have the concentrated intensity of television drama, and Ford seems to have conceived them, and much else in the play, in a stage version of close-up. The duologues invite the audience simply to alternate its attention rhythmically from one speaker to the other, following a delicately phrased contest in which subtext and disguised feeling are as important as text. Again there is much here for the Stanislavskian actor.

The encounter in II, iii between two people crippled by their thwarted love for each other is a small masterpiece of private theatre writing. The characters are unable to approach each other in the embrace their love demands and their pain causes them to attack, accuse and rend in a way quite harrowing for the audience. Each word is measured as Penthea, her motives often misunderstood by the scholar but patent to the actor and spectator, forces Orgilus by strength of will (over herself and him) to leave her physically and emotionally.[8] Note here that stoicism does not imply an unlovely *apatheia*: far from it. But for the two King's actors, only a restrained and realistic manner of playing would have released the proper charge of the dialogue, with its reined-in tensions and high emotion.

The realism and restraint proper to these scenes, together with the psychological patterning of the *dramatis personae*, by no means make the play austere in effect and monochrome, although it is uniquely homogeneous in tone. The almost gaudy emotions of the characters ensure this. But also Ford's baroque imagination conjures a series of florid scenes in the last phase of the play which act out the fate of the protagonists in a bravura style and so provide a counter-pull to the realism elsewhere. The characters are products of the union of 'historical' Sparta and Henrietta Maria's court, and they contrive to end their lives in theatrical splendour. Nothing becomes these people like their deaths.

Penthea's last scene alive is her madness scene of IV, ii, although, characteristically in this play, she will continue to be eloquent in death (IV, iv). Madness is a kind of mental collapse, a breakdown of that rational control the stoic man prides himself on, and in IV, ii Penthea is 'a prey to words' (l. 44). But her lines have an artful quality and an air of conscious design. In her painful delirium, the apparent free association of her wandering mind leads to an allusiveness, a recourse to concrete reference and a metaphorical cast that we associate with formal poetry. In her language, Orgilus sees not madness but something oracular (l. 133) as her subconscious fashions a chain of linked images that explore and judge her situation and the parts that others have played in it.

The actor of Penthea moves amongst the six others on stage, 'Her hair about her ears', in a kind of surreal performance, touching one, gesturing towards another and drawing them, unwilling, into her playlet. In the performance, the character is refined by art into a metaphysical lament (Penthea= 'Complaint'), a ritual apology for her life. She begins with the sirens' song, proceeds by way of the rose garden where happiness is briefly tasted and rudely lost, and ends in contemplation of a leprous soul which has only griefs as friends.

Penthea's madness scene has method in it and her final act, offstage, is to order the dirge which catches and sublimates her predicament as an endless matryrdom to love:

> for now Love dies,
> Now Love dies, implying
> Love's martyrs must be ever, ever dying.
> (IV, iv, 151–3)

The other three death scenes with which the play ends also take the form of ceremonies staged by the protagonists in acts of calculated effect.

In IV, iv, Orgilus's three chairs symbolise the deadly triangle for three of the characters – contracted lovers parted by the tyranny of a brother. An elaborate stage direction describes how the scene is set:

Enter CHYRYSTALLA *and* PHILEMA, *bringing in* PENTHEA *in a chair, veiled; two other* Servants *placing two chairs, one on the other side, and the other with an engine on the other. The maids sit down at her feet mourning.* The Servants *go out.* ITHOCLES *and* ORGILUS *meet them.*

After a brief exchange between one of the servants and Orgilus, Orgilus and Ithocles contemplate the careful tableau arranged before them, a piece of funeral statuary, in which the empty chairs invite the young men to join it. The discovery-space is not used because all the action will centre on the chairs and Ford needs it on the main stage and in full relief.

The playwright risks the machiavellian trick chair because Ithocles's death, as he and Orgilus intend, is to be a ritual slaughter and not the result of a contest. Such chairs were used in real life, however melodramatic they seem to us,[9] and Ford may have known of a stage version that appeared in 1607 in *The Devil's Charter* by Barnabe Barnes. Here the trapping device is operated by the murderer some time after the victim has sat down and it is clear from the dialogue that the victim is caught by the arms by some spring mechanism.[10] In Ford's play, it seems that the trap operates automatically as soon as Ithocles sits – 'ITHOCLES *sits down and is catcht in the engine*' – and we may assume that again the victim's arms are caught, for it is important that he should not be able to resist the knife. Perhaps the actor of Ithocles operated the device himself as he settled in the chair, as this would be a reliable way of making sure that this piece of business worked properly.

At once, Ford and Orgilus gain an effective irony from the chair '*With an engine*' – ''Tis thy throne of coronation, Thou fool of greatness' says Orgilus (ll. 23–4). But Ithocles's noble nature will sublime the event into heroic art: 'By Apollo', exclaims the admiring avenger, 'Thou talkest a goodly language' (ll.51–2); and he will later describe to the court that Ithocles

> Was murdered; rather butchered, had not bravery
> Of an undaunted spirit, conquering terror,
> Proclaimed his last act triumph over ruin.
>
> (V, ii, 41–3)

Ithocles's last act, his piece of acting, is indeed a 'triumph', for the word means not only a victory but a spectacle staged to celebrate a victory ('triumph' in its original and court-ceremony use).

In this sequence, in fact, several ceremonial acts are neatly conjoined. Orgilus presents a show to Ithocles which is both a funeral for Penthea (with dirge, orations and ceremonial observances) and also a ritual revenge on Ithocles himself. (A duel would preclude a ritual element vital to Orgilus's design – certainty of outcome.) Then Ithocles, playing a manly part in the show, claims back a part of the initiative by his undaunted response and heroic language and so creates a triumph for himself. And his end becomes a self-fulfilment as his breath 'On the sacred altar Of a long-looked-for peace – now – moves – to heaven' (ll. 69–70).

Just as the delivery of the words is carefully controlled by the playwright's punctuation, so the whole scene has been carefully staged in Orgilus's imagination, and he now foretells a fitting apotheosis for brother and sister, martyrs of love: 'Sweet twins, shine stars for ever!' (l. 74). So ends an episode in which violence is ritualised and solace, even peace, achieved. Through dialogue and stage imagery, Ford goes boldly for a baroque effect and the moment is completed, as it began, with music, for the scene ends the act. Here perhaps, and it would certainly be tempting in a revival today, the Blackfriars band played a reprise of Penthea's dirge. Curiously, Ford makes no provision in the text for the removal of the bodies in their chairs; he merely writes in Orgilus's exit. Perhaps he vaguely has in mind the idea that the bodies can be concealed in the discovery-space by the arras (although it was argued earlier that the first stage direction seems to suggest that the chairs are placed on the open stage). Instead, and during the interact music, the servants must re-enter and carry out the chairs with their burdens with the chaste decorum in which the entire scene has been played.

V, ii comprises two elaborate ceremonies, the revels, which is the celebration ordered by Amyclas for the marriage of Prophilus and Euphrania, and the execution of Orgilus. The scene begins with a formal procession on to stage, two men leading the bride, two women the bridegroom, and accompanied by *'loud music'*. There follows the extraordinary sequence in which, during the dancing, Calantha is informed at three appropriate pauses in the music of the deaths of Amyclas, Penthea and Ithocles but refuses 'to interrupt the custom of this ceremony' (ll. 26–7), thus incurring for Ford the wrath of later commentators who deplore her behaviour. Eloquent in this vein is William Archer:

> The whole thing is a piece of funereal affectation. No one is helped by it: no one is served: no decency is maintained. On the contrary, decency is outraged when a daughter goes on dancing by the bier, so to speak, of her father. The imagination which conceived the scene is warped by that bias towards the unnatural which led the author to found another play on the passion of a brother for a sister.[11]

The standpoint here, as always with Archer, is the natural expectation of the reasonable behaviour of credible human beings – a realism of the emotions. But Calantha's unnaturalism is precisely the point. According to her taste, she observes decorum, not nature; the dictates of culture, not those of an untrammelled sentiment. The effect is almost the opposite of Orgilus's ceremony of IV, iv, for here, art has been contrived to mark a social endorsement of a favoured marriage and Calantha's concern, a stoic one, is to refuse to allow private grief to intrude upon public ceremony. Through this, *pace* Archer, something very important is served.

The passage reads awkwardly but the effect on stage is exciting theatre. In Ford's mind, probably, there were two germs for the sequence. Historically, the episode reflects the story Plutarch tells about the Spartans' reception of the news of the battle of Leuctra, for the leaders would not allow the people 'to break off their dance in the theatre' during a day already ordained as a public feast. Theatrically, Ford remembered Marston's *The Malcontent*. In V, vi of that play, Malevole and Pietro reveal themselves to their wives in a dance.

At Blackfriars, and despite the Spartan setting so carefully observed in many aspects of the play, we can be sure there would have been no careful archaising of the dance. No doubt the band played a familiar dance tune popular at court so that the meaning and tone of the occasion were clear to the audience, and the four couples danced a well-known, contemporary dance. Almost certainly this was either a Pavan or Almain, each of them stately, walking dances in pairs, suitable for a ceremonial occasion such as this. The Almain employed a kind of goose-step, in a rhythm of four stresses to the measure, and with a processional effect. Arbeau in his *Orchesography* (1589) describes it in such a way as to make exact theatrical sense of Ford's handling of the episode in which the news arrives at specific intervals in the dance, though *The Broken Heart* needs one extra change before that final, faster movement which Arbeau refers to and Calantha calls for (l. 17):

> The Almain is a simple, rather sedate dance. . . . You can dance it

in company, because when you have joined hands with a damsel
several others may fall into line behind you, each with his partner. . . .
When the musicians finish this first part each dancer stops and
engages in light converse with his damsel and then you will begin all
over again for the second part. When you come to the third part you
will dance it to a quicker, more lively duple time with the same steps
but introducing little springs in the coranto.[12]

The audience knows of two of the deaths and will be unsurprised (and
unmoved) by the news of the third, that of Amyclas. Consequently, its
attention is directed entirely towards the unfunny irony of the counter-
pointing of tragic news and joyous activity. Particularly, it will watch
Calantha's astonishing responses, and do so with a detachment confirmed
by the Princess's own denial of emotional involvement. The moment is
not heart-warming but it is thrilling, particularly as the audience is cheated
of what it might normally expect here, the sight of a character overwhelmed by tragic news. Ford, of course, like Archer, knows what
is 'natural', and so he writes for Armostes an acknowledgment of the
egregiousness of Calantha's behaviour: ''Tis strange these tragedies should
never touch on Her female pity' (ll. 94–5). But better information awaits
him and the audience at the end of the play and her masculine toughness
is not at all a kind of callousness.

Before then, a second death ritual takes place, the execution of Orgilus,
ordered by Calantha but devised by himself. Bleeding to death looks first
like a late example of the characteristically sensational violence that marks
the end of many Jacobean tragedies and no doubt the company needed
to order a deal of blood from the shambles. But this execution/suicide
shares the theatricalised quality of much else in this play and by its very
staginess invites its audiences inside and outside the play to ponder on
its emblematic significance. Afterwards, Bassanes will observe that
Orgilus has 'shook hands with time' (l. 156), for the ceremony is a
performance through which Orgilus bids farewell to the phenomenal
world and contentedly leaves this life: with Penthea, he knows his 'home
is in the grave' (see II, iii, 146–8). The event, like Calantha's death, has
the pictorial eloquence of the masque. Archetypal imagery gathers around
the suiciding figure and the fundamental elements of earthly existence are
defined and interpreted through a slow-motion pantomine of mortality.
It is an art-work for the curious onlooker, another eloquent tableau, and
Calantha has properly deputed Nearchus, Bassanes and Armostes to be
'spectators of [his] end' (l. 87).

In Davenant's play *The Cruel Brother*, printed in 1630 and played at
the Blackfriars, there is a death by blood-letting that Ford probably knew.
Corsa, dishonoured by the Duke, is killed by her brother, Fores. He sits

her down, ties her arm to a side of the chair with a scarf and then cuts her wrist, and she bleeds to death during several minutes of stage time. Near the end, recorders play 'sadly', and Fores hears the music of the spheres as her soul ascends to heaven. Ford would have appreciated the sense of sacrifice and martyrdom that Davenant had built into the episode and especially the vaguely religious atmosphere created.[13]

However, another blood-letting also informs Ford's idea, for he would have known of the death in that manner of Seneca, whose brand of stoicism so pervades Ford's play. Indeed, this may be the incident in history referred to in the Prologue in lines never satisfactorily explained:

> What may be thought a fiction, when time's youth
> Wanted some riper years, was known a truth.[14]

Nero had condemned Seneca to death and the philosopher-playwright, in Tacitus's account, chose blood-letting as the manner. When he cut his arm, however, his old body released its blood too sluggishly and so he also cut his ankles and slashed behind his knee, still to no avail. Finally, he died of suffocation in a vapour-bath.

Orgilus's piece of theatre, however, is not bungled. This, by contrast, has the orderliness and grave (though unsolemn) effect proper to ritual art. Through Bassanes, Ford, perhaps remembering Seneca's untidy attempt, comments with satisfaction on Orgilus's vital blood:

> It sparkles like a lusty wine new broached.
> The vessel must be sound from which it issues.
>
> (II.126–7)

This energetic outflow of Orgilus's life occupies two or three minutes of stage time.

The business is stage-managed by Bassanes for whom the whole action is a joyous artifice and a triumph (ll. 131–4). Orgilus stands centre-stage with Bassanes busying round in close attendance, while Nearchus, Armostes, Lemophil and Groneas make up the stage audience. The actor of Orgilus supports himself first on one stave and then on a second. (Presumably these are brought on by an attendant, but Ford has not written into the text any provision for the various properties needed here.) His arms are bound with strips of cloth to aid the process and it seems inevitable, in such an elegantly unhurried piece of business, that on the Blackfriars stage actual blood was seen to flow. Presumably, the simple device of a blood bag about the actor's body with tubes run down the inside of his arms allowed the illusion to be convincingly managed. The falling blood would have created a problem, making the stage floor dangerously slippery for the next scene were it not caught. In *The Cruel Brother*, Corsa's blood is caught in a basin ('Here In this basin bleed') and we must imagine there were two receptacles for Ford's play, perhaps held by servants in such a way as to contribute to the symmetrical shaping of the tableau that the dying Orgilus makes with the two staves.

Whatever the mechanics, Orgilus stands while the blood flows and pronounces his own elegy, reaching a kind of *anagnorisis* as he remembers Tecnicus's prophecy that '*Revenge proves its own executioner*'. He sees the ironic circularity here, the Elizabethan joke of being hoist with one's own petard; but he matches it with a commentary on his impending death that bypasses any simple, moral charge:

> When feeble man is bending to his mother,
> The dust 'a was first framed on, so he totters.
>
> (ll. 148–9)

The staves fall with a startling crash and Orgilus collapses, while Bassanes points up the elemental frame of reference with 'Life's fountain is dried up' (l. 150). And now Orgilus, lying centre-stage, speaks his last words in a calm tone:

> A mist hangs o'er mine eyes. The sun's bright splendour
> Is clouded in an everlasting shadow.
> Welcome thou ice that sittest about my heart;
> No heat can ever thaw thee.
>
> (ll. 152–4)

There are echoes here from the death of Flamineo in *The White Devil*. But we are a world away from the agnostic nightmare of Websterian grotesque, all the distance between Jacobean and Caroline, or between mannerism and baroque. Flamineo is a villain and his last lines are restless, fearful and neurotic. He is lost in a mist and his vague awareness of an ethical reality fills his last moments with conventional, moral thoughts expressed in a sardonic manner. Orgilus's lines, on the other hand, have no ethical content or nervous energy and they are not at all sardonic. They are of a piece with the extravagant but simple imagery of his self-execution. His mist is not an intellectual one but that of failing eyesight, and in his anticipation of the coldness of death there is no existential shiver but a perception of frozen stasis, death fashioned in art, and a sense of welcome oblivion. The frozen heart is an image of the escape from feeling, and Taylor, if it were he, played these lines not with groans, sighs and rolling eyes but with a glacial calmness as he lay half-supported by Bassanes. To the latter's charge falls the funeral urn, death again as art-work.

V, iii is Calantha's death scene, contrived like Orgilus's as a fitting, final gesture. We may infer that before the scene opens she has ordered her dirge, prepared her requiem mass with appropriate costumes and furnishings, and written her obituary: and so a play of ceremonious behaviour ends ceremoniously, as a 'high-tuned poem'. Ford's own care in this is witnessed again by a full stage direction for the scene opening which details not only the stage dressing but a preliminary blocking and several minutes of elaborate stage action:

> An altar covered with white. Two lights of virgin wax. Music of recorders; during which enter four bearing ITHOCLES *on a hearse, or in a chair, in a rich robe, and a crown on his head;* [they] *place him on one side of the altar. After him enter* CALANTHA *in a white robe and crowned;* EUPHRANIA, PHILEMA, *[and]* CHRYSTALLA in white: NEARCHUS, ARMOSTES, CROTOLON, PROPHILUS, AMELUS, BASSANES, LEMOPHIL *and* GRONEAS.
> CALANTHA *goes and kneels before the altar. The rest stand off, the women kneeling behind. Cease recorders during her devotions. Soft music.* CALANTHA *and the rest rise, doing obeisance to the altar.*

By the manipulation of visual and aural effects, Ford aims at a powerfully sacramental atmosphere, half Christian and half pagan, at once chaste and sensuous. Once again, as with IV, iv, the discovery-space is not used though we might imagine it would have been easier and neater to set the altar there with Ithocles's body beside it before the scene opens. In fact, Ford's licence to the King's Men over Ithocles's form of transport, hearse or chair, recognises that the company would have had to experiment with and rehearse carefully on stage the details of the processional entry and the establishing of the scene to get them exactly right, and also the business of Calantha's embrace in death. We might assume that the altar, with its white cloth and candles, is set upstage and a little off-centre with the hearse/chair to its side. Together with the extras who carry Ithocles on as part of the opening and perhaps remain on stage as the singers, there are sixteen actors in all whose movements must be blocked. Once the altar is set, they enter probably from both doors and their subsequent movements, as well as their costumes, underline the consistent concern with sexual roles that the play has shown. Partly, Ford's imagination seems to turn here on a notion of vestal virgins, and Philema, whose name, ironically, means 'kiss', will shortly be dedicated to Vesta's temple (ll. 52–3).

The processional entry complete, Calantha kneels before the altar facing upstage, her attendant ladies downstage of her, also kneeling, the principal men in line upstage/downstage on either side and in front of the stage-sitters, the four hearse-bearers upstage of the altar. Now the recorders cease their gentle but solemn music and Calantha's devotions are made. The music begins again, the women rise '*doing obeisance to the altar*' and the attendant ladies move left and right, Euphrania joining Prophilus, leaving centre-stage for Calantha who turns downstage for her first speech. She will now hold this upstage centre position for the rest of the scene, gesturing to the individuals whose fates she determines and then engaging in her wedding ceremony with dead Ithocles. What the Blackfriars audience saw – and heard – was a passage of simplicity and power. The white dresses and flickering candles were highlights in a carefully composed tableau that organised itself, spatially, first in relation to the altar and then to Ithocles, as Calantha, martyred womanhood at the focus of the scene, assumed her position as the centrepiece of a baroque picture.

Calantha's series of revelations about herself and Ithocles offer no surprises to the audience outside the play. The impact of the final sequence, with the placing of the ring, the kiss, the song and the death, is not one of shock and violence, nor even of the clarification of a story-line. Instead, what has always been hinted becomes explicit and what the song talks of is rendered almost literally through the stage imagery:

> Love only reigns in death, though art
> Can find no comfort for a broken heart.

The song itself, unlike Penthea's, is sung by men, both in solo voice and in chorus. Penthea's death was soft, passive and womanly, but Calantha's toughness of spirit belongs in the world of Spartan heroism. So the song is a tribute in tenor and bass voices, and it sadly speaks of a transient world where pleasure is hard to find, felt only when 'the mind is untroubled, or by peace refined'[15] (1.84). But the special peace here is death itself. So Calantha dies in an embrace with her dead husband and Bassanes notes the histrionic nature of her final moment: 'O royal maid, would thou hadst missed this part. Yet 'twas a brave one' (ll. 96–7).

The last moments of the play are tactfully brief, the unriddling of Tecnicus's riddle and Nearchus's assumption of the crown; for it is Calantha's assumption (in the religious sense) that is the play's proper end. So *The Broken Heart* ends quietly, almost quietistically, and the action itself hovers precariously on the edge of sentimentality. At Blackfriars, however, and within the protective atmosphere of a coterie theatre, a careful observance of the scene's rhythms and an unironic 'belief' by the actors in the truth of their parts must have ensured a moving effect. Lamb sensed the sublimity here (he had no opportunity to see the play performed) in words that later offended with their sacrilegious overtones but which nicely express the sense of mystical martyrdom that Ford aimed at:

> I do not know where to find in any play a catastrophe so grand, so solemn, and so surprising as this. . . . Who could be less weak than Calantha? Who be so strong? The expression of this transcendant

scene almost bears me in imagination to Calvary and the Cross: and
I seem to perceive some analogy between the scenical sufferings which
I am here contemplating, and the real agonies of that final completion
to which I dare no more than hint a reference.[16]

The Broken Heart is a logical development of Jacobean Private Theatre
and an English version of European baroque. We have no way of telling
if it was notably successful but it seems to have started a small fashion
in plays about Spartan women[17] and it inspired a play, intended for royal
entertainment and printed in 1640, entirely on the subject of Calantha
dying for love.[18] Ford's play seems now a curiously unEnglish piece and
has not received the constant twentieth-century revivals of *'Tis Pity*. Even
when baroque theatre was in vogue in the Restoration period it was not
played, although three others of Ford's plays were. For its first revival
after Ford's own time, by William Poel in 1898, Edmund Gosse wrote a
perceptive programme note stressing the 'severity' and Frenchness of
Ford's achievement:

> The performance tonight can scarcely fail to emphasise that severity,
> we might almost say rigidity, which distinguishes Ford from all
> other English playwrights, and draws him nearer to Corneille and to
> Rotrou in their devotion to dramatic discipline.
>
> There is no play in the English language which gives the impression
> of fine French tragedy so completely as *The Broken Heart*. The
> spectator should be prepared more for a performance in the French
> than in the English taste, and for a piece perhaps the most classic
> in our repertory.[19]

It is a mark of the play's distinctive style that one commentator emphasises
its discipline and classical quality, another, Lamb, its mysticism and
emotionalism. It is this unusual mixture that gives *The Broken Heart* its
special theatrical tone, a tone the King's Men would have striven hard to
perform. If they achieved it, no doubt the tragedy played like 'some high-
tuned poem'.

Part Three

The King's Theatre

8 · Court Theatre, 1603–42

The interrelation of theatre and court during the Tudor and Stuart periods is an intricate one. It was earlier stressed (pp. 56–7) that the Stuart court became increasingly involved in theatrical affairs, by the time of Charles exerting considerable pressure on the style of drama and invading the processes of theatre in a variety of ways. Officially, commercial theatre in London was traditionally tolerated only so that a royal taste for theatrical entertainment might be supplied at short notice by expert writers and performers with well-rehearsed plays. At the Caroline court, an art once professed by rogues and vagabonds was being transformed, by way of the specialisation inherent in the developing private theatre, into an aristocratic pursuit. In the masque, Charles and Henrietta Maria could be most themselves by appearing on stage as idealisations of themselves, projecting their image in sublime pantomines.

Court theatre is both theatre for the court (visiting professional shows) and theatre of the court (mimetic pageantry with royal actors). For the most part, the two were quite distinct. But professional playwrights had always been drawn to a kind of courtly play of masque and allegorical compliment (e.g. Lyly's *Endimion*, 1588, Jonson's *Cynthia's Revels*, 1600 and Heywood's *Love's Mistress*, 1634). Also, plays and pageants became inextricably meshed, in content, form and auspices, in the stylised pastorals that Henrietta Maria introduced from a French court tradition and, in the first two cases, herself played in: Racan's *L' Arténice* (1626 in the Hall, Somerset House), Montagu's *The Shepherd's Paradise* (1633, in the Paved Court, Somerset House), and *Florimène* (1635, in the Hall, Whitehall).

In this atmosphere, Fletcher's pastoral *The Faithful Shepherdess*, which failed at the Blackfriars in 1608–9, might be revived for the court in 1633 with Inigo Jones's scenery and be extremely successful. Aristocratic participants in masques and pastorals looked increasingly like actors (Buckingham was criticised in 1626 for playing a master of fence 'too histrionical to become him') and professional women performers, brought in by 1632 to sing in the masque, anticipated the actresses of the Restoration professional stage. In effect, the Caroline court became a laboratory for theatrical development and experimentation and it inevitably affected the ideas and the ambitions of the professional theatre people brought within its ambit. At the Restoration, the cavalier theatre of Davenant and Killigrew, first tried out at Charles's court, would predominate and determine the course of British professional theatre for many decades.

A play-performance by a visiting, professional company was a standard feature of court recreation. The court season officially began on 1 November, All Saints' Day, when the sovereign would mark the end of his summer progress by officially taking up residence at Whitehall for the winter months. There was a concentrated period of celebration during the Twelve Days of Christmas, and Candlemas (2 February) and Shrovetide were also important occasions for revels. James ordered many more plays to be given at court than had Elizabeth. Though he seems not to have had a particular interest in drama, he sometimes allowed performances to continue after Easter or to be given on Sundays. The lowest total of plays in one season at court throughout his reign was eleven, except in the winter of Prince Henry's death. During 1609–10, he saw a total of twenty-three plays and even during his absences from court, other members of the royal household were entertained by the play companies.[1] Charles had a greater literary interest in the drama than his father (and a well-thumbed copy of Shakespeare). He developed the Cockpit-in-Court as a regular royal playhouse and in its first winter season, 1629–30, seventeen plays were presented there by his own company, the King's Men, while about the same number were performed by the Queen's company. In all, thirty-seven plays were performed at Whitehall or Hampton Court in four and a half months by these two companies alone during that winter season.

The summons to play at court presumably could not be resisted. For the major companies, the element of court performance evidently played an increasingly large part in company affairs. Performances were generally given at night and so did not interfere with the companies' public playing in the afternoons, and though the financial rewards seem to us not to have been great (£10 for all the work involved in transporting a play for one performance) it was almost all profit, and the exercise conferred special status on the players: as liveried servants they were fulfilling their special function. (When a daytime performance was given, there was adequate compensation for the loss of income.)

The choice of play lay with the Lord Chamberlain. His important office was responsible for a wide range of court activities including court entertainments, and his white staff on the night of court revels would magically clear the appointed hall of its throng of courtiers so that the masque, play or dance might take place. He exerted great influence over court politics as well as court theatre and his historic post, which remained in the personal gift of the sovereign, was highly prized. The officers for the period concerned were: Thomas, Lord Howard (later Earl of Suffolk), 1603–14; Robert Carr, Earl of Somerset, 1614–15; William Herbert, Earl of Pembroke, 1615–26; Philip Herbert, Earl of Montgomery, 1626–41. In the next chapter, it is argued that the Lord Chamberlain chose *Bartholomew Fair* for production at court in somewhat unusual circumstances.

Under the general supervision of the Lord Chamberlain was the other office directly related to the operation of the court theatre, and so in turn to professional London theatre: the Office of the Revels.[2] The Master of the Revels was responsible for the licensing of plays for performance in all theatres, and at Court his office was responsible for the 'soft furnishings' of theatrical events such as scenery, costumes, gloves for the boy companies, and stage hangings, as opposed to the stage and seating scaffolds erected by the Office of Works. The Revels Office had for many years provided the scenic 'houses' of stretched canvas on wooden frames that graced many a court play under Elizabeth, and it became increasingly involved in the developing elaboration of masque scenery. It kept a stock of costumes, props and other scenic materials and had workshops for the storing and refurbishing of this stock or for new making as the occasion required. After 1607, the offices and workshops were located at St John's and performance materials (and people) were regularly transported from there to Whitehall and to the other royal residences for court performances. The premises also provided space for rehearsal and the office carried a technical staff of carpenters, prop makers, tailors, embroiderers and wire-drawers. The masters during the period were: Sir George Buck, 1603–22; Sir John Astley, 1622–3; and Sir Henry Herbert, 1623–42.

Until 1630 when the converted Cockpit-in-Court was ready, theatre at court had no permanent home. Professional plays and court 'shows' alike were accommodated in a number of fit-up rooms at Whitehall. The range of imported entertainment extended from serious drama to circus-like acts and animal baiting, and the same playing areas were for some time used interchangeably. The main performance areas were the Great (or Tudor) Hall, The Great (or Guard) Chamber, the Cockpit, the Banqueting House and, late in the period, the Masquing House. Their geographical positions relative to each other and to the royal apartments are shown in figure 8.1.

Much has already been said about the Cockpit and its conversion into a regular playhouse in Chapter 3 where it is quoted as a witness to the fact that Jacobean private playhouses and their managers resisted the

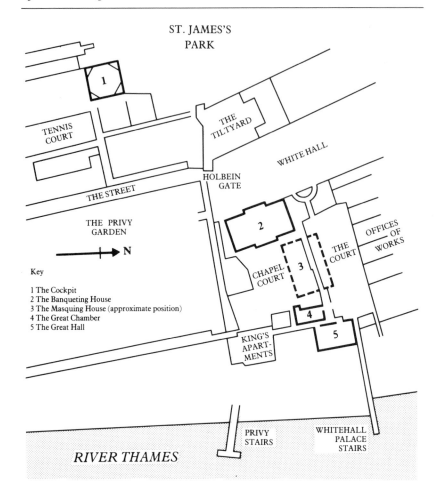

Figure 8.1:   The Palace of Whitehall, showing the principal performance areas
(based on a print of Fisher's map of Whitehall, 1670)

accommodation of the new ideas of scenic theatre tried out over many
years by the very man who designed the Cockpit conversion, Inigo Jones.
Plays were performed in the Cockpit long before the conversion, usually
several times each season (e.g. five times in 1607–8, three times in
1618–19). After the conversion, although our records of court performances get scantier, it is evident that the Cockpit regularly housed royal
command plays to the near exclusion of the other available spaces. Its
dimensions appear in Chapter 3. It was situated on the west side of the
palace, adjacent as its origins dictated to the tennis court on one side and
the tilting-yard on the other.

The Great Chamber, not to be confused with the Presence Chamber, was used occasionally for plays in the Jacobean period but more regularly for dance. It was situated on the east side of the Chapel Court opposite the Banqueting House and, adjacent to the Hall, was originally the place where the Yeomen of the Guard waited in attendance on the sovereign. But it had long been taken over, also, for semi-public functions and ceremonies. No dimensions survive, but it was probably too small to serve adequately for the more spectacular kinds of court theatre and it played only a minor and irregular role as far as the subject of this chapter is concerned.

The Great Hall, on the other hand, was an imposing space for theatre, a Tudor Hall, 89 feet by 40 feet, with a musicians' gallery 10 feet deep above and behind the screen at the lower end. A plan of the Hall set out for a performance of *Florimène* survives, drawn by Inigo Jones (see Plate 12). It shows what must have been a regular arrangement of the auditorium, with tiered seating on three sides in eight degrees, parts of it partitioned to provide boxes (annotated on the plan 'the lady marquess her box' and 'The Countess of Arundell's box'). There is evidently a balcony above (the posts can be seen), and there is an open space in the middle of the floor in front of the stage, dominated by the King's state. The stage, 40 feet wide, runs across the width of the hall and backs on to the buttery screen, but it is fitted out as a scenic stage and so does not represent the normal arrangement for 'straight' (commercial) plays. The seating and stage were undoubtedly fashioned out of stock materials which had been used previously (and would be again), and the work of fitting-up was carried out by the Office of the Works. The materials were stored in Scotland Yard to the north of the palace.

The other major performance space at court was the Banqueting House, or rather the succession of Banqueting Houses and their temporary replacements that housed a variety of court ceremonials under Elizabeth, James and Charles.[3] At first these were temporary structures devised for special occasions. However, the building ordered by Elizabeth for the reception of the Duc d'Alençon in 1581, although flimsily constructed out of canvas with wood supports, was refurbished and strengthened from time to time so that it lasted a quarter of a century. It was finally demolished by James in 1606 when it was 'old, rotten, slight-builded'; but it was here that the first masque on which Jones and Jonson collaborated, *The Masque of Blackness*, was performed on Twelfth Night, 1605. A stage 40 feet square was built for that occasion.

The first Jacobean Banqueting House was built on the site of Elizabeth's. It was a substantial structure of brick and a plan drawn by Robert Smythson in 1618 shortly before its destruction by fire shows its layout and dimensions (see Plate 13). In fact there were ten, not nine pillars

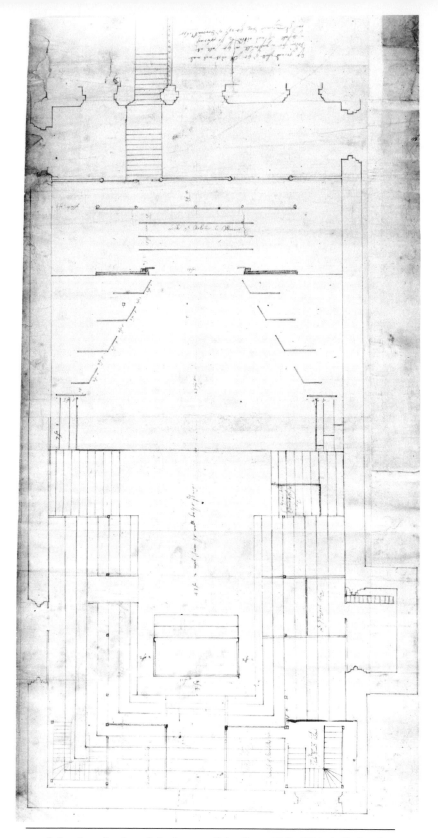

12 Inigo Jones's plan of the layout of the Great Hall, Whitehall, for the performance of *Florimène*, 1635

down each side of the hall,[4] but otherwise Smythson shows clearly what its unknown architect had designed, a basilican hall, 120 feet long (externally) by 53 feet wide (internally) with, in place of the screens passage normal at the lower end of a hall, an 'ante-room' created by a further two pillars at the north end. These presumably supported a musician's gallery above. The pillars along the length of the hall formed 8 feet deep aisles on either side. There is no firm evidence to tell us which end was converted to stage-end and which to house-end.[5] The 'ante-room' would have provided an effective tiring-house if the stage were at the lower (northern end) but that end was the major access to the hall by way of the 'close-walk' marked on Smythson's plan. At the upper end, the apartments adjoining might provide the tiring-house, but these presumably connected with the King's quarters, and his presence was the *raison d'être* of the Banqueting House itself. In the Second Jacobean Banqueting House, the stage, as custom had long dictated, was at the lower end, and it is probably safe to assume that this was generally the case in the first. (*Florimène* in the Hall was also, as we have seen, played at the lower end.)

> The house was built for the sumptuous entertainment of foreign princes and ambassadors, for the ratification of diplomatic treaties and agreements, for the gracious reception of the Houses of Parliament, for public audiences, for ceremonies connected with the creation of new peerages, for the pomp of St George's Feast, and for the solemn rite of touching for the 'King's Evil'. In short, it was built as a stage for the display of royal might and glory.[6]

Also, for eleven years from 1608 and *The Masque of Beauty*, it was the setting for most of the Whitehall masques and from 1610 (though why not before we do not know) it regularly housed the imported commercial plays. If the list above stresses its solemn usages, it is worth noting that it was also prepared on occasion for such entertainments as bearbaiting, tumbling and 'to see the dancing ass and goat'.

A splendid description by the Italian visitor Busino (see p. 110) records the scene in the First Jacobean Banqueting House on the occasion of the masque *Pleasure Reconciled to Virtue*, performed on Twelfth Night, 1618:

> A large hall [the Banqueting House] is fitted up like a theatre, with well secured boxes all round. The stage is at one end and his Majesty's chair in front under an ample canopy. Near him are stools for the foreign ambassadors. . . . Whilst waiting for the king we amused ourselves by admiring the decorations and the beauty of the

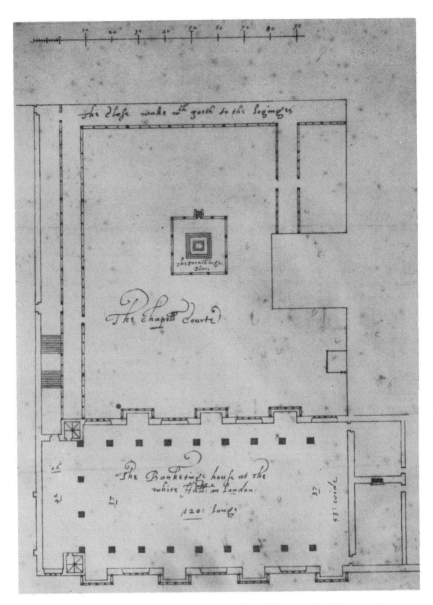

13   Robert Smythson's plan of the first Jacobean Banqueting House and
its environs, drawn between 1608 and 1618

house with its two orders of columns, one above the other, their distance from the wall equalling the breadth of the passage, that of the second row upheld by Doric pillars, while above these rise Ionic columns supporting the roof. The whole [of the internal structure] is of wood, including even the shafts, which are carved and gilt with much skill. From the roof of these hang festoons and angels in relief with two rows of lights.[7]

Ten or more Jones/Jonson masques were performed there. Then on 12 January 1619 the Banqueting Hall burned down, a victim, contemporary gossip maintained, of a thief poking around amongst the masque materials at night and accidentally setting fire to them with his candle. Ironically, court records show that in 1613–14 and again in 1616–18 the building had been guarded at night against the risk of fire.

Plans to replace the Banqueting House were rapidly set in motion but it was not until 1622 that Jones's fine Palladian building, which still stands, was completed. James and Charles both planned to give Whitehall a major face-lift but financial restrictions defeated them. Only in the Banqueting House itself, in the royal collections of paintings, statues and tapestries and particularly in the extravagant masques which the building housed between 1622 (*The Masque of Augurs*) and 1635 (*The Temple of Love*) and the ones performed in the Masquing Room thereafter did the Stuart court express its 'magnificence' in the blatant way it intended.

The Second Jacobean Banqueting House is 110 feet by 55 feet by 55 feet internally, a double cube in the spirit of Vitruvian mathematics. It is divided by wall pilasters into seven bays, Ionic below, Corinthian above. Gone are the aisles of its predecessor. Instead, Jones created a huge, austere box in which the pageantry of state, in its most sumptuous accoutrements, could be accommodated, especially the masque. Again, there was no permanent stage or auditorium; this would be supplied as needed. And again, the space would play host to bearbaiting as well as to court rituals.

In fact, for all its austerity, Jones's Banqueting House (see Plate 14) provides an aesthetic vocabulary for the Stuart masque as a whole. Outside, its chaste classicism must have been in stark contrast to the medieval gothic of the palace setting; but underneath the hall, a part of the vaulted undercroft was fitted out as the 'King's Privy Cellar' and decorated in the 'grotesque' manner by Isaac de Caux. He was paid in 1623–4 'for making a rock in the vault under the Banqueting House' and later 'for making an addition of shellwork to the outside of the work'. His father or uncle was Solomon de Caux, tutor to Prince Henry, mathematician and engineer, who had published books on water pumps, fountains and grottoes. Isaac laid out the famous gardens of Wilton House

14   Inigo Jones's Banqueting House, 1622: (a) exterior today; (b) interior
today (restored); (c) the Rubens ceiling

and made a grotto there. In the work of the two de Caux, the Stuart
court cultivated that association of mechanical invention and the bizarre
typical of the grotesque element in contemporary baroque and of the
palpable ingenuity of the theatrecraft of the masque.

On the ceiling of the Banqueting House was eventually installed the
great series of Rubens paintings that is there today. Rubens consulted

(b)

with the English court over the commission as early as 1619 but its final
form was not reached until after James's death when it became Charles's
memorial to his father: in the great, central, oval panel is the apotheosis
of Rex Pacificus as saint and emperor. The entire work makes up an
allegorical programme describing the blessing conferred on the united
kingdoms of England and Scotland by the wise rule of James. The three

central paintings are *tableaux vivants* centred on James himself, and the third contains an unmistakable allusion to the Judgment of Solomon as well as a representation of Minerva as presiding spirit over the joining of England and Scotland. Each of the corner ovals figures an allegory of the restraining of a vice by an heroic virtue, one of them picturing another Minerva, here defeating Ignorance. The ceiling *in toto* is a sublime and theatrical statement about Stuart politics. It combines filial piety with a distinctly Caroline assertion of the doctrine of Divine Right.

Classical exterior, 'grotesque' cellar and sublime ceiling; these represent the various elements of Caroline court style which combine most express-ively and dynamically in the court masque. In the masque performance there was a serial display of visual and aural imagery carrying the spectator from the world of comic grotesque to a ritual assertion of extravagant sublimity. At the climax, the masquers superimposed on the everyday life of the court an ideal world of exemplary courage and selfless heroism; their arrival, gods visiting the earth, was the climactic moment of the evening. In *Coelum Britannicum*, the masque featured in Chapter 10, Jones as designer and Carew as writer contrived a pasteboard and verbal web of imagery which would receive constant echo in Rubens's brush-strokes on the ceiling next year. The clouds issuing around the ascending James broke dynamically forth in Jones's 'racks' of wood, canvas and rope to convey deities to the stage floor and back into the heavens; Minerva, guiding the union of the two nations, was echoed by Carew's Genius who oversaw the selfsame event in the masque; and just as the infant, Herculean Charles of Rubens's design is presented a double crown as guarantee of concord, so in the masque, as the King who has just played Hercules rejoins his consort, Eternity affirms the future of a Stuart Kingdom blessed by the personification of Concord. Paintings and masque communicate through the standard iconography of baroque art.

Ironically, the Rubens ceiling was responsible for the banishment of the masque from the Banqueting House. On its installation in 1635, Charles feared that the smoke from the many lights that were a necessary feature of the masque would damage the canvases, and no more masques were played there. Eventually, a Masquing Room was constructed nearby (only ten feet away according to one report), over the terrace which connected the Banqueting House and the Great Chamber. It was a temporary structure built largely of wood, and though dismissively referred to as 'the Queen's dancing room', it was huge, as large as the Banqueting House itself at 112 feet by 57 feet (externally), and expensively fashioned. The last three royal masques of Charles's reign were performed there with Jones's scenery and costumes: *Britannia Triumphans* and *Luminalia*, 1638, and *Salmacida Spolia*, 1640.

When the sovereign was present at a court performance or masque, there was inevitably generated a kind of double theatre. Elizabeth had known that in public a ruler necessarily played a royal role: 'We princes, I tell you, are set on stages, in the sight and view of all the world daily observed'[8]; and James echoed her: 'a King is as one set on a stage, whose smallest actions and gestures, all the people gazingly do behold'.[9] In court ceremonies, the state itself, where the King sat on a throne under a canopy, was a kind of miniature theatre, as contemporary visitors observed. When a play was performed for James at Oxford in 1605, the state had to be moved from its first position because, so anxious functionaries were aware, the King would not be properly seen by the audience. That, as a result of the move, he himself could but poorly hear and see the play was of less account.

For the imported play at court and for court theatricals, the King, consequently, was not only the chief spectator but a rival performance. At the court presentation of *Bartholomew Fair*, indeed, he seemed to the playwright the only spectator, placed by his superior judgment at the exact spot where the moral perspective of the play would work to best advantage. That play, it is suggested in Chapter 9, took its being from the King's presence, ended only in the King's indulgence and gathered up its royal patron, to whom it was offered as a present, into its very action. At the masque, if he were not its chief actor, the King observed the scene from literally the exact spot where the pictorial perspective contrived by Jones would best work.

A prologue written by Carew for an unnamed and untraced play in the 1630s suggests that the King might in fact temporarily abdicate his central role. The play was presented in the Great Hall by the Lord Chamberlain, and the prologue addressed the King thus:

> Sir,
> Since you have been pleas'd this night to unbend
> Your serious thoughts, and with your Person lend
> Your palace out, and so are hither come
> A stranger in your own house, not at home,
> Divesting state, as if you meant alone
> To make your servant's loyal heart your throne . . . [10]

In what was presumably a similar vein, the queen visited the Middle Temple in 1636 to attend a masque written by Davenant and given in honour of the Prince Elector: 'the queen was pleased to grace the entertainment by putting off majesty to put on a citizen's habit, and to sit upon the scaffold on the right hand amongst her subjects'.[11] Such modesty has a distinctly theatrical air about it and the situation was in any case unusual because the Elector was the guest of honour. At *Flori-*

mène, Jones's plan shows how the King's state dominated the auditorium, providing the audience with a cynosure that competed with his wife's ladies' performance on stage. In the adaptation of the Cockpit-in-Court into a regular playhouse, the orientation of the house exactly divides attention between the stage and the King's box directly opposite. In effect, private theatre at court served a most public funtion: the King, displaying his sacred presence, fulfilled his public role as the divinely-appointed sovereign. When Charles chose to appear in the masque, he became 'public' twice over.

To us, the Stuart masque is a peculiarly inaccessible form of historical theatre. The printed page offers sketchier remains of the original perform-ance than does a playscript – perfunctory dialogue, stage directions which are often lengthy and self-congratulatory but which offer few clues to actual staging techniques employed, and the lyrics of a handful of songs. To these we can add a little of the original music and, for a number of masques, particularly the later ones, Jones's designs of costumes and scenery. The values expressed by the masques, concerning monarchical virtue and chivalric heroism, couched in a language of unqualified flattery, are scarcely to our taste. Even the scale of the masque as art-work, unreconstructable through its very cost, is difficult to grasp. Indeed, the masque texts do not invite reconstruction or revival. They reach us as memorials, for the masque was essentially occasional, for the most part unrepeatable and completed in performance only by the presence of the sovereign or his consort for whom they were a gift.

The masque eludes, too, our critical vocabulary. It brings with it a vexed *auteur* problem, one indeed it had already at Charles's court, for Jonson, the librettist, and Jones, the designer, quarrelled over the ques-tion of whose creative talent was most responsible for the finished product. Critical insights relevant to the drama and based on notions concerning dramatic unity, narrative flow and conflict-centred action do not apply. In its own period, the masque in principle was not to be confused with the play. So Middleton introduces his *A Courtly Masque*, 1620, with

> This is our device we do not call a play,
> Because we break the stage's laws today.
> There's one hour's words, the rest is songs and dances.

On the other hand, a masque might be a failure for seeming like a play. *The Lord's Masque*, 1613, was criticised for being 'more like a play than a masque'. Increasingly, it is the splendour of the scenic display that predominates in the spectators' experience and Jones, secure in the court's approbation, could claim: 'These shows are nothing else but pictures with light and motion' (*Tempe Restored*, 1632). Others, though not Jonson, had said as much before: 'In these things, the only life consists in show; the art and invention of the Architect gives the greatest grace and is of most importance.'[12] Today's reader of the masque 'book' can catch only distant echoes of a lost art-form.

Jones, Craig-like, increasingly dominated the whole process of the making of the masque once the partnership between him and Jonson, responsible for all the major masques at Whitehall between 1604 and 1631, broke up. He became in fact the *'dominus do-all'* that Jonson sneeringly labelled him, working with a succession of poets to contrive the banquet of the senses the masque was intended to be. Bacon, hard-headed and sceptical as he was – 'these things are but toys' – responded with Renaissance enthusiasm to the variety of delights the masque offered, the chief one residing in that very variety. In the masque, he says,

> Dancing in song is a thing of great state and pleasure. . . . Acting in song, especially in dialogues, hath an extreme good grace. . . .
> Several choirs, placed one over against another, and taking the voice by catches, anthem-wise, give great pleasure. . . . The alterations of scenes . . . are things of great beauty and pleasure; for they feed and relieve the eye before it be full of the same object. Let the scenes abound with light, specially coloured and varied. . . . Let the songs be loud and cheerful. . . . Let the music likewise be sharp and loud, and wellplaced. . . . Let the suits of the masquers be graceful, and such as become the person when the vizards are off. . . . Let the music [of the antimasque] be recreative, and with some strange changes. Some sweet odours suddenly coming forth, without any drops falling are . . . things of great pleasure and refreshment.[13]

Nevertheless, as well as royal recreation, the masque was a political statement. It was 'a compliment of state' and foreign ambassadors were inevitably a part of the invited audience. Through the conspicuous consumption that marked the spectacle, the King expressed his court's 'magnificence'. This was a quality that was more than sumptuous display for it had a politico-moral value, an aspect and demonstration of royal virtue, and as such, it was at the centre of Renaissance and baroque ideas of state-craft. Moreover, in its iconographic power and allegorical mode the masque was supremely able to make clear statements about royal prerogative and the magical, mystical power of the divinely appointed ruler. It is no coincidence that the ten great Caroline masques at court were all composed and performed during the 'eleven years' tyranny' while Charles ruled without a Parliament – 1629–40. In the last of them, *Salmacida Spolia*, the royal pair uniquely appeared on the same stage. Their union, so often the preoccupation of the late masques attuned to neo-platonism in their political philosophy, perfectly expressed the idea of a nation achieving its perfect state of peace and plenty within the spiritualising force-field of the royal love match.[14]

The origins of the Stuart masque, too complicated to trace through here, lay in court pageantry and ceremonial, in the medieval mummings and disguises of popular tradition and in the artistic innovation of neo-Vitruvian stagecraft. Out of this mix was developed a form constantly embellished but never radically altered: on a stage of unified settings and within a slight but idealised fiction, a group of aristocratic masquers make a triumphal entry that banishes a grotesque, antimasque world of ugliness and strife. The masquers come down from the stage to dance their Entry dance and then, after a song sung by musicians, they take partners from the audience in the hall for the Revels, a suite of court dances that is in effect the centrepiece of the evening's entertainment. After more songs, the masquers return to the stage, the fiction is completed and the masquers disappear. Finally, the important guests partake of a banquet. The masquers were aristocrats, led by one of the royal family (Queen Anne or Prince Charles in the time of James, Queen Henrietta Maria or King Charles in Charles's own reign); the other performers, musicians, singers and antimasquers, were professionals, drawn from court service and from the play companies.

The artistic intention was never less than sublime and heroic. But the political stance was increasingly at odds with the country. Several masquers in *Coelum Britannicum* were destined to fight on the republican side in the Civil War; and only a few years after *Salmacida Spolia*, Charles stepped out of a specially-prepared doorway at first-floor level in the Banqueting House to his death on a scaffold of a different kind from the one he had graced as chief masquer inside.

Where Jones learned his scenographic skills remains a mystery. We are certain of his first-hand experience of advanced theatrecraft in Italy only in 1613–14 on his continental tour with Arundel. But in 1605, he had already created his first unified or single-locality setting for *The Masque of Blackness*, dismissing at one blow the long tradition of dispersed scenery in court pageantry and in effect introducing the picture-frame stage. By 1611, if not earlier, he was experimenting with sliding scene-flats to effect the scenic transformations that provided the central action of the masque, and already he had mastered the perspective setting that created the illusion of great depth on a shallow stage. In the masques of 1613, the use of ariel machinery for sophisticated descents had been brought to high pitch and moving scenery on the upper stage level was a regular feature. To the increasingly complex stage machinery was added the provision for the rapid flying-up of a front curtain and at the same time, with increasingly ambitious lighting, weather changes could be made in an existing scene (1631). In *Coelum Britannicum* (1634) the full repertoire of scenic effects was available: three stage levels worked in integrated fashion and flying reached a new ingenuity. Thereafter, Jones was forced to strive to out-do himself. In *Luminalia*, of 1636, he devised a symphony of lighting effects, 'the invention consisting of darkness and light'; and in the last masque of the era, *Salmacida Spolia*, the text made the claim that 'it was generally approved of . . . to be the noblest and most ingenious that hath been done here in that kind'. Inevitably, perhaps, such was the limitation of apt imagery available decorously to express through allegory the Caroline sense of royal autocracy, Jones began to repeat himself. Increasingly, it has been noted, he plagiarised in scene and costume design from the Italian engravings of court *intermezzi*. His theatrical effects were not always properly understood or appreciated. But we see him, in scribbled notes on the designs and elsewhere, negotiating with his aristocratic patrons over colour and style of costumes, ordering candles, talking to painters and carpenters about how to realise the scenes and generally supervising the considerable detail that goes into the devising and managing of an immensely complicated theatre performance. It is difficult, even at this distance, not to marvel that he completed one of these masques, yet alone the thirty-odd that are associated with him. In him, the Caroline court had its greatest baroque artist, a match, in stature, with Rubens in the world of visual arts, or with Jonson in the world of theatre. But his art, unlike theirs, was supremely perishable. Only by a considerable effort of historical imagination can we gauge his immense talent as a scenographer.

The audience at Whitehall was as brilliant as the performance, sometimes, no doubt, more so; it dressed the occasion as much as the play or masque did. Busino, again, is an energetic witness. After his account of the Banqueting House quoted earlier, he continues:

> Then such a concourse as there was, for although they profess only
> to admit the favoured ones who are invited, yet every box was filled
> notably with most noble and richly arrayed ladies, in number some
> 600 and more according to the general estimate; the dresses being
> such variety in cut and colour as to be indescribable . . . strings of
> jewels on their necks and bosoms and in their girdles and apparel
> in such quantity that they looked like so many queens, so that at the
> beginning, with but little light, such as that of the dawn or evening
> twilight, the splendour of their diamonds and other jewels was so
> brilliant that they looked like so many stars.

The general estimate of audience number was probably about right. In the 8 foot side aisles of the First Jacobean Banqueting House it was possible to erect four tiers of seats with a 2 foot passageway behind. The *Florimène* plan for the Great Hall has a similar arrangement on the wall side of the balcony posts, and then there are another three rows towards the middle of the hall, but this arrangement leaves scant dancing space. At the masques there was often a problem of crowd control and at least once the performance was cancelled because of the crush. Busino gives us a glimpse of the Lord Chamberlain in his traditional role: 'The Lord Chamberlain then had the way cleared [after the King and ambassadors had taken their positions] and in the middle of the theatre there appeared a fine and spacious area carpeted all over with green cloth.' This was the dancing space.

The audience was an invited one and at some stage it became customary to issue tickets to control entry. This too proved insufficient, and in the accounts of *Coelum Britannicum* we hear of some kind of turnstile being operated in conjunction with the tickets: 'They have found a new way of letting them in by a turning chair, besides they let in none but such as have tickets sent them beforehand, so that now the keeping of the door is no trouble.'[15] As early as 1613, farthingales at the masque were banned (though Busino noted some in 1618). The bench seating in the *Florimène* plan is only 18 inches wide and the wheel farthingale would have contributed in large measure to overcrowding. (Did court theatre thus promote the farthingale's rapid decline in popularity in the 1620s?)

A number of the brilliant audience participated in the action of the masque in a special manner. At a particular moment well into the masque, the masquers came down from the stage and chose partners from amongst the assembly to dance the revels. The choosing was evidently (and unsurprisingly) not left to chance. When the male masquers of *Pleasure Reconciled to Virtue*, led by Prince Charles, went to collect their partners, those, already chosen, 'were standing ready to dance'.

As a species of court ceremonial, the masque became one of the most private of occasions. The select audience, by invitation only, comprised only courtiers, for the pageantry was not concerned to present the monarch to his people but to act out ideal images of courtly behaviour by and for the court itself. King Charles became an actor within the protective atmosphere of a flattering coterie, 600 or so members of the enclosed world of court life, and so it is possible to see the court theatre of the Stuarts as an index of the loss of the common touch the Tudors had pragmatically and skilfully cultivated.

Masques took months to prepare. When the initial 'device' had been decided upon, the book had to be written, costumes and scenes designed and prepared, music and dances composed; then a good deal of rehearsal was necessary for both amateur and professional participants; and finally the stage had to be built and the auditorium fitted up. The results were not always wholly successful. *The Masque of Beauty* (1608) had to be postponed because all was not ready (although the recurrent problems of friction between the foreign ambassadors may also have been to blame). Chaotic behaviour often marked the occasion. Of the last masque of Charles's reign, *Salmacida Spolia*, a commentator wrote: 'They say it was very good, but I believe the disorder was never so great at any.' During the masque Busino saw, James became bored when the dancing flagged and shouted, 'Why don't they dance? What did you make me come here for? Devil take you all, dance.' (Buckingham saved the day with his athletic capering.) One particular *débâcle* was the masque presented at Theobalds in 1606 in honour of the Danish King.[16] Spectators and participants alike were picturesquely overcome by drink. One lady masquer tripped and dropped into the royal visitor's lap caskets she was presenting to him, other masquers were sick or unable to speak their lines, and the two kings themselves were too inebriated greatly to mind. The chaos in which masque evenings ended was constantly deplored by visitors.

The high expense of masques also troubled many a court observer. *The Masque of Blackness* cost £3000 and James tried to limit *Queens* to £1000. But inevitably the spending on masques was difficult to contain and extravagance was in any case a necessary feature of the form. *Pleasure Reconciled to Virtue* cost £4000, and no less than £21,000 was spent on the elaborate *The Triumph of Peace* which the Inns of Court produced in 1634 (and the costs of which they shared). The true cost of masques is probably irrecoverable, insofar as the masquers themselves often paid for their own costumes. James had difficulty in finding money for his wife's funeral (it was delayed two months on that account) and never erected a tomb for her. Similarly, Charles was unable to afford a coronation procession for himself and never commissioned a monument to his father. But for masques, and the houses to contain them, it was always possible to find the money, however financially embarrassed the court happened to be. Even Jonson, in the great poem *Penshurst*, could see the vain extravagance of the art-form he himself helped to develop over twenty-five years. He called the masque 'the short bravery of the night'.

A 1642 pamphlet reflected, in mournful mood, on a king's theatre of Cockpit and Masquing Room left deserted by its aristocratic patrons:

> In the Cockpit and Revelling Rooms, where at play or masque the
> darkest night was converted to the brightest day that ever shined,
> by the lustre of torches, the sparkling of rich jewels. . . . Now you
> may go in without a ticket, or the danger of a broken pate, you may
> enter at the King's side, walk round about the theatres, view the
> pullies, the engines, conveyance, or contrivances of every single

scene, and not an Usher of the Revels, or Engineer to envy or find fault with your discovery, although they receive no gratuity for the sight of them.[17]

The Masquing House was pulled down in 1645 so that its materials might be recovered, and though the Cockpit was refurbished in 1660, it was replaced in 1665 as a permanent court playhouse by the Hall and had been demolished by 1675. The masque returned briefly to Charles II's court, but it never reached its former splendour or popularity. Its politics were a thing of the past and the opera and operatic play stole its energy and much of its form. It survived for a little as fashionable entertainment but no longer made sense as court ritual theatre.

9 · 'Excellent Creeping Sport': *Bartholomew Fair* at the Banqueting House

Bartholomew Fair, first performed in 1614, occupies a special place in Jonson's stage career. His previous play *Catiline* (1611) had received, in his own words, 'all vexation of censure'; but far from retiring from the fray, he next composed his most audacious, in many ways his most ambitious, piece for the Jacobean stage, and the circumstances of its first two performances in themselves challenge our attention (and will occupy much of this chapter). The play is a kind of epic farce designed on an immense scale. It is nearly 4,000 lines long (compared to the average Jacobean play of 2,500) and the dramatist himself concedes in the Induction that he printed with the play that its playing time is also necessarily long – 'The space of two hours and an half, and somewhat more'.[1] Moreover, *Bartholomew Fair* evidently requires a much larger cast than the Jacobean play company normally furnished.

When in 1616 Jonson published those parts of his writings to date that he wanted to preserve, the play was held back to provide the opening work for the second volume. (It went into print in 1631 although the volume it formed part of was only published posthumously in 1640.) It is possible, therefore, to regard the play as a hinge work of the two folios and a summation of the author's work up to 1616, and Jonson himself very probably saw it as that.[2] For many readers and theatre critics of our own period, it is his dramatic masterpiece, a play conceived on the scale and with the profundity of *King Lear*,[3] and, like Shakespeare's great tragedy, a sombre, essentially pessimistic indictment of the human animal in a fallen world. Its surface is farcical, but just as Quarlous and Winwife visit the fair to see 'excellent creeping sport', so the play's audience is ambushed by the infectious and eye-catching vitality of the play into an uneasy connivance with the venalities and grosser crimes portrayed. As Quarlous ruefully recognises, '*Facinus quos inquinat, aequat*' (IV, vi, 29) – those whom a guilty act pollutes, it stains equally. By 'creeping', Quarlous means 'stealthy', but it also means 'ignominious', and a surrender to the fair is a kind of ignominy an audience must avoid.

The circumstances of the play's first two performances are precisely known and offer apparently ambiguous witness to the playwright's intentions. The Induction printed with the text tells us that the play was first performed on 31 October 1614 at the Hope on Bankside, for in it a fictive Scrivener reads out

> Articles of Agreement, indented, between the spectators or hearers, at the Hope on the Bankside, in the county of Surrey, on the one party; and the author of *Bartholomew Fair* in the said place and county, on the other party: the one and thirtieth day of October 1614. . . . (ll. 64–8)

The acting company is conspicuously absent here because the Induction, characteristically of a private playhouse play but not, one would have thought, of a Hope play, is obsessively concerned with the relation of the dramatist, and not the actor, with his audience. (In a cameo in the Induction, he himself, or his man, is imagined to be lurking offstage as he probably in fact had been – ll. 7–8.) The players were the Lady Elizabeth's Men, and on the evening of the next day after this opening, 1 November, All Hallows, they acted the play at Whitehall in front of the King and his courtiers. That occasion we hear of in court records, and the fact that Jonson placed special emphasis on this royal command performance is advertised in the Prologue and Epilogue, both specifically addressed to the King and published with the play in 1631.

The performance at the Hope has attracted attention from historians and critics, partly because we know a good deal about that playhouse (more, perhaps, than about any other public house of the period) and partly because *Bartholomew Fair* is the only play known certainly to have been performed there. In the autumn of 1614, the Hope was still relatively new, possibly brand new. Henslowe had had it built on the site of the Beargarden and the extant builder's contract gives information about its size and in particular discloses that its stage was to be removable so that the arena might be used also for animal-baiting. The Induction jokes with heavy disapproval about this facility, for the Stage-keeper's judgment, according to the Book-holder, is fit only for 'gathering up the broken apples for the bears within' (ll. 52–3); and the poet notes the special decorum of playing a play set in Smithfield in such a place, 'being as dirty as Smithfield, and as stinking every whit' (ll. 161–2).

If we identify the play as a Hope play (which we almost certainly should not) as opposed to a play incidentally performed at the Hope, we may easily conclude that the playwright had learned caution from the buffeting which *Catiline* had received and had devised a tolerant and genial play calculated to appeal to a popular Bankside audience; and we may even suspect, as has often been the case, that *Bartholomew Fair* was specially written as an opener for the new house. (In fact, the Hope was almost certainly in use by the Lady Elizabeth's Men somewhat earlier in the year.[4]) However, even if we were to ignore the sheer unlikelihood of Jonson ever compromising his artistic integrity in that way, and even if we were oblivious to the extended mockery of a popular audience's understanding which he develops throughout the Induction, the 1631 title page makes abundantly clear who was Jonson's real audience: 'Acted in the year 1614, by the Lady Elizabeth's Servants and then dedicated to King James, of most blessed memory; by the Author, Benjamin Jonson.' 'Then' evidently refers to the time of playing, that All Hallows evening.

Jonson included also on the title page an adaptation from Horace which invokes Democritus, the laughing philosopher, who 'were he alive now would find more to laugh at in the audience than in the play'. No genial tolerance here in 1631, and in 1614 it is likely that far from searching at the Hope for the mass audience he always scorned, Jonson looked for an understanding audience at court (the understander at the Hope, as the Induction seems to say, being deficient precisely in that quality of judgment that distinguishes the discerning spectator).

The key performance, then, is that at Whitehall, and the play may even have been a kind of royal commission. With that performance (or at least at that time), Jonson as man-of-letters reaches his zenith; just thirteen months later he received a life pension from the King of one hundred marks a year – poet laureate in all but name. It is on the court performance that we must concentrate.

Were *Bartholomew Fair* merely a standard repertory piece at the Hope, the summons to play it at court on 1 November would be decidedly unusual. The King, who disliked London, was in the habit of ending his summer progress at Windsor or Hampton Court and then at the end of October proceeding to Whitehall for the winter season which officially began on 1 November. The opening entertainment was customarily staged that evening and would be a special occasion, a homecoming for the King who would play host to his courtiers. He, as much as the entertainers, would be on view.

Command plays were normally repertory pieces that had been tried out and polished in the commercial theatre. Indeed, that had traditionally been the reason that playhouses were licensed – to provide adequate rehearsal facilities for companies who might then entertain the sovereign when summoned to court. New plays, as far as we can tell, were never played at court (though in a small number of plays such as *Macbeth* critics have seen evidence, never conclusive, that plays were specifically written for a royal audience). Of the 144 new plays presented before the King or other members of the royal family between 1590 and 1642, only eight were composed specially for court perfomance and seven of these date from 1620 and later.[5] The Lord Chamberlain's Office, which was responsible for the choice of court plays, no doubt felt more confident with repertory pieces that had been checked out for quality and for possible offensive matter; and the court was not subjected to 'first night' problems.

Furthermore, far from being the kind of playwright whose work could be confidently accepted by the court officers on trust, Jonson had already had several scrapes with the authorities over his playwriting. In 1597 he had been imprisoned for his part in the collaborative, now lost play, *The Isle of Dogs* in which Nashe had had the main hand; then he had been called before the Privy Council in 1603 to explain what were evidently taken to be treasonable ideas in *Sejanus;* and in 1605 he was again imprisoned and only narrowly escaped having his ears and nose cut off for satirical allusions to James and his court in *Westward Ho!* which he wrote with Chapman. Even after *Bartholomew Fair* he would again incur royal disapproval over *The Devil is an Ass* (1616), according to Drummond, his Scottish host. So this was not a safe playwright with a proven track record, rather the reverse.

However, *Bartholomew Fair* must have been booked for its All Hallows performance long before its premiere at the Hope. There had been time (see p. 196) for the Revels Office to build scenery for the occasion, and in all probability, with such a complicated play to stage, the company was given some opportunity to rehearse at court before the Hope opening. It seems likely, therefore, that Jonson wrote *Bartholomew Fair* expressly for that court performance and the Hope premiere was in the nature of a public dress-rehearsal. Perhaps the financial interests of the company could only be served if the play then became a regular, repertory piece; but there is no other reference to a performance of the play before the Restoration and the title page refers only to its being acted in 1614. It is possible, in fact, that because of the play's uniquely heavy demand on acting personnel, it was never feasible, logistically, to mount it again, so that besides the customary ten pounds fee the company received for their performance at court, prestige and royal favour was all their reward for doing the play, plus one gathering.

For Jonson, the play might have been a royal commission – and this would explain why a new play by a contentious playwright opened the festive season, 1614–15. The content of the play, with its enthusiastically anti-Puritan stance, would be especially congenial to James. Before succeeding to the English throne he had complained bitterly of the 'rash-heady preachers' who 'think it their honour to contend with [God] upon their fingers'.[6] He recognised that they challenged both the established church and the civil magistracy, and so they posed a political threat he was ever wary of.

In the court Prologue addressed to James, Jonson eagerly advertised the anti-Puritan thrust of the play (which in fact is much more than merely a satire against the Puritans) and of the King's well-known attitude. Summarising the play's contents, he refers to

> the zealous noise
> Of your land's Faction, scandaliz'd at toys,
> As babies, hobby-horses, puppet-plays,
> And such like rage, whereof the petulant ways
> Yourself have known, and have been vex'd long.

But Jonson can tease his royal spectator as well as flatter. In Overdo, the magistrate that Puritan Zeal deplores, the court might well have seen a burlesque portrait of James himself. Monarch and magistrate share a tendency towards pedantry, an easy familiarity with classical quotations, an urge to inveigh against tobacco and its evil effects, and even, perhaps, a notably protective attitude towards young favourites.[7] (On the 1614 summer progress, James had met George Villiers, who was shortly to be introduced at court and become the latest *protégé* as Somerset's star waned.) It is indicative both of Jonson's confidence in his relationship with the King and of the kind of 'creeping' strategy the play habitually employs that such ironies can be deployed. James, as we shall see, was a conspicuous part of the performance in a physical sense as well as through the personal address of Prologue and Epilogue. And the playwright seems to include the King yet again in the character of Solomon.

Solomon, almost a ghost character, is Littlewit's clerk in the first act. His function is rendered nearly redundant by Win, but in a play about the true operation of understanding his wisdom is inevitably referred to (I, iv, 27) and thus his name 'explained', and he is invited to accompany the Littlewit group on their outing to the fair (I, vi, 87). But he fails to arrive and in 1613 Jonson forgot to include him in the *dramatis personae*. It is not too far-fetched, however, to see here yet another allusion to James who is also invited to the fair. For Solomon was James's favourite nickname for himself and the flattering reference stuck to him through life and into death.[8] At the Hope, Solomon the Clerk was an irrelevance; at Whitehall, a witty allusion.

'Solomon', one may speculate, commissioned the play. In Aubrey's brief life of Jonson, the biographer claims that 'King James made him write against the Puritans, who began to be troublesome in his time', and Jonson would have found nothing uncongenial in tackling once again a theme already notably explored in *The Alchemist*. This in turn may have suggested the brilliant vehicle for what would be the playwright's most comprehensive anatomy of the world's folly – the festive celebration of St Bartholomew's Day, 24 August, held since the twelfth century as a civic fair in Smithfield.

Jonson's choice of the Lady Elizabeth's Men to mount the play is as intriguing and possibly almost as significant as the venues of the first two performances. He worked freelance and was not contracted, as the regular professional playwrights were, to a particular company. But four of the five plays composed before *Bartholomew Fair* and four of the five plays composed afterwards were performed by London's most prestigious troupe, the King's Men. The Lady Elizabeth's Men had been licensed in 1611 and were managed by Henslowe (in whose business papers Jonson first appears in connection with London theatre[9]). By October 1614, the company had gone through two years of instability, refashioned several times by Henslowe in order, the players complained, that he could keep them in debt and therefore under his control. In 1613, the original company was amalgamated with the Children of the Queen's Revels, a semi-juvenile troupe which had performed two of Jonson's plays at the Blackfriars under the name of Children of the Chapel and a third as Children of the Revels at the Whitefriars.[10] Then in March 1614, there was a further reconstruction of the company and the importation of more players. The company had performed three times at Court in 1611–12 and three times in 1612–13, but *Bartholomew Fair* was their only court offering in 1614–15 and already, perhaps, Henslowe had new plans for them, for they were disbanded some time in 1615 and their place at the Hope and in Henslowe's operation was taken by Prince Charles's Men, a company with whom they had had some form of association during the first part of that year and possibly earlier.[11]

During their short London period (after 1615 they appear only in the provinces) the company played at the Swan, they were the first lessees of the Hope, and they probably also performed at the Whitefriars. Henslowe, it was suggested earlier (see p. 28) was looking for a private house to run in tandem with the Hope when the Whitefriars lease expired and it is interesting in this connection that the Induction of *Bartholomew Fair*, so tied as it is to the Hope performance, provides some evidence that the play was intended to be performed in a private house as well as at court; for the prices which the audience is supposed to have paid for entrance could never have applied to the Hope, even for a new play, but are in fact the standard ones for the private house (see p. 15):

> it shall be lawful for any man to judge his six pen'orth, his twelve pen'orth, so to his eighteen pence, two shillings, half a crown, to the value of his place. . . . (ll. 88–91)

Two factors might have steered Jonson towards the Lady Elizabeth's Men. Firstly their company leader was Nathan Field who, with the Children of the Chapel, had played in three of Jonson's plays, first as a child actor. By 1614 he was a highly experienced, 'private theatre' performer, but in his youth he had been a *protégé* of the playwright, for Drummond reported that 'Ned Field was [Jonson's] scholar, and he read to him the Satires of Horace, and some Epigrams of Martial'. In turn, Field wrote puff poems for the printed texts of *Volpone* and *Catiline* and he was himself embarked on a playwriting career. In 1616 he was recruited by the King's Men as a replacement for Shakespeare.

In *Bartholomew Fair*, in a passage that will bear further comment later, Jonson pays tribute to his former pupil, registering Field's high standing in his profession by comparing him with Burbage:

COK	Which is your Burbage now?
LEA	What do you mean by that, sir?
COK	Your best actor. Your Field?

(V,iii,79–82)

Coincidentally, it was Field, the court's account books show, who received the ten pounds payment for the performance on behalf of the company.

Jonson's esteem for Field may have been one reason for selling the play to the company, but there was a bonus for the playwright in that the actor's father, it was well known, was John Field, a Puritan preacher of the 1570s and 1580s who had been a radical reformer and an effective publicist for the cause. Jonson, as we have seen, makes the 'sanctified assembly' a special target in his play and he sharpens the attack by weaving into Zeal's sermonising, at least once, well-known words from Field senior. So for the Puritan attack on the puppets, Jonson writes a clever pastiche contrived out of a famous admission of defeat by Field – 'Seeing we cannot compass these things by suit or dispute, it is the multitude and people must bring the discipline to pass' – together with a prophecy from Giles Wiggington, another reformer – 'We look for a bickering ere long and then a battle, which we cannot endure' – plus a simile from a Puritan prayer – 'Our souls are constantly gaping after thee, O Lord, yea verily, our souls do gape, even as an Oyster'.[12] Zeal's lines run:

I have long opened my mouth wide, and gaped, I have gaped as an Oyster for the tide, after thy destruction: but cannot compass it by suit, or dispute; so that I look for a bickering, ere long, and then a battle.

(V,v, 20–3)

For a knowing court audience, such writing is wittily allusive. With Field junior on stage, the effect is fiercely comic.

If Field is one reason for Jonson's choice of company the second may lie in that company's unusual size. The conventional twelve men and four boys of the Elizabethan-Jacobean acting troupe would have found the casting of Jonson's play severely daunting, probably impossible. Not including the Induction (the parts of which were easily doubled), and not including the puppet voices (Leatherhead seems to indicate that he provides them – V,iii,74), there are thirty-three speaking parts in the play. Though a few could have been doubled, a large number of them are more than speaking extras and there are eighteen principal characters onstage together in the play's finale. Assuming, as we do, that Jonson composed with performance in mind and that the 1631 text represents the original version, then he clearly wrote for an unusually large company. Either because of the amalgamations of 1613 and 1614, or because, as evidently was the case in 1615, the company was able to associate easily with Prince Charles's Men, the Lady Elizabeth's Men offered Jonson the opportunity of writing the kind of large-cast play that seldom occurred. In his comedies prior to *Bartholomew Fair*, *Volpone* (King's Men, 1606) had a cast of thirteen, *The Silent Woman* (Children of the Queen's Revels, 1609) fifteen, and *The Alchemist* (King's Men, 1610) twelve. In composing for a huge cast, Jonson created a new kind of play.

Four different rooms in the Palace of Whitehall were used regularly for theatrical entertainment in the period around 1614. These were: the Banqueting House, built in 1607 and able to house the elaborate court masques written by Jonson and staged by Inigo Jones; the Great Hall; the Cockpit, not yet converted into a permanent playhouse but used intermittently for plays; and the Great Chamber (see pp. 149–51). *Bartholomew Fair* was evidently played in the first or last of these, but there is conflicting evidence as to which it was. In the Chamber Accounts for September and November 1614, there is an entry of payment to one John Heborne for the work of ten assistants in preparing the Banqueting House 'for plays', the operation lasting eight days.[13] (The same accounts for later in the season show the Great Hall being readied for plays while the Banqueting House is occupied with a masque.) But in the Declared Accounts of the Office of Works for the period 10 October 1614 to 30 September 1615, there is an entry: 'diverse works and reparations in making the Great Chamber for plays, the Banqueting House for a masque and the Hall for revels and shows'.[14] It was the Office of Works department that was responsible for the construction of stages and auditoria for such occasions, but this entry has a bureaucratic neatness to it that is suspicious. The general pattern of the Chamber Accounts shows that the Great Chamber was used very little during the five season period with 1614–15 as the middle one. We can assume that it was a much smaller hall than the Banqueting House and would have allowed only an exiguous stage space for Jonson's epic play (a fit-up theatre in Richmond's Great Chamber in 1588 had a stage 14 feet by 14 feet). Furthermore, as will be discussed, specially prepared scenery had to be accommodated. If, too, we assume that the audience for the first night of the season would be large, it is probably safe to trust the Chamber Accounts and conclude that on All Saints' evening of 1614, *Bartholomew Fair* was performed in the Banqueting House.

Some account has already been given of the 1607 Banqueting House and its lay-out for performance (see pp. 151–3 and Plate 13). For this reconstruction, it is assumed that the stage was erected at the north end, with the vestibule area behind the four pillars forming a tiring-house with some kind of screen in front. (Curtaining would be adequate for Jonson makes no specific use of practical doors, though other plays following hard on might well have done so.) Around the walls, between the pillars and under the balconies, scaffold seating was set up providing accommodation for about 600 spectators. In the middle of the auditorium directly opposite the stage was the King's state and around it were placed stools for the royal family, important visitors and high-ranking courtiers. The ground plan for *Florimène* in the Great Hall (Plate 12) provides a likely lay-out for the auditorium.

A stage fitted between the pillars would be 37 feet across and allow spectators to sit on either side, making it a thrust stage as was conventional in the commercial playhouses. (The stage for *Florimène* was 40 feet across but its perspective scenery allowed no spectators alongside.) If we allow a stage-depth of 31 feet, which is the distance between four of the side pillars, that would leave an auditorium of 73 feet long and 53 feet in width. Into that goes the state which, if it is in the middle of the auditorium, is about 36 feet from the stage, allowing the King to be easily visible to many of the audience, at least in profile.

This of course is a principle essential to court theatre. Jonson, as we have seen, has already made James a notional actor in his play; he is to be the arbiter, both morally and aesthetically, so conspicuously missing on the stage proper. But the King in fact is on his own stage, solo actor in a play of sovereignty which runs alongside, as well as meshing in with Jonson's play. In the Epilogue, James is gracefully re-assigned to his role of chief, even sole, spectator; but during the course of the evening's performance, he played his part in public view as enthusiastically as the Lady Elizabeth's Men.

The occasion and the audience must have been dazzling. The hall was brightly lit by candelabra strung on wires running across the hall, and the candlelight was reflected back by the sumptuous costumes of the courtiers present; and here there was a fine irony that Jonson was intent on exploiting. With its rueful references to the smell and squalor of the Hope providing a decorous setting for the play's first outing before a public, the Induction to *Bartholomew Fair* acts as an 'alienating' device, drawing attention to the play's artifice, not its realism. In it Jonson spells out overemphatically that the play is insulated from the real world and that the proper response from the audience is not an indulgent engagement in the action but a discriminating and detached judgment upon it. And so the frame play of Stage-keeper, Book-holder and Scrivener asserts the inner fiction of the main play with heavy irony:

> Gentlemen, have a little patience, they are e'en upon coming instantly. He that should begin the play, Master Littlewit, the Proctor, has a stitch new fallen in his black silk stocking; 'twill be drawn up ere you can tell twenty. (ll. 1–4)

At court, and for the same purpose of 'alienation', the playwright trades off the paradox, even the tongue-in-cheek audacity, of inviting the sovereign (and his fine courtiers) to a fair – 'Your Majesty is welcome to a Fair. . . . The Maker . . . hopes tonight to give you a fairing [= a present from a fair], true delight' (Prologue). For in life such demotic pursuits as fair-going would be anathema to the upper class. In the play itself, Grace (who is surnamed Wellborn) knows that she demeans herself by going to a fair: 'There's none goes thither of any quality or fashion' (I, v, 28–9). Modern criticism has often branded her a snob, a charge she does not really deserve. Half a century later, Pepys (who was certainly a snob) was to marvel at Lady Castlemaine's visiting a puppet-booth at the real Bartholomew Fair, 'thinking the people would abuse her'. Assuming a lofty superiority to the fair and its visitors, Quarlous and Winwife go there seeking 'creeping sport' and, as gentlemen, are assumed to be 'too fine to carry money' to spend on fair merchandise (II,v,165); though Quarlous recognises 'our very being here makes us fit to be demanded' (II,v, 16–17). Indeed, Jonson soon demonstrates their inability, at least on Quarlous's part, to maintain their distance, and Whit embarrasses him acutely by even recognising him. So Jonson, Brecht-like, invites the audience to consider its own attitude to what is shown. A gentle audience may visit a play-fair but, with Quarlous, can be implicated in the action.

Just as the frame play at the Hope invited an awareness of the play's detachment from real life, so the play-within-the-play of *Hero and Leander*, and indeed much of Act V, does the same thing. The whole episode of the puppet-play is a sustained passage of 'alienation' in which the courtly audience, watching a sophisticated, 'difficult' play is invited to observe another audience watching a crassly populist piece of dramatic entertainment. In fine, mannerist style, Jonson introduces the puppets themselves in a passage of ironic in-jokes that flattered his audience's knowingness as patrons of the theatre. In it, characters handling the actor-dolls of the play within remind the outer audience that the characters are themselves

actors inside their roles. Leatherhead brings the puppets out in a basket
to show them to Cokes:

COK   Do you call these players?

LEA   They are actors, sir, and as good as any, none disprais'd, for
dumb shows: indeed, I am the mouth of 'em all!

COK   Thy mouth will hold 'em all. I think, one Taylor would go
near to beat all this company, with a hand bound behind him.

LIT   Aye, and eat 'em all, too, an' they were in cake-bread.

COK   I thank you for that, Master Littlewit, a good jest! Which is
your Burbage now?

LEA   What mean you by that, sir?

COK   Your best actor. Your Field?

LIT   Good, i' faith! You are even with me, sir. . . .

LEA   And here is young Leander, is as proper an actor of his inches,
and shakes his head like an ostler.

(V, iii, 71–99)

Some allusions are probably irrecoverable (and little of this will work
in a modern revival), but the Whitehall audience was reminded here of
four contemporary actors, two currently performing the play and probably
on stage at the time, that is Field and Joseph Taylor, and two from the
King's Men, Burbage and Ostler. Taylor, if that is the reference here,[15]
had been a founder member of the Lady Elizabeth's Men and would
shortly move on to the King's Men and perform in *The Duchess of Malfi*
(see p. 102). Ostler, who perhaps had a trick of shaking his head, had
been a fellow actor with Field in the Children of the Chapel, and he too
played in *The Duchess of Malfi*. He would survive this stage reference by
only two months.

The passage would work best if Field and Taylor were on stage and
commentators have suggested that Field played Littlewit, though the
jokes here work better if he played Cokes. In fact, the play lacks an
obvious lead part, but Cokes's is the largest by line-length (Littlewit's is
the fourth largest) and Field was evidently the principal actor. Also, as
burlesque lover of the outer play, Cokes parallels Leander, chief lover of
the puppet play who is in turn to be played by the puppet company's
'best actor'. However, if Field played Cokes, this tells us that he had an
unusual physique (see p. 178).

A fifth actor evidently referred to in the puppet-play sequence is
Thomas Basse who was, like Taylor, a founder member of the company
(he had moved to Queen Anne's by 1617). Wrangling with the puppet
Dionysius, Zeal is warned: 'You cannot bear him down with your bass
noise, sir' (V,v,69–70), so probably Basse played Zeal.[16]

It is important to stress the 'alienation' in Jonson's play because reader and performer are likely to be struck forcibly by the play's apparent absorption with and grounding in the actuality of a real fair, both in its operation and in the behaviour of its clients and customers. No Elizabethan-Jacobean script is so prescriptive in its presentation of the physical appearance of its characters. Jonson displays an extraordinary eye for detail and his imagining of the minutiae of physique and costume shows his considerable control over the apparently anarchic energies of the play's action. It shows too that Jonson was writing with a particular group of actors firmly in mind, for they need to have amongst their number the following:

A small actor able to play an old man (for Wasp: I,iii,111; I,iv,43,5; III,v, 250).

A young, tall, thin actor with grotesquely long legs (for Cokes: I,iv, 85–6; I, v, 96–7; V,iv, 76).

A young, thin, diminutive actor (for Mooncalf: II,ii, 66–7; II,ii,138; II, v,57).

A large actor to play a dame part (for Ursula: II,v, *passim* – see p. 188).

A middle-aged actor nearly bald (for Overdo: II, vi, 3–4).

Two boy-actresses paired for their contrasting heights (Mrs Overdo and Win: V,iv,25–6).

Jonson intends a theatre of grotesques, even making Joan Trash 'a little crooked o' my body' (II,ii,24–5), and he needs a company that can play this with some ready aptitude.

The physical specificity is carried through to those elements of hair-style and colouring in the power of the make-up department to effect, but in part, again, Jonson probably utilises the natural assets of particular actors: Zeal is 'sorrel'-haired and has a beard (I,vi, 32; III,ii, 129); Knockem has a 'dibble' beard and is long-haired (II,iii, 45; III,vi,27); Win is dark chestnut (IV, v, 21); and Trouble-All has a long and ragged beard that reminds people of Old Testament prophets and is sufficiently distinctive that it can be faked by Quarlous over his own beard (IV, iv,131).

Such detailed imagining by the playwright extends to costume, and the script, again uniquely, yields an extraordinarily full list for the wardrobe and the tiremen:

WASP: satin doublet, old-fashioned sword (fox) with basket hilt (II, vi,33, 56).

COKES: beaver hat with feather, sword, cloak, gloves, doublet and hose (III,v,184; IV,ii, 36–7, 62; V,iii,158–9; V,iv,89).

WIN: velvet cap with 'custard' embroidery, laced or striped habit; fine high shoes; later, green dress and mask (I,i,20,24; I,ii,7; I,iv,54; V,iv,44; V,vi,48).

MISTRESS OVERDO: French hood of velvet; tuft-taffeta, silk dress; later, green dress and mask (I,v,15; IV,iii,117; IV,iv, 149, 182, 201–2; IV,v,65).

TROUBLE-ALL: ragged gown or robe and cap, the habit of a madman (V,ii,14–15, 111).

ZEAL: costume of a schoolmaster, in furred gown, with buttons (I,ii,68; III,ii,25; V,iv,344–5).

DAME PURECRAFT: strait stomacher; small, printed ruff; velvet hat (III,ii, 75,138; IV,vi,170).

OVERDO: the habit of a fool, which is a guarded coat, as Arthur; later, a porter's outfit (II,i,9; II,vi,16; V,ii, S.D).

RAMPING ALICE: ruff, waistcoat and petticoat, of green and scarlet (IV,v,82,91).

The costume detail is not incidental or whimsical. Dress denotes social status and several characters are upwardly mobile (as Wasp constantly observes). Also, in a play of hypocrites, appearances can deceive, as Ursula points out to Quarlous and Winwife: 'I ha' seen as fine outsides, as either o' yours, bring lousy linings to the brokers, ere now, twice a week!' (II,v, 106–8). Through change of dress, characters translate themselves or, ironically, reveal their true identities. Trouble-All in the last scene has only Ursula's pan to cover his nakedness, while Quarlous is mad 'but from the gown outward' (V,vi,66–7). On the other hand, Dionysius the puppet, beneath his garment, has no sex (V,v,after l. 99).

Just as the characters are defined exactly, provided we can read the signs, by physique and dress, so are they by a parallel specificity of 'dialect'. The actors of the play are given little autonomy, small opportunity to interpret their roles, and the language they are given is precise verbal costuming, definitely (that is, with exact definition) determining their personalities (as with physique and costume) from the outside, each one's verbal set fixing his or her view of the world as though in aspic. So Zeal can only judge through his Old Testament prejudices and Overdo's laboured classicism precludes a sensitive response to what he hears and sees. For Knockem, the house-courser, his vocational jargon reduces all the world to an equine nightmare in which man is only identifiable as the animal he constantly degenerates into. His describing of Win in value terms appropriate to horseflesh is two-edged because that is as she allows herself to be bartered for and disposed of: as horseflesh (IV,v,20–8).

The dialogue is supremely gestic and Jonson 'sees' the characters in dynamic action as he writes their words. He leaves no ambiguity about a character's inner life, and the subtext of a speech belongs to the writer and not to its speaker. In effect, the characters' language is wholly dramatic; they live in and through it, not behind it. They are created as much by what they say as by their actions, and in the densely demotic hubbub which is the important scenery of the fair, Jonson's fine ear for linguistic mannerism allies in his characteristic way with comic distortion to dazzling effect. For the modern actor, the lack of space between the words might prove frustrating and the seventeenth-century idioms are difficult. For the Lady Elizabeth's Men the script was certainly taxing to master (verse, in any case, is easier to learn), but the strong identity of their parts imparted by their speech habits was no doubt reassuring in a play bristling with difficulties in its practical *mise en scène*.

We generally assume that staging practices in the commercial playhouses and at court were standardised, allowing the easy transference of productions with a minimum of difficulty over restaging. If the general line of this account of the first performance is correct, then the restaging in the players' minds was done in the opposite direction from normal, as they prepared first for the Whitehall performance and then (before in time but after in intent) performed the play at the Hope.

Nevertheless, moving the play must have been a headache to the stage manager. As with physique, costume and language, *Bartholomew Fair* is a densely specific play with regard to the stage properties it calls for. It probably requires more props than any other contemporary play, 'such ware' that Jonson promises in the Prologue. There are the inevitable key items around which the story revolves – the black box with Cokes's marriage license, Overdo's black book, Cokes's purses, Ursula's firebrand and pig-pan, and the pair of tables by which Grace chooses a husband. But in addition there is the paraphernalia of the fair itself – the countless objects on Leatherhead's stall, Joan's gingerbread-men, the trinkets which Cokes has bought elsewhere and which weigh Wasp down, Nightingale's song-sheets, the pipes, tobacco, bottles and ale deployed around Ursula's booth, the basket of pears which proves Cokes's downfall, and the puppets and other equipment of the *Hero and Leander* play. None of these things can be left to the audience's imagination. Characters point at them and identify them, drop them, lose them and attack them; and the stagecrew perforce must have collected them, set them, struck them and then, during All Saints day, transported them to Whitehall and reset them. *Bartholomew Fair* is a play full of objects, which is part of its great density of physical presence, an astonishing particularity that gives it its special flavour.

Many a reader of the play and, one suspects, some recent directors, have been overwhelmed by this richness of texture into overlooking the play's form and shapeliness and its disciplined development, and we can best observe these qualities through the staging. At the Hope, in their trial run, the Lady Elizabeth's Men played on a thrust stage with an audience on three sides, and upstage of them was a tiring-house screen with two doors and a centrally hung arras (Induction, 1.8). It has been suggested that the Hope's impermanent stage was not in fact used, so that an authentic fairground atmosphere could be created in the arena with players mingling with audience in a kind of promenade or environmental theatre. But this is again to miss the 'alienation' of the play that Jonson works so hard to achieve.

At the court, the distance created literally by working on a stage was probably enhanced by the space left vacant between the stage itself and the King's state, though, it was suggested earlier, a seated audience might stretch along the short sides of the stage. For the Hope performance, we have little to guide us in judging how far scenic units were provided to support the action. Clearly, Leatherhead's shop and Joan Trash's basket require physical embodiment. But Ursula's booth, a central controlling image in the play, was easily provided by simply dressing up (with the sign referred to at III,ii, 8–9 and stage direction, and the boughs which provide shelter outside) the arras itself, which evidently concealed the discovery-space. Jonson conspicuously makes little use of the physical features of the playhouse. (He had made great play with doors and discovery-space in his previous play, *The Alchemist*, and would make telling use of the upper level in his next play, *The Devil is an Ass*, both at the Blackfriars.) For *Bartholomew Fair*, both because of the needs of his story and perhaps because the play was principally to be played at court, staging demands are confined to simple movable structures which can be placed in front of a tiring-house screen which itself is impermanent; and we hear of these structures in an entry in the Revels Accounts: 'Canvas for the booths and other necessaries for a play called *Bartholomew Fair*.'[17] (For the operation of the Revels Office see Chapter 8.)

The 'booths' of the entry evidently refers to the business premises of Ursula and Leatherhead and to the puppet-booth, and the 'other necessaries' might refer to extra costumes for this exactly costumed play and to some of its great profusion of props. (Again, we are inevitably left with the feeling that by comparison with the court performance, the Hope presentation of Jonson's play was an unfinished thing rather like a rehearsal.)

In employing a canvas structure for Ursula's booth, of course, the court production was by no means breaking new theatrical ground. The military tent, of a practical nature and even providing if necessary a stage within a stage, had been a regular feature of the Elizabethan theatre. It seems to be required for *1 Henry VI*, *Richard III* (two on stage simultaneously?) and *Troilus and Cressida;* and Thomas Platter describes the use of a tent in an unknown play of 1599: 'Meanwhile the Englishman went into the tent' (and stole his daughter out of it).[18] In *The Devil's Charter*, played at court by the King's Men in 1607, separate stage directions read: 'Barbarossa *bringeth from* Caesar's *tent her two boys*', and '*He discovereth his tent where her two sons were at cards*' (in IV, iv; the Prologue with its dumbshow also has two tents).

Zeal, through his Old Testament spectacles, sees Ursula's booth as one of 'the tents of the unclean' (III,ii,83–4), but elsewhere, and by other characters, it is referred to as 'lodge', 'mansion', 'bower', 'pigsty', 'pig-box' and 'the great woman's house': a 'pathetic fallacy' place that nevertheless had a firm theatrical shape. Overdo, as mad Arthur, can refer to but not necessarily see, the smoked appearance of its backside (II,vi, 40–1), and it has a practical entrance by which are brought on to stage the tankards, bottles, tobacco and so on of Ursula's trade and through which visitors exit to sample the pork. Chairs set in front of the booth, including Ursula's own, provide a sitting-out area for customers and the pig-woman's cronies, and above the entrance is the elaborate sign of the pig's head (III,ii, 58–9 and following stage direction). But the whole play does not take place around the booth, and it is necessary to examine Jonson's handling of locale before we can determine more precisely what the Revels Office actually provided.

In seeing the play into print (in 1631, seventeen years later), Jonson provided a copy-text improved for the reader with explanatory side-notes, and he divided it into five acts, each act in six scenes. The five-act structure marks a careful articulation of the plot and, to a large extent, shadows the practical staging. But one must be aware that the scenes are not staging units of a conventional kind – that is, pieces of continuous action which end when the stage empties – but are 'classical', literary units defined, for the most part, by the entry of a new, important character. (In fact, Jonson handles this somewhat arbitrarily.) Divided in the customary way, the play has either nine or ten scenes (compared with Jonson's thirty-six). Act I is all one scene, and so are Acts II and III; Act IV is three scenes or four; and Act V is three scenes.[19] The effect on stage, consequently, is more fluent and dynamic, less staccato than the reader may imagine from a text printed according to Jonson's own. From II on, there is a constant flow of fair people and visitors as the various groups arrive, meet, split up and eventually reunite at the puppet-play at the end of the day.

Act I's single scene takes place, narratively, in one room of the Littlewits' house. Offstage, and to be imagined, is the study from which the licence and its box are fetched, the kitchen where Zeal is discovered sleeping and the street-door by which the visitors arrive. But the staging requirements are nil: the action develops in a neutral space and only one entrance for the actors is required. A few stools might usefully dress the scene and help the actors, but the domestic ambience is created and sustained by the dialogue and needs no literal presentation. It is even possible that scenic elements of the fair are already present on stage at the beginning of the play, set upstage of the action and ignored until brought into use; for, starting with the Prologue (or at the Hope, the Induction), the fair is already forcibly present in the play in the minds of the characters. Later, they will be physically taken over by it as soon as they allow this to happen. Only a through-going realism, of the kind that Jonson consistently eschews, requires that during Act I the stage should represent convincingly the Littlewit household.

If the fair's booths were not already set, this is done between acts I and II. It is attractive to see Overdo's opening peroration of II,i as the opportunity to do this, but Jonson communicates important ideas in the speech and no actor enjoys playing in front of frenetic business carried on by the stagecrew. There are three practical structures that will remain on stage through Acts II and III – Ursula's booth, Leatherhead's stall and Joan Trash's gingerbread business. These last two are evidently set close together because Leatherhead urges Joan to 'sit farther off with your gingerbread-progeny there, and hinder not the prospect of my shop' (II,ii, 3–5). She has a basket to contain her produce (later it is called a 'flasket') and perhaps it is set on a table, because it will be turned over by Zeal (III,iv). Before that, she sells the whole of the business, with the ground rent, to Cokes for four shillings and eleven pence.

Leatherhead calls his business a shop (see earlier) and it contains a great many gew-gaws for sale, but like Joan's it is readily mobile. When he and Joan have sold up to Cokes (he charges twenty shillings sevenpence halfpenny plus three shillings ground rent), they take the opportunity of Cokes's absence to '*plot to be gone*' (side-note after III, vi, 18) and Leatherhead urges 'Let's pack up all, and be gone, before he find us'. Joan counsels delay, with the result that Zeal attacks her gingerbread, and at the end of the scene Leatherhead says: 'Let's away; I counsell'd you to pack up afore, Joan.' And so they exit with their things and we do not see Joan again, nor Leatherhead except translated into puppeteer. Evidently, Leatherhead's shop is a stall on wheels, perhaps with canvas sides, and he pushes it off, upstage, so that Cokes loses all his purchase.

Even with booth, stall and basket set on stage during Acts II and III, the stage, in Jonson's mind, is not seriously incommoded. When Busy enters in III, ii, he ushers in his flock with

So, walk on in the middle way, fore-right, turn neither to the right hand, nor to the left; let not your eyes be drawn aside with vanity, nor your ear with noises.

(III,ii, 28–30)

and the party is seen approaching over eight lines of dialogue. As Zeal homes in on the smell of roast pork issuing from Ursula's booth he '*scents after it like a hound'*. When Cokes arrives back on stage two scenes later, he *'runs to [Joan's] shop'* (III,iv,93) and, next scene, *'runs to the ballad man'* (III,v, after l. 15). The whole episode of the stealing of Cokes's purse while the ballad is sung requires a great deal of stage space so that the action can be generously blocked and so made clear to the audience. There are eleven speaking characters on stage plus extras. Winwife and Quarlous are physically detached but in a position from which they can see the theft of the purses and direct the audience's attention. With, let us say, Ursula's booth upstage left, its chairs in front of it and Leatherhead's stall and Joan's basket up right, there needs to be space enough downstage and centre to allow this complicated episode to work. It seems doubtful that the Whitefriars, had it been available, could offer a sufficiently large stage (though the Hope probably did). A stage at court of 37 feet by 31 feet (see earlier) would be none too big. Again, the last moments of the play, when first Overdo and then Quarlous deploy on the stage eighteen characters including themselves so that they can all be seen, require a large stage: 'stand there . . . stand by her . . . stand you both there, in the middle place . . . stand forth you weeds of enormity . . . First . . . next . . . then . . . stand you there . . . stand you there . . .' (V, vi, 6–68). No 'cheese-trencher' will serve the playwright's turn (see p. 41).

In Act IV, it appears that Ursula's booth, at least as it was first presented, is no longer visible and Jonson clearly regards the location as somewhere else from that of II and III. When Nightingale makes off with Cokes's sword, hat and cloak in IV,ii, he should logically exit into the booth where the stolen goods of the play are customarily cached. But instead of some such direction as 'Get you in', Edgworth orders him 'Away, Nightingale: that way' (IV,ii, 45) and he runs off stage. In the next scene, Edgworth informs Quarlous that they are 'o' the backside o' the booth already, you may hear the noise' (IV,iii, 125–6), which is a studied indication that the next scene takes place outside the back entrance of Ursula's establishment. Edgworth and Quarlous then exit, Knockem and the others engaged in the 'vapours' game (plus Mistress Overdo) enter, and only after nineteen lines of the new scene do Edgworth and Quarlous re-enter. The booth here needs no representation. It is, as it were, behind an upstage entrance, as the dialogue has carefully indicated. And through the rest of the scene, that entrance will serve to convey the women to Ursula's makeshift toilet or allow Knockem and Whit to impress them into prostitution; and so the backside, symbolically and literally, represents the other face of Ursula's trade.

With the booth no longer physically present on stage in Act IV, its place as a focus of the action is partly taken over by the stocks. They symbolise society's faltering attempts to discipline its wayward members and become the occasion for much comic business that demonstrates the law is an ass. They evidently sit one side of the stage and are used in the first and last scene (first for Overdo, and then, with comic propriety, for Overdo, Zeal and Wasp, the three who are most censorious of their fellows' behaviour). But scene iv is elsewhere ('carry him away to the pigeon-holes' – IV, iv, 165–6) and scene v is a continuation of the action; so during these two scenes either the stocks remain on stage but ignored or they have been taken off and are brought back for scene vi. Together with Trouble-All, crazed victim of the judicial process, the stocks express, as a potent stage-image, ideas concerned with licence and constraint.

In Act V, and for the whole act, a new stage-image dominates – the puppet-booth. The stocks have been cleared and no other stage-dressing is now necessary or pertinent. It has been suggested that Ursula's booth is still on stage, referred to in Cokes's 'by that fire' (V,iii,28–9) and Littlewit's 'I left her [his wife] at the great woman's house in trust yonder' (V,v, 15–16).[20] But there plainly could never have been a practical fire left burning on stage for four acts (Cokes probably swears, poetically, by the sun); and Littlewit's 'yonder' is possibly accompanied by a gesture offstage to an imagined locality nearby. The puppet-booth is set between IV and V or by Leatherhead and his doorkeepers in V,i. It is a small structure (the little tiring-house referred to jocularly by Leatherhead at V, iii, 56–7) to provide the staging for the puppets. The puppets themselves were either glove puppets or rod puppets.[21]

Booth, banner and bill-board, together with chairs, form the puppet theatre. Speculation that the whole stage now represents the inside of a larger booth in which the audience is to watch a puppet-play is incorrect because this is an open-air 'playhouse'; at the end of the play the sick Mistress Overdo is to be taken to 'out o' the air, it will make her worse else' (V,vi,99). In any case, Winwife and Grace and Overdo and Zeal can all be on the real stage during the puppet-play without actually being noticed by the others, and they remain unaccosted by the door-keepers.

Probably, chairs around the puppet-stage define the playhouse's area and Sharkwell and Filcher allow entry to and receive money from would-be spectators who draw near. It is in effect a miniature public playhouse, though Edgworth's suggestive joke to Win converts it for a moment: 'This is a very private house, madam' (V,iv,39). At the play's end, the puppet-booth, which is as transitory as the other shows of the fair, can be carried, lock, stock and barrel, to the Justice's house for a private entertainment at a supper party.

'The booths and other necessaries', therefore, are all movable feasts, and as act succeeds act, they operate as emblematic devices: II and III have booth and stall; IV, the stocks; V, the puppet theatre. In this way, and with a clarity imposed by staging, *Bartholomew Fair* works, during

II-V, through a series of related ideas: temptation and greed, excess and beastliness, inverted correction, and finally illusion and disillusion. The sense of design, an elegant articulation, is strong in the staging, correcting any superficial impression gained by the reader that Jonson is intent merely on dramatising with photographic fidelity the chaotic activity of a day at the fair.[22] Jonson's keen sense of actuality is at the service of an image not of a fair, but of Vanity Fair. The farcical business is overlaid on a morality play armature, but the staging is sequential and not simultaneous.[23]

Indiscipline is a key idea of the play, symbolised in the running motif of 'vapours'. For Knockem, 'vapours' is a nonsense word-game in which any proposition might be refuted (IV, iv); but it has a general reference in the play to the state, in the modern idiom, of losing one's cool. In that state, induced by alcohol, tobacco, aggression or simple vanity, the judgment is befogged, chaos comes again and a man quickly loses his wits, his possessions, his wife or his bearings. In a well-ordered society, indiscipline is eliminated by the warrant or licence of the civil magistracy; but Overdo's failures (an overzealousness as pernicious as Zeal's) register Jonson's growing disillusion (traceable through the previous comedies) with the idea that the detached moralist is capable of reforming others.[24] At the end of the play only the King, and by implication the poet, has the right to judge his fellow man (and the Epilogue spells this out).

However, if indiscipline is a major informing idea, the key to playing is discipline, and Jonson expected it in great measure of the Lady Elizabeth's Men if they were to manage effectively this immense script, with its frenetic stage business, demotic and demanding dialogue and great profusion of props. The action demands the most careful of pacing as the interlocking stories, which are all one story, are complexly organised. Act I introduces us carefully to the visitors and their various relationships, kinship, courtship and mercenary. In II, equally cautious in tempo, we first meet the fair people (plus Overdo) and see how they operate, and then the first visitors reach the fair. By III,ii, all the visitors have arrived and the fair business quickens. Through III and IV, a disintegration of the various visitor groups proceeds and that movement is complete by IV, v with the abandonment of Win. And then in Act V, with a total grasp of the internal rhythms of the play, Jonson assembles the characters around the puppet play and allows a lengthy unmasking to take place, conducted firstly by Overdo and then by Quarlous. At the end, the stories are resolved: four characters have found marriage partners but not the ones they expected; three self-appointed moralists have learned humility; two wives have narrowly escaped prostitution; and of the visitors, only Cokes, whose head is full of the worthless gew-gaws he so delights in at the fair (see I, v,88–94), has evidently learned nothing. If the successive stages of this audacious plot are carefully marked and the minor climaxes given due weight, the play has both momentum and shape.

The discipline required from the Lady Elizabeth's Men is two-fold. Firstly, the stage-action demands the careful timing of classic farce and is built on a series of comic encounters, surprises, *coups de théâtre*. The stage constantly empties and refills, and set-piece (of sermon, song, puppet-play) is watched, ignored, applauded and interrupted. Live emblems, a kind of wit that James no doubt enjoyed, abound: Zeal scenting like a dog, Ursula with a firebrand, Cokes on piggy-back, the overthrowing of the gingerbread-men, three wise monkeys in the stocks, Grace playing handy-dandy and puppet Dionysius lifting his gown. Noise follows quiet, crowd scene succeeds an intimate duologue, fighting (and yet more fighting) comes on the heels of wooing. As the pace quickens, overwatching (and overhearing) scenes proliferate, rigorously exercising the audience's own faculty of judgment about what it hears and sees. The opening of V,ii is an outrageous example of Jonson's demanding stage craft (and, incidentally, of his use of stage space):

> *The JUSTICE comes in like a porter*
>
> JUS This later disguise, I have borrow'd of a porter . . . Two main works I have to prosecute: first one is to invent some satisfaction for the poor, kind wretch, who is out of his wits for my sake; and yonder I see him coming; I will walk aside, and project for it.
>
> [*Enter*] WINWIFE, GRACE.
>
> WINW I wonder where Tom Quarlous is, that he returns not; it may be he is struck in here to seek us.
>
> GRACE See, here's our madman again.
>
> [*Enter*] QUARLOUS, PURECRAFT. QUARLOUS *in the habit of the madman is mistaken by* Mistress PURECRAFT.
>
> QUAR [*Aside*] I have made myself as like him, as his gown and cap will give me leave.
>
> PURE Sir, I love you, and would be glad to be mad with you in truth.
>
> WINW How! my widow in love with a madman?
>
> (V.ii, 1–18)

A passage like this makes poor, staccato reading but is brilliant theatre. The playwright juggles the various plots and involves the audience in a deadly serious game of truth-detection. In fact, two-thirds of the lines here are addressed to the audience (did the actors at Whitehall constantly speak only to the King?), twice so that an entering character may identify himself in his new disguise. There are three separate entries and two of these are noticed by a character already on stage who each time fails to identify what he sees. And there is an overhearing (Winwife of Purecraft) promptly reported to the audience.

The blocking is necessarily complicated and requires careful rehearsal. Overdo enters, moves downstage away from the puppet-stage, sees Quarlous approaching and moves 'aside'. Before Quarlous is properly on, however, and from another direction, come Winwife and Grace who also see Quarlous entering but (as does Overdo and, incidentally, the audience) mistake him for Trouble-All. In fact, the audience has already been alerted to expect this mumming of Quarlous. He and Purecraft reach stage-centre and only then does Quarlous reveal the trick. The effect is two-fold: the audience is forced to assess its ability to 'read' the situation and simultaneously is made aware of the characters' own vulnerability and isolation. For these farcical manoeuvres enact a near tragic short-sighted-ness on the part of the fair visitors who see what they expect to see.

To play *Bartholomew Fair*, Jonson's cast needed to be disciplined in the sense of being able to work as an ensemble. Many of the parts are virtuoso roles, grotesques and caricatures which are fine vehicles for the kind of actor that today we call 'Brechtian', able to play a part with gusto but at the same time express a critical attitude to it. So the Ursula role is a kind of pantomime dame, a grotesque woman almost certainly played by an adult male (as she was on the Restoration stage and has been generally since); Zeal is the most spectacular of Jonson's line of pious, button-bursting Puritans; and Trouble-All is a brilliant burlesque of the prophetic, stage madman. These and many others are eye-catching parts. But while playing with a due sense of grotesque style, the players had not to fudge the delicacy of Jonson's writing by inventing stage business (the playwright writes in what is necessary), by upstaging or by losing a sense of teamwork. Probably amongst the Lady Elizabeth's Men, many of whom had trained in satirical theatre as boy actors and had worked together over many years, teamwork was one element that the playwright could count on.

Dryden, in an age that found much merit in Jonson's play, could see the artistry through which the fair was rendered by the playwright into an art object. In the play, he explains,

> he does so raise his matter . . . as to render it delightful; which he
> could never have performed had he only said or done those very
> things that are daily spoken or practised in the Fair: for then the Fair
> itself would be as full of pleasure to an ingenious person as the play;
> which we manifestly see it is not. But he hath made an excellent lazar
> of it; the copy is of price, though the original be vile.[25]

No doubt James thought so too. He prided himself on his scholarship and learning and on his moral seriousness, but he enjoyed slapstick. He was a man of licentious personal habits, but he was much given to melancholy. And Jonson, without making artistic consessions, caters accurately for that kind of chief spectator. In a play about the controls on human nature, the Epilogue nominates James as the final arbiter.

Bartholomew Fair is not tolerant at the end. The final ambush of the audience is the ironic finale in which the visitors are invited in a spirit of humane forgiveness to supper with Overdo. But the 'excellent creeping sport' must instruct as well as entertain; and Jonson seeks the consolation not available to Democritus that someone at least, a private audience of one, will understand his high expectations but small hopes of mankind.

10 · 'The Crystal Mirror of your Reign': *Coelum Britannicum* at the Banqueting House

Coelum Britannicum was presented in Inigo Jones's Banqueting House on the evening of Shrove Tuesday, 18 February 1634. The chief masquer was King Charles and the chief spectator was his consort, Henrietta Maria. She had presented the pastoral *The Faithful Shepherdess* to Charles at Somerset House on Twelfth Night and the King's masque was understood by a Venetian observer to be a reciprocal offering: 'in return for the entertainment given him by the Queen a few days ago', he wrote on 24 January; he anticipated that it would be 'very solemn and stately'.[1] But the new masque was also intended to be a response to the great pageant presented by the Inns of Court, *The Triumph of Peace*. This was given on 3 February, also in the Banqueting House, and beneath the customary flattery of the monarch could be discerned suggestions that royal power should be circumscribed by the processes of law. The King's masque would celebrate Charles's own views of Stuart absolutism and provide an ideal and improving view of courtly virtues. It would be, in a phrase from the masque itself, 'the crystal mirror of your reign' (l. 85).[2]

Amongst the audience Shrove Tuesday night was Sir Humphrey Mildmay (see p. 21) who expended sixpence on the visit. It seems unlikely that this was the price of entry, though tickets were issued and some kind of turnstile had been installed to control entry (see p. 164). Probably the money was for his transport. Otherwise, we know little of the audience for this occasion though we can be confident it was glittering in costume and social distinction, the 'gay people' (l. 126) and 'this trim audience' (ll. 186–7) referred to in the masque itself.

There was some thought of repeating the performance – 'the King intends to have this masque again in the Easter holiday'[3] – but no indication that this ever happened. However, it was highly successful. Sir Henry Herbert, the Master of the Revels, who was responsible amongst other things for the provision of many of the costumes, purred his pleasure at its royal reception:

It was the noblest masque of my time to this day, the best poetry, best scenes, and the best habits. The king and queen were very well pleased with my service, and the queen was pleased to tell me before the king, 'Pour les habits, elle n' avait jamais rien vu de si brave'.

Shortly after, the text of the masque was published. There is no author's name on the title page, but Thomas Carew is known to have written the book and lyrics. At the end is given a list of masquers and their torchbearers. The masquers, led by the King, were fifteen in all. They included a duke, four earls, a viscount, and no one under the rank of lord. The torchbearers were all 'young lords and noblemen's sons'. There were ten and they included the Earl of Bridgewater's two sons, Lord Brackley and Thomas Egerton, who in September of that same year would play speaking parts in Milton's *Comus*. For the latter, Henry Lawes wrote the music and we can be reasonably confident that he or his brother William, or both, wrote the music for *Coelum Britannicum*. The Lawes brothers were both King's Musicians and William (with Simon Ives) had just supplied the music for *The Triumph of Peace*. No music for *Coelum Britannicum* survives.

Preparations for the masque no doubt occupied some months. We first hear of it seven weeks before the performance night when Inigo Jones is issued with a warrant for 'a scene to be made in the Banqueting House for the King's masque at Shrovetide next'. The Works Accounts record payment to John Damport, carpenter, for overseeing the building of the auditorium degrees and three other carpenters were paid for building the stage. This, in fact, was the same stage as that used for *The Triumph of Peace*, though embellished, of course, with new scenes and machines. Jones, conscious that only fifteen days separated the two performances, no doubt designed both with the rapid turn-round in mind. The Revels Accounts tell us that eight men worked eight days and two nights fitting up the masque, but long before that an army of costumiers had been busy preparing the costumes. The Wardrobe Accounts name thirteen people paid for supplying materials for, and for making up, the King's own costume and they included in their number the redoubtable Nicholas Stone, master mason and sculptor who had worked under Jones on the Banqueting House itself. (For the masque, he embossed patterns of lion's heads for the simulated shoulder armour of the masquers.)

If we add to this army of artists and artificers a choreographer and dancing master (unknown), we complete a team of multiple talents brought together to create a 'crystal mirror' of Charles's reign and one of the most ingenious and brilliant of the Caroline masques.

There is a contemporary manuscript account of *Coelum Britannicum* which provides a useful synopsis of the masque and a good deal more.[4] It is anonymous and is evidently not in Carew's or Jones's handwriting, but it is not a post-production account by a spectator. Rather, it is written like a programme of the masque, to assist either its royal spectators or its aristocratic participants (or both) to follow it. Some of its actual language is reproduced in the printed version of the masque, elsewhere it shows a vagueness that suggests that some details were still to be settled in rehearsal; and generally its language and address are highly respectful, in a style appropriate to the occasion itself. Additionally, it provides insights into the aesthetic intentions of the masque and into its artistic techniques. Headed 'The Design' it is given here in full, transcribed into modern spelling, to serve among other things as a plot summary. (The italics draw attention to some of the points above.)

The scene is a globe, supported by Atlas, the hemisphere beautified with stars. Mercury descends to their Majesties, declaring the resolution of the gods to purge the heavens of those constellations which antiquity had fixed there as eternal registers of their luxuries, which they renounce, and intend a reformation in conformity to their Majesties' exemplar court, made such by the sedulous imitation of the unparalleled, conjugal love and other heroical virtues of so royal precedents. To him Momus is joined, *with intent (as he is feigned a privileged scoffer) to interweave with the more serious passages a continued thread of mirth.*

The disbanded stars fall into three antimasques: the first expresseth natural deformity, emblemed in the Bear, the Hydra and other monsters; the second, obliquity in motion, danced in retrograde paces, referring to the Crab; the third, a deviation from virtue, in the several vices proper to distinct stars. Momus proclaims the banns; and Riches, Poverty, Pleasure [and] Fortune plead right of succession to the vacant heavens, each attended by his antimasque – the first of ploughmen and shepherds and miners treading to rural music, with a cornucopia and other country vats, *such morrices or other rustic measures as are usual at their sheepshearings and other harvest homes,* as the inexhausted fountains of wealth; the second of Gypsies; the third of the Five Senses, as the seats of all pleasure; the fourth (*because though all estates have an immediate dependence on fortune, yet the events of war beget the greatest revolutions*) of a skirmish or umbratic fight, performed by soldiers to martial music. Their several reasons are refuted and they (*that the dramatic and mimic part be equally mixed*) successively alternate their speeches and dances.

Mercury, having reserved the instauration of the heavens for his Majesty and those selected spirits which he had dignified with the glory of waiting upon his perfection, so to appropriate to their sphere the title of 'Coelum Britannicum', calls out the last antimasque of Picts and other nations anciently inhabiting this island. Atlas ariseth out of the earth, transformed into a rocky mountain, in the midst whereof are seated three persons representing three kingdoms, on the top their Genius, upon the stage a Chorus of Druids and Rivers. They sing, the rock breaks, [and] the masquers are discovered in a cave.

They issue and dance their Entry; which finished, the Genius ascends singing, the three Kingdoms and Chorus below alternatively answering. The Main dance succeeds; which ended, Eternity is discovered sitting on a sphere, illustrated with that excess of light which his Majesty in the most glorious place and form with the rest of the stellified masquers are supposed to impart. On the one side Eusebia, Alethia, Sophia, on the other Homonia, Dicaerche, Euphemia, pendant in the air, sing the Assumption and Goodnight.

The idea of the masque-Jupiter's expulsion of the wicked stars and the subsequent installation of Charles and his courtiers had been borrowed from a little-known dialogue piece, written in Italian by Giordano Bruno during a visit to England and published in Paris in 1584 as *Spaccio de la bestia trionfante*. This tells in three dialogues of Jupiter's attempt to reform himself and his court and of his summoning a council to sit in judgment on each star in the firmament so that those found to be disreputable might be replaced by appropriate symbols of moral virtue. The work is allegorical in form and is generally concerned with the moral reformation of man and society. Jupiter, Bruno explains in the dedication to Sir Philip Sidney, 'represents each one of us'.

Jones, Carew or perhaps even Charles himself saw in this odd, serio-comic work a useful application to Caroline court pageantry. The allegory fitted the customary mode of the masque, and Jupiter's reformatory zeal could be held to reflect, even to be inspired by, a parallel activity in Charles's court. In Momus, one of Bruno's interlocutors, was a figure well-suited to preside over the antimasque elements of the adaptation and provide the opportunity, as 'The Design' notes, 'to interweave with more serious passages a continued thread of mirth'. Above all, Bruno's fable, slight as it was, would serve perfectly as the inspiration of Jones's sceno-graphic imagination.

Carew wrote the masque's book and lyrics. Presumably he worked closely with Jones. He also worked with one eye on the Bruno source, borrowing verbally from it. How he was chosen for the job we do not know. He was not a dramatist as most other masque-writers were, but he had been given a number of minor court appointments on Charles's accession and he belonged to the court circle of wits that included Suckling, Cotton and Waller. As far as Herbert was concerned, he produced the 'best poetry' in a masque up to that time (and Jonson's demise was being resolutely unlamented). A quotation from Ausonius on the title page of the published version suggests the poet's modesty: 'I have not the talent, but Caesar ordered, so I will have. Why should I deny my ability when *he* thinks me able.' It tells us, too, that the poet was Charles's choice.

What Carew conspicuously provided was dialogue sufficiently dramatic for the professional players who played Mercury, Momus and the antimasquers to create an air of theatrical vitality. But all this comes in the first half before the masquers appear. Thereafter, from Carew's point of view, the dramatic was necessarily replaced by the lyric, speech by song, conflict by celebration, for that is the way the masque worked. But the songs, too, are finely written and Carew shows a judicious awareness, as writer, of the rival or even greater claims of the visual and danced parts of the masque. Curiously, successful as he seems to have been, he was not asked again. The next and last four Whitehall masques of the reign were all written by Davenant, and none has *Coelum Britannicum*'s literary accomplishment.

Jones had been designing masques for nearly thirty years. What he contrived for the visual part of *Coelum Britannicum* – scenes, machines and costumes – survives in the 'stage directions'[5] of the published texts and in a series of about ten designs which are associated, with varying degrees of certainty, with the masque. We may begin with the costumes if only because, semantically at least, 'masque' referred to the masked figures of the performance, and some sense of elaborate, disguising costumes remained central to the word's meaning. The high point of any masque was the arrival or discovery on stage of the masquers. If, increasingly, the force of Jones's artistry was to transfer the meaning of the show to its scenes, nevertheless aristocratic personages got up in elaborate and dazzling costumes to tread a series of solemn dances remained the excuse for the whole affair.

The text tells us what the chief masquers looked like. Halfway into the masque the rock opened and out of a cave came the fifteen exotic figures 'richly attired like ancient Heroes, the colours yellow, embroidered with silver, their antique helms curiously wrought, and great plumes on the top' (ll. 948–51). The baroque splendour of these costumes, barely suggested by the words, is preserved in a small series of designs culminating in a finished or final version (see Plate 15). Here we see a suit with a scalloped, falling collar, gathered sleeves with reversed and petalled cuffs, a drop-waisted doublet suggestive of a cuirass and a bell-shaped skirt falling to mid thigh. Sleeves and skirt are slashed and richly embroidered in scroll shapes, and the whole costume is completed by

15 Inigo Jones's design for a masquer (an Ancient Hero)
for *Coelum Britannicum*, 1634

high-heeled shoes with rosettes and plumed helmet. The Wardrobe Accounts detailing the King's costume[6] give us further detail. The chief fabric was satin, with sarcenet for lining and calico for stiffening; the embroidery was 'all over with fine silver pearls, plates and silver o's'. For the King, the colour of the satin was not yellow but 'aurora', presumably to mark him out from his fellow masquers, and he had a mask of 'sweet white leather'.

The design principles were fourfold. There is a basic iconographic shape which suggests 'antique hero', made up of part Roman and part Ancient Briton. The choice of colours and materials is determined by the need to catch, reflect and be enhanced by candle- and torchlight. The style is intended to promote physical ease for the dancing and to show off the leg. And the cost of material and the richness with which it is decorated must suggest magnificence. '*Pour les habits*', Sir Henry Herbert confirmed, the Queen '*n'avait jamais rien vu de si brave*'.

At their entrance, the masquers were accompanied by a troupe of torchbearers. These were given an old-fashioned look:

> apparelled after the old British fashion in white coats, embroidered with silver, girt, and full gathered, cut square collared, and round caps on their heads, with a white feather wreathen about them.
> (ll.953–6)

A design (see Plate 16) again complements the text, and the picture is completed by a bill for the suit of one of the bearers, Lord Cranborne, which survives in the Hatfield House papers. The materials are itemised as satin carnation and white taffeta, and the costume cost over twenty pounds. Evidently the torchbearers' families paid for their scions' costumes, and we may assume that the masquers also had to pay for their costumes.

The costumes for the professional performers on the other hand were provided by the Revels Office. These included the featured characters such as Mercury, Momus, the chief antimasquers and the solo singers, Genius and Eternity; and also the antimasque dance troupes, the chorus of Druids and Rivers and other singers. Some costumes undoubtedly came out of stock, such as those for the soldiers or gypsies. Others, more specialised, such as those of the Five Senses, would have to be modelled specially. Mercury's dress was probably available complete, left over from one of the several masques in which that figure had already featured. Nothing novel would be wanted here if the character were to be quickly identified and the text gives us the conventional details: 'Upon his head a wreath, with small falls of white feathers, a caduceus in his hand, and wings at his heels' (ll. 44–5).

For Momus, however, no costume was instantly available and the

16 Inigo Jones's design for a torchbearer for *Coelum Britannicum*, 1634

17   Inigo Jones's design for Momus for *Coelum Britannicum*, 1634

figure would be unfamiliar to a masque audience. The text describes this 'privileged scoffer' in careful detail:

> Enter *Momus* attired in a long, darkish robe all wrought over with poniards, serpents' tongues, eyes and ears, his beard and hair parti-coloured, and upon his head a wreath stuck with feathers, and a porcupine in the forepart.
>
> (ll. 104–7)

This is a walking hieroglyph, and Jones was obliged to produce a design for the Revels costumiers (see Plate 17). It is a rapid pen-and-ink sketch, rough in its draughtsmanship, but it no doubt served its purpose. We see a bust-length figure, turning to look at us from deep-set, quizzical eyes over a beaked nose, and his character as railer is evident. For this is the most truly dramatic of the masque's characters, first cousin to the bitter fool or malcontent of the Jacobean play. But his costume is allegorical, for he is not, formally, a man who detracts and inquisites: he is the very spirit of detraction and inquisition itself. Perhaps the actor himself was shown the sketch; it would instantly have motivated his performance.

The action of *Coelum Britannicum* is built on five scenes, where 'scene' means an integrated set in the modern sense, or a visual statement dominating the stage space. That space itself, and the stage structure which provided a practical frame for the settings and the machines, is detailed in the task work accounts referred to earlier. There the carpenters are paid

> for framing and setting up a stage of 40 foot one way and 27 foot another way and 7 foot in height, with double stairs, in the Banqueting House; enclosing the same and covering it overhead with fir poles and deal boards 42 foot in height . . . it being made to serve both the masque performed by the Inns of Court gentlemen and also for the King's masque afterwards to be presented there . . .[7]

Dimensions for scenic stages were fairly standardised by this time. Here we have a stage 40 feet wide, 27 feet deep and 7 feet high, with a flying grid 42 feet above the stage. The *Florimène* stage (1635) was also to be 40 feet wide (built from wall to wall) and 7 feet high at the downstage end (though raked to 8 feet upstage). It was shallower (23 feet to the backstage shutters) but had space for 'relief' scenes beyond. The *Salmacida Spolia* stage of 1640 (in the Masquing House) was a little larger, 42 feet by 28 feet, but it also was 7 feet high. So it was presumably no limitation to Jones to design two quite different masques for the same stage; he was working to dimensions at which he had arrived over many years of experiment.

The 'double stairs' of the Accounts refers evidently to two flights leading from the stage to the dancing space on the hall floor. In the published accounts of *The Triumph of Peace* they are 'a descent of stairs in two branches landing into the room'. The arrangement may have been that shown on a design for *Florimène* of a standing scene (though not shown on the groundplan). There are few extant designs of *The Triumph of Peace*: a frontispiece, a design for a back shutter for the first scene and a rough sketch of the 'delicious arbour' on which the masquers appeared; not much to inform us about the stage. But the arbour sketch carries the inscription 'not to draw the upper shutters' which tells us that the upper shutters were a part of the machinery of the stage for the two masques. The text of *The Triumph of Peace* confirms what we should expect, that the stage was at the lower end of the Banqueting Hall. The grid, 42 feet above the stage, was evidently floored in with firpoles and deal boards, and the whole contraption, we must assume, was hung from the Hall's timbered roof. It provided anchorage for and access to the upper stage works, including the sky borders, clouds and flying devices so vital to the masque's physical imagery.

The two masques set one after the other on the same stage each had its individual frontispiece or 'ornament', the frame for the scenic picture. The design for *The Triumph of Peace* has vertical pillars approximately 3 feet wide and an entablature 4 feet deep. This gives an opening of 30 feet wide and 27 feet tall. We should expect these dimensions to apply to *Coelum Britannicum's* frontispiece of which there is only a rough sketch. The 'ruined city' design associated with this masque, however, is squared off in units 34 wide and 30 tall. If we take each unit to represent one foot, this design would fit neatly into a frontispiece 30 feet wide but it seems somewhat tall. However, we may take it that the scene opening for *Coelum Britannicum*, inside the frontispiece, was probably 34 feet across and 30 feet tall.

The frontispiece itself is carefully described in the published text and appears roughly drawn in a design (see Plate 18). The central compartment carried the masque's title, while the two ovals, one on each side, carried respectively the emblem and motto of the King and Queen. 'All this ornament', the text reports, 'was heightened with gold, and for the invention and various composition, was the newest and most gracious that hath been done in this place' (11.28–31). Before the masque began, a curtain of watchet (pale blue) concealed the stage. It was rapidly raised by means of a roller and counterweights (*The Triumph of Peace* began in the same way) and stayed out of sight until the end.

The transformation of each scene into the next, the true action of the masque, propelled the audience's mind through a series of linked ideas rendered visually: 1. a ruined city – civilisation decayed back into a state of nature; 2. Atlas bearing a globe – the heroic force that sustains heaven and earth; 3. a mountain landscape – harsh nature from which civilisations grow; 4. a garden and a princely villa – civilisation and gentle nature in harmonious counterpoint; and 5. Windsor Castle – British sovereignty, with a reference to the Order of the Garter. 'The Design', surprisingly, makes little of the scenes: only Atlas and the Rock which rises in the mountainous scene (another manifestation of Atlas as the manuscript notes) are specifically referred to. But the printed text is fulsome on the 'bodily part' of the masque, and extant designs for scenes 1, 2 and 3 enable us to speculate on their engineering and the effect they were to produce.

The ruined city, the text says, comprised

old arches, old palaces, decayed walls, parts of temples, theatres,
basilicas and therme, with confused heaps of broken columns, bases,
cornices, and statues, lying as underground, and altogether
resembling the ruins of some great city of the ancient Romans, or
civilised Britons.

(ll.34–9)

18   Inigo Jones's design for the Proscenium and Mountain Scene for
     Coelum Britannicum, 1634

The design associated with this (see Plate 19) is more modest. Here are
four pairs of wings, copied mostly from a design of Giulio Parigi for *Il
Guidizio de Paride* (1608). Jones had already plundered the engravings
from this Medicean pageant for *Britannia Triumphans* and they served as
inspiration for other scenic elements of *Coelum Britannicum*. The wing
pieces seem, surprisingly, to be serlian, angled wings (incapable of that

19 Inigo Jones's design for The Ruined City for *Coelum Britannicum*,
1634

easy changeability afforded by the straight wings in grooves Jones increasingly employed). The background is empty, to be completed by back
shutters designed separately. It is all fairly routine, seemingly less
impressive than Carew's (or Jones's) words in the text, but it was no mere
background: 'This strange prospect detained the eyes of the spectators
some time', the text tells us (ll. 39–40) for it was intended to be eloquent
with moral and political ideas: from decay, it is implied, renewal is
possible.

For the second scene we have a moving, visual witness in Jones's design
for the Atlas and Globe (see Plate 20). The change is made in full view
of the audience, and the text tells us what happened:

At this [Momus's announcement that he will describe the state of
Jupiter's heaven] the Scene changeth, and in the heaven is discovered
a sphere, with stars placed in their several images; borne up by a
huge, naked figure (only a piece of drapery hanging over his thigh)
kneeling, and bowing forwards, as if the great weight lying on his

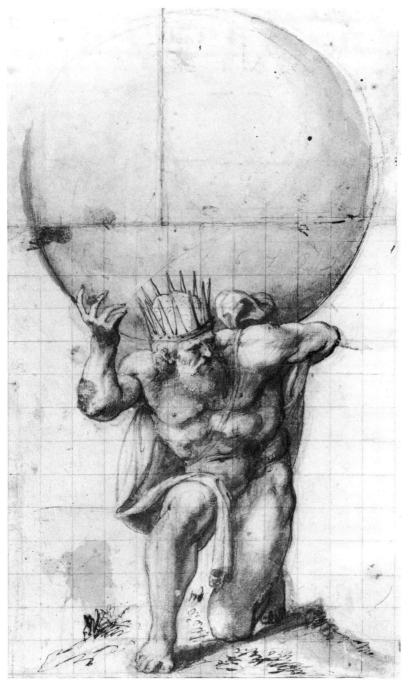

20   Inigo Jones's design for Atlas for *Coelum Britannicum*, 1634

> shoulders oppressed him, upon his head a crown, by all which he
> might easily be known to be *Atlas*.

(ll. 188–94)

If the ruined city was routine work, Atlas and his globe must have
appeared a spectacular novelty, deserving and probably receiving a round
of applause. The beautifully composed design shows a monumental figure
under its great load, but not the detail of 'the stars in their several images'.
The whole tremendous icon was probably a back scene, 22 feet in height,
12 feet wide (estimated from the squaring lines on the drawing).

Both the design and the description quoted above suggest the image
was created in two halves. The bottom half only of the design is squared
off for transferring to its full size form, and this includes all of Atlas and
his spiky crown and only the small segment of the globe contained behind
his head, hand and looped drapery. All this was probably painted on
black shutters and concealed, until this moment, behind the shutters that
completed the ruined city. Meanwhile above, on upper back shutters or
as a 'relief' flat (that is a cut-out) was the globe, with the upper stage
balcony behind. The globe was pierced through with appropriately placed
holes, behind which were candles. As the antimasques proceeded, stage
hands on the balcony extinguished the candles, carefully matching their
work to the dialogue and dance on the main stage so that at the end of
the third antimasque, '*All the stars are quenched, and the sphere darkened*'
(l.399). What happened to the city wings we cannot tell. Perhaps they
were darkened or covered with cloths. Certainly, Atlas with his globe
dominated the stage both in size and in imaginative power, an heroic
figure easily associated with the political force of the Caroline dynasty.

For the third scene, two designs are extant. One is evidently a rejected
idea for the mountain landscape with its rising rock in the midst. The
other is a comprehensive sketch of proscenium and scene shortly before
the rock rises but already showing the musicians, as Druids and Rivers,
sitting about the stage (Plate 18). Impressionistic, and even confusing, as
this seems (the proscenium is borne up on rocks to the height of the first
stage level and the whole design seems too tall for its width), it is squared
off for use by the scene painter and so is at once a creative realisation of
a climactic moment in the masque and a working design for the scene
painters. In addition, it shows clearly that Jones did not compose stage
pictures solely in wood and canvas but included performers. He is
'directing' in the modern sense, creating a dynamic moment of visual
theatre with all staging means available to him.

In the text, the mountainous scene and the rising rock, in the middle
of which are eventually seen the chief masquers, are described in four
separate episodes, the whole account concluding with a statement of ill-

concealed self-congratulation at the ingenuity of the machinery that had produced the effect. First of all,

> *Atlas* and the sphere vanisheth, and a new scene appears of mountains, whose eminent height exceed the clouds which passeth beneath them; the lower parts were wild and woody.
>
> (ll. 878–80)

The Picts occupy this scene of mountains as a setting for their martial dance; and then,

> When this antimasque was passed, there began to arise out of the earth the top of a hill, which little by little grew to be a huge mountain that covered all the scene. The underpart of this was wild and craggy, and above somewhat more pleasing and flourishing.
>
> (ll. 883–7)

Three figures representing the kingdoms of Britain sat in the middle part and above them, on the top, Genius. Eventually the climax of the action is reached: 'the under-part of the rock opens, and out of a cave are seen to come the Masquers' (ll. 947–8). After the Genius's farewell song and the masquers' Entry dance,

> the rock with the three kingdoms on it sinks, and is hidden in the earth. This strange spectacle gave great cause for admiration, but especially how so huge a machine, and of that great height could come from under the stage, which was but six foot high.
>
> (ll. 996–71)

(The Works Account says the stage was 7 feet high. There may merely be a discrepancy here, or perhaps the stage was raked, reaching 7 feet at its upstage limit.)

This spectacular *coup* is primarily achieved by the rock 'machine', so huge eventually as to dominate ('cover') all the scene. The initial landscape is evidently made up of wings and back shutters. The rising mountain was, we must assume, made in flat sections and drawn up through a trap at the rear of the stage. As the top section passed the upstage upper balcony so Genius entered from behind and appeared sitting there, and similarly with the three kingdoms as the middle section came level with the balcony over the stage. Then as the rock is complete, extending over 20 or more feet upwards, the chief masquers entered behind at stage level through the back shutter area and awaited the moment when 'the under-part of the rock opens' to reveal them in their cave. They then issued on to the stage and Genius was flown out. Finally, the reverse process took the rock back beneath the stage to applause from the marvelling audience.

The fourth scene change was less ambitious. After the masquers had danced their main dance, they returned to the stage (we may surmise) and then the Garden with the Princely Villa appeared, an attractive but relatively simple exercise in perspective illusion:

> a new and pleasant prospect, clean differing from all the other, the nearest part showing a delicious garden with several walks and parterres set round with low trees, and on the sides against these walls were fountains and grots, and in the furthest place a palace . . . and all this together was composed of such ornaments as might express a princely villa.
>
> (ll. 1012–20)

Here, Jones celebrates his own sympathy for, and importation of, the new (Italian) architecture and does so, evidently, with the standard perspective device of side-wings and back shutters. (Two designs associated with this scene, however, are unconvincing.)

For his last scene (and the design is not extant) Jones emphasises the self-reflexive quality of the masque ('in the crystal mirror') by picturing Windsor Castle, afar off, while above, completing the symbolic narrative, 'was a troop of fifteen stars, expressing the stellifying of our British heroes'. The iconography is at once simple and abstruse, for Charles's sustaining heroism, the masque has said, is that of Atlas, Hercules and Arthur, all types of each other in the myth of Britain; and in popular genealogy, the Order of the Garter, conferred at Windsor, was derived from Arthur and his Round-Table Knights. But if some spectators saw merely a gratifying allusion to the royal household, which had the effect of anchoring a sublime story in a local reality, that would have been good enough. Always, the masque in its semiotic complexity could work on a number of levels simultaneously.

'Machines' are not really detachable from the scenes in which they appear, as we have seen with the rising rock. The last two scenes are relatively simple in their engineering to leave room for complicated cloud effects. Much, in fact, of the sophisticated machinery of *Coelum Britannicum* is devoted to flying (and it is worth mentioning again that Jones had only fifteen days to install his new scenes and machines, train his stage crew to operate them precisely and then rehearse with them with the performers). The 42 feet of height to the grid was extensively utilised.

The first machine, early in the masque, was a flying chariot for Mercury which descended to deposit the actor on stage and was then, presumably, winched up out of the way. By the 1630s such descents were routine, but there was much more to come. Most spectacular was the rising Rock, Jones's masterpiece in a masque of continuous stage inventiveness. For Genius's exit, 'a pleasant cloud' came down on the top part of the rock to embrace Genius, 'but so as through it all his body is seen' (ll. 926–3).

It then rose up with him and disappeared into the heavens. Evidently the cloud had diaphanous material held out in front which dropped on the downstage side of the actor while he slipped on to the machine's supporting frame behind him. After the Revels, and leading into the masque's final brilliant sequence (including the scene of Windsor Castle), a more elaborate cloud episode was staged. First a great cloud appeared 'coming forth from one of the sides, as moving by a gently wind' (ll. 1053–4). This evidently was not, strictly speaking, flown but moved across stage on a beam, and it was of colossal size, 'so great it covered the whole scene' (l. 1056), where 'scene' most probably refers to the upper back shutters. It was, if we may judge from the squaring lines, 14 feet across and 10 feet high. The two smaller clouds appeared from above, each bearing inside three singers; and there then followed another breathtaking effect:

> These [the smaller clouds] being come down in an equal distance to the middle part of the air, the great cloud began to break open, out of which struck beams of light; in the midst sat Eternity on a globe. . . . In the firmament about him, was a troop of fifteen stars, expressing the stellifying of our British heroes; but one more great and eminent than the rest, which was over his head, figured his Majesty.

A design for the Great Cloud survives (see Plate 21). It is inscribed 'The cloud which opening Eternity was seen' and the square opening is clearly marked on it, behind and in which sat Eternity with his globe and the fifteen new stars. Perhaps this whole inner scene was placed on the balcony stage, to be revealed as the central sections of the cloud slid aside. Lighting here is a vital part of the effect and this is underlined by the corresponding account in 'The Design' (see p. 193).

So Eternity and the six moral personifications in the two smaller clouds sang 'the apotheosis and goodnight' and then the stage crew worked the last piece of scenic illusion:

> the two clouds, with the persons sitting on them, ascend; the great cloud closeth again, and so passeth away overthwart the scene, leaving behind it nothing but a serene sky.

> (ll. 1140–2)

There then followed the masquers' last dance. When it was finished they re-entered the stage (we may presume) and 'the curtain was let fall' (l. 143).

'The best poetry, best scenes and the best habits', said Herbert. But until Jones and Jonson reinvented the masque in the early years of James's reign, music and dance traditionally expressed the soul of the masque

21 Inigo Jones's design for the Great Cloud for *Coelum Britannicum*,
1634

and those elements still featured importantly in *Coelum Britannicum*.
Besides the Revels, when the masquers joined the spectators for an
extended suite of court dances, the masque presented twelve dance
episodes, eight by the professional antimasquers during the first half, one
by the torchbearers and three (Entry, Main and Final) by the masquers
themselves. The antimasque dances were 'mimic', expressing in stylised
movements or histrionic representation the meaning or appearance of the
character or characters portrayed (in 'natural deformity', 'retrograde
paces' and 'deviation from virtue'). Costume and movements for the first
three were angular and droll, the effect grotesque. For the next three
dances, the choreographic principle was different – something more
formally dance-like was presented. First came the country dances, then
an exotic, perhaps Moorish, sequence 'of Gypsies' and, finally in this trio,
a miniature ballet representing a battle. The dance of the Five Senses
returned the mood to the comic and exaggerated, but after it was danced
'a more grave antimasque of Picts' which allowed the masque to move
from the burlesque to the sublime.

The torchbearers' and masquers' dances were not so histrionic as those
of the antimasquers. Charles enjoyed, and was conspicuously good at,
dancing, as were some of his retinue. Lord Wharton, for example, was a
handsome twenty-one year old with fine legs and the inclination to show

them off to best advantage. The masquer design (Plate 15) catches the figure dancing, his weight thrown forward on to the right foot, the legs promoted by the short skirt, high heels and ankle rosettes, the left hand and arm elegantly spread, the right hand jauntily placed on the hip. We see here a deliberate anticipation of Charles or Lord Wharton in action and, dramatically lit, an action photograph from the show.

For their three dances, the masquers left the stage by the two staircases to take their place on the green carpeted floor in front of the state. (At some point the King had been cued to move from the state where he watched the opening part of the masque to behind the stage where he awaited his entry as the chief masquer. After the Revels, he returned to the state, and to the Queen's side, to watch the final moments.) Their carefully choreographed ballets combined rhythms, steps and shapes to express abstractly but complexly ideas about idealised nature. These might be 'read' by the sophisticated spectator so that their performance was at once ethically ennobling and aesthetically pleasing. The song which followed the Entry dance describes the effect aptly, stressing that perfect concord of musical notes and dance steps which symbolised neo-platonic virtue. The lines were shared between the Kingdoms, Chorus and Genius:

> Here are shapes form'd fit for heaven,
> These more gracefully and even,
> Here the air and paces meet
> So just, as if the skilful feet
> Had struck the viols. So the ear
> Might the tuneful footing hear.
> And had the music silent been,
> The eye a moving tune had seen.
>
> (ll. 927–9)

We cannot tell if the dancing was that perfect, but the song was intended to make it so. For in a dance the masquers expressed in 'a crystal mirror' the ideals of Caroline courtly behaviour.

Sixteen separate pieces of music were required for the eight dances of the antimasquers, the four of the masquers and torchbearers, and the four songs. In addition, there was probably a good deal more incidental music used for covering scene changes, to drown the noise of wooden frames drawn in grooves and of pulleys and hinges, as well as of the communication signals between members of the stage crew (traditionally the stage manager used a whistle). Only once is this referred to in the text, the 'loud music' (1.40) which is played during Mercury's descent near the beginning; but there was certainly more. Much of the music was traditional or currently popular, but some of it no doubt had especially to be composed. Henry Lawes, if he was the chief musician, probably had a very large task to score the masque, rehearse the instrumentalists and singers and co-ordinate the playing during the performance. Possibly, he also sang the role of Genius.

The musicians, mostly from the King's Music, were deployed in three different ways and were correspondingly located in different parts of the hall. There was an 'orchestra' (in the modern sense) situated in the auditorium alongside the proscenium, if we may take the *Florimène* plan as evidence of typical court theatre practice. This would play before the masque began and serve, most importantly, as a dance band during the Revels. Behind the scenes, more musicians would provide special musical effects and, as necessary, supplement the main orchestra. Finally, there were musician performers who as Druids, Rivers and named parts had specific roles in the masque's story. We see some of them with instruments in Plate 18. (Whether the soprano parts were sung by boys or women we cannot tell.) Some overlap between the second and third group is likely, but in any case there must have been several dozen musicians in all. For the masque of a fortnight earlier (which was an unprecedentedly lavish affair) eighty musicians had performed under the supervision of William Lawes. For *Coelum Britannicum*, he or his brother devised not so much a series of settings for individual dances and songs but a coherent score drawing the masque towards opera.

The masque at its height of artistic development – and *Coelum Britannicum* represents that height – was not in fact an embryo opera but a special kind of performance art. In it, and this is different from our experience of most versions of music theatre today, the various performance strands, while contributing in coherent manner to the artistic and political statement of the piece, were kept curiously distinct. So the scene was to be observed in its own right, not as a locale for the action which would ensue; and a song was followed, not accompanied, by a dance, or a scene change was provoked by, rather than supported, a passage of dialogue. All was variety of effect, a banquet of dishes served serially, not simultaneously. Occasionally, the different effects were mutually enhancing – Genius sang while being carried aloft on a cloud machine as we learn from 'The Design'. But more typical was the discrete 'action' – involving some simple effect of scenery, song, dialogue or dance. The principle is well-expressed in 'The Design' which describes the passage of the main antimasquers: 'they (that the dramatic and mimic parts be equally mixed) successively alternate their speeches and dances'. So the various art-forms converged, their statements cohered; but they did not mesh. If a single artist could be said to have created *Coelum Britannicum* it was certainly Jones. But although he designed the production (with all the modern connotations of 'design'), he probably did no more and no less than co-ordinate the other artistic inputs.

'A crystal mirror' of court life, the masque was indeed a glorious if ephemeral product of the court itself, a combination of effects by artists and artisans, professionals and amateurs, and a unique experiment in ritual theatre. The other plays described in this book live on through our need to reinterpret them on today's stage. In our revivals, past and present intersect, and *The Tempest* and other plays renew themselves in performance. *Coelum Britannicum* belonged to 18 February 1634. As Bulstode Whitelocke commented elegiacally on *The Triumph of Peace:* 'Thus was this earthly pomp and glory, if not vanity, soon past over and gone, as if it had never been.'

Notes

Abbreviations

E. S.   E.K. Chambers, *The Elizabethan Stage*, 4 vols, Oxford, 1923
J. & C.S. G.E. Bentley, *The Jacobean and Caroline Stage*, 7 vols, Oxford,
          1941–8
S. S.   *Shakespeare Survey*
T. N.   *Theatre Notebook*

1 Introduction: Jacobean Private Theatre

1 The petition is quoted in full in *E.S.*, IV, pp. 319–20. One of the petitioners
was Lord Hunsdon who already was, or was about to become, the Lord
Chamberlain.

2 An excellent and succinct summary of information about the pre-
Commonwealth private theatre is W.A. Armstrong's *The Elizabethan
Private Theatres: Facts and Problems*, London, 1958.

3 *J. & C.S.*, VI, p. 18.

4 W.J. Lawrence, *Those Nut-Cracking Elizabethans*, London, 1935, pp.31–2.

5 See Hiram Haydn, *The Counter-Renaissance*, New York, 1950.

6 Analyses of mannerist theory and style appear in A. Hauser's *Mannerism:
The Crisis of the Renaissance and the Origin of Modern Art*, trans. Eric
Mosbacher, London, 1965, and J. Shearman's *Mannerism*, London, 1967.

7 Attempts to relate mannerist art and seventeenth-century drama are: Wylie
Sypher, *Four Stages of Renaissance Style: Transformations in Art and
Literature, 1400–1700*, New York, 1955, especially chapters II and IV;
Cyrus Hoy, 'Jacobean Tragedy and the Mannerist Style', *S.S.*, XXVL,
1973, pp. 49–67; G.R. Kernodle, 'The Mannerist Stage of Comic
Detachment', *The Elizabethan Theatre*, III, ed. D. Galloway, Montreal,
1973, pp. 119–34. The relationship of the work of John Ford to baroque
art is excellently explored in R. Huebert's *John Ford: Baroque English
Dramatist*, Montreal, 1977.

2 The Audiences of the Jacobean Private Theatre

1 For descriptions of the private theatre audience, see W.A. Armstrong, 'The Audience of the Elizabethan Private Theatres', *Review of English Studies*, n.s.X, 1959, pp. 234–49; A. Harbage, *Shakespeare and the Rival Traditions*, New York, 1952, pp.49–57.
2 A. Harbage, *Shakespeare's Audience*, New York, 1941.
3 See A.J. Cook, 'The Audience of Shakespeare's Plays: A Reconsideration', *Shakespeare Studies*, VII, 1974, pp.283–305. Her extended account, *The Privileged Playgoers of Shakespeare's London, 1576-1642*, Princeton, 1981, probably goes too far in blurring distinctions between 'popular' and 'private' audiences in the Stuart period.
4 *J. & C.S.*, I, pp.4–5, 31–4.
5 *J. & C.S.*, VI, p.80.
6 *J. & C.S.*, VI, p.76.
7 It is reprinted in *The Seventeenth Century Stage*, ed. G.E. Bentley, Chicago, 1968, pp.28–37 and discussed in *J. & C.S.*, VI, pp.109–12.
8 The Mildmay records are reproduced in *J. & C.S.*, II, pp.673–81.
9 An account of the Inns is given by W.R. Prest, *The Inns of Court under Elizabeth I and the Early Stuarts: 1590-1640*, London, 1972.
10 From Francis Lenton's *The Young Man's Whirligig*, 1629.
11 E.M. Symonds, 'The Diary of John Greene (1635–57)', *English Historical Review*, XLIII, 1928, pp.385–94.
12 Prest, *op.cit.*, pp.155,169.
13 The account seems a little inconsistent, as a few details are more appropriate to the public houses.
14 In his Preface to the 1647 *Beaumont and Fletcher* Folio.
15 Quoted and discussed in *J. & C.S.*, VI, p.33.

3 Jacobean Private Playhouses

1 There is some dispute over how closely the Globe reproduced the form, as well as reusing the timbers, of the theatre. But in all probability, the reusing to a large extent dictated the form.
2 For accounts of the boy companies, see: C.W. Wallace, *The Children of the Chapel at Blackfriars, 1597–1603*, Lincoln, Nebraska, 1908; and H.N. Hillebrand, *The Child Actors: A Chapter in Elizabethan Stage History*, Urbana, Illinois, 1926.
3 The story is obscure and difficult to piece together and some of this account is deduction, not demonstrable fact. But see: *J. & C.S.*, VI, pp. 77–86; J.Q. Adams, *Shakespearean Playhouses*, Boston, 1917, pp.342–7; F.P. Wilson, 'More Records from the Remembrancia of the City of London,' Malone Society *Collections*, IV, 1956, pp.55–65.
4 The diarist is Thomas Crosfield. His theatre notes are reprinted in *J. & C.S.*, II, pp.688–9.
5 W.A. Armstrong, *The Elizabethan Private Theatres: Facts and Problems*, London, 1958, p.7, uses an engraving in the 1634 edition of *A Maidenhead Well Lost* to speculate about the 'inner-stage' at the Phoenix. E.A.

Langhans, in 'A Picture of the Salisbury Court Playhouse', *T.N.* XIX, 1964–5, pp.100–1, associates a tiny sketch on a 1706 map of London with the Salisbury Court.

6　The first identification is by C. Walter Hodges in *The Globe Restored*, rev. edn, London, 1968, p.108. The second, evidently correct, is by John Orrell, in *The Quest For Shakespeare's Globe*, Cambridge, 1983, pp.18–19. Orrell suggests that Hodges's building is in fact Bridewell.

7　See I.A. Shapiro, 'Robert Fludd's Stage-Illustration', *Shakespeare Studies*, II, 1966, pp.192–209. F.A. Yates, in 'The Stage in Fludd's Memory System', *Shakespeare Studies*, III, 1967, pp.138–66, disputes Shapiro's contention and makes the claim, developed in her *Theatre of The World*, London, 1969, that it represents the Globe.

8　Accounts of the Worcester College designs for the unnamed playhouse are: D.F. Rowan, 'A Neglected Jones/Webb Theatre Project, Part II: A Theatrical Missing Link', *The Elizabethan Theatre*, II, ed. D. Galloway, Montreal, 1970, pp.60–73; and R. Leacroft, *The Development of the English Playhouse*, London, 1973, pp.70–3. John Harris dates the designs 1616–18 in *The King's Arcadia: Inigo Jones and the Stuart Court*, London, 1973, pp.107–8.

9　For arguments that the designs relate to the Phoenix, see Iain Mackintosh, 'Inigo Jones – Theatre Architect', *Tabs*, XXXI, No. 3, 1973, pp.95–105; and John Orrell, 'Inigo Jones at the Cockpit', *S.S.*, XXX, 1977, pp.157–68. See also John Harris and A.A. Tait, *Catalogue of the Drawings by Inigo Jones, John Webb and Isaac de Caus at Worcester College Oxford*, Oxford, 1979, p.15. Mackintosh argues ingeniously, but wrongly in the present writer's opinion, that the Phoenix was designed so that it might operate as a scenic theatre.

10　Accounts of the Cockpit-in-Court designs are: D.F. Rowan, 'The Cockpit-in-Court', *The Elizabethan Theatre*, I, ed. D. Galloway, Montreal, 1968, pp.89–102; *J.&.C.S.*, VI, pp.267–84; G. Wickham, *Early English Stages II*, Part Two, London, 1972, pp.117–22; and R. Leacroft, *The Development of the English Playhouse*, London, 1973, pp. 73–7.

11　R. Hosley, 'The Second Blackfriars Playhouse (1596)', *The Revels History of Drama in English*, III, ed. C. Leech and T.W. Craik, London, 1975, esp. pp.217–26; T.J. King, 'Staging of Plays at the Phoenix in Drury Lane, 1617–42', *T.N.*, XIX, 1964–5, pp.146–66; and David Steevens, 'The Staging of Plays at the Salisbury Court Theatre: 1630–1642', *Theatre Journal*, XXXI, 1979, pp.511–25.

12　The whole matter of scenery in the private playhouses is summarised in John Freehafer's 'Perspective Scenery and the Caroline Playhouses', *T.N.*, XXVII, 1972–3, pp.98–112.

13　Although Shakespeare's *Henry VIII* is associated with the burning down of the Globe, there is much internal evidence, and the tone and detail of the prologue, to encourage the idea that this was intended as a Blackfriars play – in which case Shakespeare's presentation of the trial in II, iv had a special piquancy, even, dare one suggest, a reason for writing the play.

14　A detailed account of the Blackfriars precinct and a history of the two theatre operations there is contained in Irwin Smith's *Shakespeare's Blackfriars Playhouse*, London, 1966, a far-ranging and scholarly book flawed only by Smith's assumption that the Second Blackfriars had an 'inner stage'. A pioneer work on staging at the Blackfriars is J. Isaacs's *Production and Stage-Management at the Blackfriars Theatre*, Oxford, 1933.

15 Herbert Berry, 'The Stage and Boxes at Blackfriars', *Studies in Philology*, LXII, 1966, pp. 163–86. Berry's conclusion that the boxes were upstage rather than at the sides of the stage is unwarrantable.

16 Smith, *op. cit.*, locates the tiring-house outside the 66 feet. R. Hosley, *op. cit.*, to whose reconstruction the present study owes much, locates it inside. See also D. Whitmarsh-Knight, 'The Second Blackfriars: The Globe Indoors', *T.N.*, XXVII, 1973, pp.94–8.

17 In fact, Jones may only have built up existing walls. See John Orrell, *The Quest for Shakespeare's Globe*, Cambridge, 1983, p. 178, n.32.

18 D.F. Rowan, *op. cit.*, p. 70; A. Harbage, *Shakespeare and The Rival Traditions*, New York, 1952, p.340; Smith, *op. cit.*, p. 297; Wallace, *op. cit.*, p. 52.

19 The point is well made in R. Graves, *English Stage Lighting: 1575–1642*, Ph.D thesis, Zerox University Microfilms, Ann Arbor, 1976, p. 243. The whole study constitutes a thorough examination of pre-Commonwealth stage lighting.

20 The accounts are quoted in *J.&C.S.*, VI, pp. 271–3.

21 Note Pepys's experience at the theatre in 1669. He sat 'in the side balcony over against the music'. He could not see the play 'because the trouble of my eyes with the light of the candles did almost kill me.'

22 See J.R. Brown (ed.), *The Duchess of Malfi*, London, 1964, pp.xxii-xxiv.

23 *The National Theatre: 'The Architectural Review' Guide*, ed. Colin Amery, London, 1977, p. 40.

24 B. Beckerman, *Shakespeare at the Globe: 1599–1609*, New York, 1962, p.169.

25 *Prefaces to Shakespeare*, Second Series, London, 1930, pp.249–50.

26 *J.&C.S.*, VI, pp.271–3.

4 The Private Theatre Companies, Their Playwrights and Their Repertory

1 Dates and auspices of plays in this chapter are mostly derived from *J. & C.S.*

2 *E.S.*, II, p.8.

3 *J.&C.S.*, I, pp.72–3.

4 *J.&C.S.*, I, pp.108–34.

5 G.E. Bentley, 'The Salisbury Court Theatre and its Boy Players', *Huntingdon Library Quarterly*, XL, 1977, pp.129–49.

6 Heton's papers are published in *J.&C.S.*, II, pp.684–7.

7 A.C. Kirsch, 'Cymbeline and Coterie Dramturgy', *English Literary History*, XXXIV, 1967, pp.285–306.

8 Fletcher, 'To the Reader', *The Faithful Shepherdess*, 1609.

5 'A Quaint Device': *The Tempest* at the Blackfriars

1 Quotations are taken from the Arden edition, ed. F. Kermode, 1962.
2 For narrative sources and the topicality of the play, see G. Bullough, *Narrative and Dramatic Sources of Shakespeare*, VIII, London, 1975, pp.237–74.
3 See Harry Levin, 'Two Magian Comedies: "The Tempest", and "The Alchemist" ', *S.S.*, XXII, 1969, pp.47–58.
4 *The Star*, 15 September 1904.
5 Quoted in David William's '*The Tempest* on the Stage', *Jacobean Theatre*, ed. J.R. Brown and B. Harris, London, repr., 1965, p.149.
6 *Shakespearean Criticism*, ed. T.M. Raysor, I, London, 1960, p.118.
7 The argument is developed in E. Law's *Shakespeare's 'Tempest' As Originally Produced at Court*, Shakespeare Association Pamphlet, London, n.d. (?1920).
8 The verbal plainness of the play is often remarked – especially a thinness of metaphor and a lack of 'fine' speeches.
9 Jan Kott, *Shakespeare our Contemporary*, trans. B. Taborski, London, 1964, p.180.
10 Prologue to the revised version of *Everyman in his Humour*, 1616. Jonson may well refer directly to *The Tempest* here.
11 A.C. Sprague, *Shakespearian Players and Performances*, London, 1954, p.157.
12 Law, *op.cit.*, p. 20.
13 I have adopted, in part, the proposed emendation of these lines in Kermode, p. 161, except I have given to Ariel 'With diligence'. The argument is unaffected.
14 See, for example, N. Frye, *A Natural Perspective: The Development of Shakespearean Comedy and Romance*, New York, 1965, p.177; and W. Farnham, *The Shakespearean Grotesque*, Oxford, 1971, p.165.
15 Quoted in J.E. Hawkins's, *Backgrounds of Shakespeare's Thought*, Hassocks, 1978, p.174.
16 Kermode, p.95n., quotes E. Welsford on 'trick' as a technical expression derived from French *truc:* 'an elaborate device or ingenious mechanism used for pageantry, etc.'

6 'A Perspective that Shows us Hell': *The Duchess of Malfi* at the Blackfriars

1 Quotations and line references are taken from the Revels edition of the play, ed. J.R. Brown, London, 1964.
2 See Inga-Stina Ekeblad's 'Webster's Realism or, "A Cunning Piece Wrought Perspective" ', *John Webster*, ed. B. Morris, London, 1970, pp.157–78.
3 Cf. French *boussole*. In *A Cure for a Cuckold*, probably by Webster and Rowley, there is a comic seaman called Compass; and Webster shows a fondness for witty naming in 'Cariola' which refers to the Italian *carriolo*, a 'truckle-bed' (see *The Duchess of Malfi*, ed. E.M. Brennan, London, 1964, p.104).

4   *Times Literary Supplement*, 24 December 1976, pp.1621–2; 11 March 1977, p.272; 24 October 1980, p.1201.

5   Forobosco is called for at II, ii, 31 but never appears. Perhaps a sequence involving him was subsequently cut but after the play's opening performance(s).

6   See J.R. Brown, *op.cit*, pp.xx-xxi.

7   T.W. Baldwin, *The Organisation and Personnel of the Shakespearean Company*, New York, repr., 1961, pp.178–81.

8   By John Davies in *Scourge of Folly*, c.1611.

9   See A. Hart, 'The Length of Elizabethan and Jacobean Plays', *Review of English Studies*, VIII, 1932, pp.147–52.

10 There is no exit in the text at this point but the action clearly demands one.

11 That this is the end of the mourning period gives special point to much of the Duchess and Antonio's exchange at the end of the scene, especially ll. 385–8 and 453–5.

12 The 'Pope-dressing' scene in Brecht's *Galileo* has a similar effect. Brecht knew *The Duchess of Malfi* well, producing various 'modernisations' of it.

13 The translation appears in *Penguin Critical Anthologies: John Webster*, ed. G.K. and S.K. Hunter, London, 1969, pp.31–2. The Italian version is reprinted in *E.S.*, III, pp.510–11.

14 *Theatre Notebook: 1947–1967*, trans. B. Taborski, London, 1968, pp.253–6.

15 Webster knew *The Arcadia* well and borrowed extensively from it in composing his play.

16 He was reviewing a performance of the play in 1893. The piece appears in *Penguin Critical Anthologies, op.cit.*, pp.74–85.

17 According to Irwin Shaw, *Shakespeare's Blackfriars Playhouse*, London, 1966, p.384.

18 The charge of 'impure art', the mixing of conventional and realistic impulses, is made against Webster by T.S. Eliot and refuted by Inga-Stina Ewbank, 'The "Impure Art" of John Webster', *Review of English Studies*, XI, 1958, pp.253–67.

19 The Duchess seeing Ferdinand in her mirror has been done in production: see George Rylands, 'On the Production of *The Duchess of Malfi*', Sylvan Press edition of the play, 1945, p.ix. For the moral pictures in Dürer, etc., see R. Van Marle, *Iconographie de l'Art Prophane au Moyen-Age et à la Renaissance*, The Hague, 1931, I, pp.396–401, 404.

20 *The Theatre and its Double*, trans. V. Corti, London, 1970, pp.6, 85. The text, presumably incorrectly, reads 'outside puppets'.

21 J.R. Brown, *op.cit.*, p. 203.

22 The idea is developed in Inga-Stina Ewbank's article referred to in note 18.

23 Johnson also wrote music for *The Tempest*; see p. 83. The music is printed in J.R. Brown, pp. 210–13.

24 That the latter was developed as a series of *lazzi* is indicated in the 1708 Fourth Quarto's two stage directions which evidently record traditional stage business: '[Ferdinand] puts off his four cloaks one after another' (V, ii, after l. 69); and '[Ferdinand] throws the doctor down and beats him' (after l. 81).

25 *The Life of the Drama*, London, 1966, p.7, following Virginia Woolf's notion of the novel as an extension of the range of our gossip.

26 The idea is developed by D.C. Gunby, '*The Duchess of Malfi*: A Theological Approach', *John Webster*, ed. B. Morris, London, 1970, p.182.

7 'Some High-Tuned Poem': *The Broken Heart* at the Blackfriars

1 Quotations and line references are from the Revels edition, edited by T.J.B. Spencer, Manchester, 1980.
2 According to the *Oxford English Dictionary*, 'high-toned', which is patently a variant of 'high-tuned', does not appear in English until 1804, and not in its metaphorical sense until 1814.
3 Crashaw's couplet was first printed in *The Delights of the Muses*, 1646, but survives in a manuscript datable not after 1634. See *The Poems Latin and Greek of Richard Crashaw*, ed. L.C. Martin, 2nd edn, Oxford, 1957, pp.xc, 181.
4 Orgilus's wild talk may be an argument with a book he is carrying or the two sides of a debate he conducts with himself, most probably the latter, though a book would add useful colouring to his disguise and prompt his request for (more) books.
5 The idea of *The Broken Heart* as a tragedy of manners is suggested in R.J. Kaufman's 'Ford's Waste Land: *The Broken Heart*', *Renaissance Drama*, n.s.3, 1970, pp.167–87.
6 The scene is often taken to be a betrothal ceremony, but this makes nonsense of Ithocles's secret disclosure to Orgilus at ll. 121–3 of the affiancement and the court's surprise at the 'wedding' in V,iii. There is certainly a previous agreement between Calantha and Ithocles about the relationship, but Ithocles is only accepted publicly here as suitor or champion.
7 See *J.&C.S.*, III, 452–53 and IV, 917–20.
8 Lines 77–107 give us the shape of Penthea's tragedy. She refuses Orgilus not out of an excessive regard for the legality of her marriage, which some have claimed, but because that marriage, which is really a rape, has made her unworthy of Orgilus and of their love. The key is ll. 119–102.
9 Spencer, *op.cit.*, discusses trick chairs in Appendix B.
10 The murderer says: 'I have devised such a curious snare as jealous Vulcan never yet devis'd, To grasp his arms unable to resist Death's instruments enclosed in these hands.' Other chairs trapped the victim's thighs.
11 William Archer, *The Old Drama and the New*, London, 1923, p.65.
12 *Orchesography*, ed. Julia Sutton, New York, 1967, p.125. I am indebted to Gillian Edmonds for this reference, in an unpublished paper, Lancaster University, 1980.
13 It seems that the whole of Davenant's scene was played in the discovery-space so that drawing a curtain concealed the body at the end.
14 Other explanations for these lines include the relationship of Sir Philip Sidney and Penelope Rich, a Dutch murder of the mid-sixteenth century involving a trick chair like Orgilus's, a tragic love story in *The Book of the Courtier*, and the uninterrupted festivities at Sparta after the battle of

Leuctra. Only the last seems to accommodate 'when time's youth wanted some riper years'.

15 The quarto and Spencer read 'Is not untroubled . . .' but I see no sense in this.

16 *Specimens of English Dramatic Poets* (first publ. London, 1808) repr. 1897, p.228.

17 In 1634, a new play, *The Spartan Ladies*, by Lodowick Carlell, was played at Blackfriars. It is not extant.

18 The play is *Sicily and Naples*, by Samuel Harding. It was apparently never performed though intended to be played before the King at Oxford.

19 Reprinted in Robert Speaight, *William Poel and the Elizabethan Revival*, London, 1954, p. 129.

8 Court Theatre, 1603–42

1 For an account of Jacobean court theatre, see *E.S..*, I, pp.1–26.

2 For an account of the Revels Office, see *E.S.*, I, pp.71–105.

3 The Jacobean and Caroline Banqueting Houses are described in *J.&C.S.*, VI, pp. 255–67 and pp.284–8 and G. Wickham, *Early English Stages*, II, Part Two, chapter xiv, London, 1972. A major study of the Second Jacobean Banqueting House, designed by Inigo Jones, is Per Palme's *The Triumph of Peace: A Study of the Whitehall Banqueting House*, Uppsala, 1957.

4 This and other information is given by R.F. Hill (ed.), in 'Dramatic Records in the Declared Accounts of the Office of Works: 1560–1640', Malone Society *Collections*, X, 1977, pp.xvi-xix.

5 R. Leacroft, *The Development of the English Playhouse*, London, 1973, pp.54–6, in his reconstruction of the first Jacobean Banqueting House, argues interestingly for the placing of the stage at the upper end, but most of the evidence points the other way.

6 Per Palme, *op.cit.*, p.120. He refers to the Second Jacobean Banqueting House, but the description suits the function of the first as well.

7 The longest version of Busino's account appears in A.M. Nagler's *A Source Book in Theatrical History*, New York, 1952, pp.148–54, from which the present extracts are taken.

8 Quoted in L.B. Smith's *Elizabeth Tudor: A Portrait of a Queen*, London, 1976, p.78. Pages 78–80 are relevant.

9 *Basilicon Doron*, 1603, ed. J. Craigie, Edinburgh, 1944, p.12.

10 *The Poems of Thomas Carew*, ed. R. Dunlap, Oxford, 1949, pp.127,270.

11 *J.&C.S.*, III, p.129.

12 Samuel Daniel, preface to *Tethys' Festival*, 1610.

13 Essay 'Of Masques and Triumphs', added to *Essays*, 1625.

14 For an account of the 'Platonic politics' of the Caroline masque, see S. Orgel and R. Strong, *Inigo Jones: The Theatre of the Stuart Court*, I, Berkeley, California, 1973, chapter iv. This fine study of the work of Jones is drawn on in this chapter and in Chapter 10.

15 *J.&C.S.*, III, pp.107–8.

16 A contemporary account is quoted in *E.S.*, I, p.172, n.1.

17 Quoted in *J.&C.S.*, VI, p.284.

9 'Excellent Creeping Sport': *Bartholomew Fair* at the Banqueting House

1 Quotations are taken from the Revels edition, edited by E.A. Horsman, London, 1960.
2 See R. Dutton, *Ben Jonson: To the First Folio*, Cambridge, 1983, pp.156–7.
3 The notion occurs in R. Ornstein, 'Shakesperian and Jonsonian Comedy', *S.S.*, XXII, 1969, p.46; and G. Parfitt, *Ben Jonson: Public Poet and Private Man*, London, 1976, p.83.
4 John Taylor, the Water Poet, arranged a trial of wit to take place at the Hope on 7 October 1614. When his adversary failed to turn up, he entertained the audience for a while until the players, evidently the Lady Elizabeth's Men, came to his rescue. See *E.S.*, II, pp. 468–9.
5 B. Beckerman, *Shakespeare at the Globe*, New York, 1962, pp.20, 219.
6 *Basilicon Doron*, ed. J. Craigie, Edinburgh, 1944, pp.14, 39.
7 The idea is carefully argued in William Blissett's 'Your Majesty is Welcome to a Fair', *The Elizabethan Theatre*, ed. G.R. Hibbard, Montreal, 1974, pp.80–105.
8 See D.H. Willson, *King James VI and I*, London, 1956, pp.63, 272, 396, 398, 446.
9 *E.S.*, III, p. 352.
10 *Cynthia's Revels* (1600), *The Poetaster* (1601), *Epicoene* (1609).
11 Field's *Amends for Ladies* was published, 1618, as acted by both companies; Rowley and Newton (with Prince Charles's Men) represented both companies before the Privy Council in March 1615; and Rosseter's patent of June 1615 was to build a playhouse in the Blackfriars area for both companies. See *J. & C.S.*, I, p.201, n.2.
12 The passage from Field senior is in *Puritanism in Tudor England*, ed. H.C. Porter, London, 1970, p. 120. In fact, Jonson's borrowing seems to have gone unnoticed. For the Wiggington and prayer borrowings, see *Collected Works*, ed. C.H. Herford, Percy and Evelyn Simpson, X, Oxford, 1950, p.213.
13 'Dramatic Records in the Declared Accounts of the Treasurer of The Chamber, 1558–1642', ed. David Cook, Malone Society *Collections*, VI, 1962, p.111.
14 'Dramatic Records in the Declared Accounts of the Office of the Works, 1560–1640', ed. R.F. Hill, Malone Society *Collections*, X, 1977, p.26.
15 It might be a reference to John Taylor and an incident at the Hope. See note 4 above.
16 The Revels edition, following the 1631 text, reads 'base' for 'bass'. No doubt a pun is intended, as well as the allusion.
17 *E.S.*, IV, p. 183.
18 *E.S.*, II, p. 365.
19 Most single editions, as well as the *Collected Works* (*op. cit.*), follow Jonson's practice. An exception is the New Mermaid edition, edited by Maurice Hussey, 1964, which divides the play into ten scenes.
20 '*Fire* – in Ursula's booth', *Collected Works*, X, p. 209.
21 G. Speaight, in *The History of the English Puppet Theatre*, 1955, pp.57–60, concludes that the puppets were of the glove variety. But rod puppets with jointed limbs are as likely (Jonson elsewhere refers to many kinds of puppet) – in particular serving best for the climax of the argument with

Zeal when '*The Puppet takes up his garment*' (after V, v, 99). A playbill for a puppet show at the real Bartholomew Fair in 1700 boasts of puppets 'as large as children of two years old'.

22　For an account of the internal coherence of the play's action, see R. Levin's 'The Structure of *Bartholomew Fair*', *Publications of the Modern Language Association of America*, LXXX, 1965, pp.172–9.

23　The argument for simultaneous staging is made by E.M. Waith, 'The Staging of *Bartholomew Fair*', *Studies in English Literature*, II, 1962, pp. 181–95, reproduced in slightly different form in the author's Yale *Ben Jonson* edition of the play, Appendix II. Waith usefully stresses the Brechtian elements of *Bartholomew Fair*.

24　See, for example chapter 3 of George Parfitt's *Ben Jonson* (*op. cit.*).

25　*A Defence of an Essay of Dramatic Poetry*, in Dryden, *Poetry, Prose and Plays*, ed. D. Grant, London, 1952, p.442.

10　'The Crystal Mirror of your Reign': *Coelum Britannicum* at the Banqueting House

1　*J. & C.S.*, III, p. 107. Discussions of *Coelum Britannicum* drawn on in this chapter are: A. Nicholl, *Stuart Masques*, London, 1938, pp.101–4; ed. R. Dunlap, *The Poems of Thomas Carew*, 1949, pp.273–83; S. Orgel, *The Illusion of Power*, Berkeley, California, 1975, pp.83–7; G. Parry, *The Golden Age Restor'd: The Culture of the Stuart Court, 1603–42*, Manchester, 1981, pp.194–6. S. Orgel and R. Strong's *Inigo Jones: The Theatre of the Stuart Court*, Berkeley, California, 1973, contains the text, designs and some account of the politics and scenery.

2　Line references are to the edition in R. Dunlap, *op.cit.*, which, however, is an old-fashioned spelling text, here modernised.

3　*J. & C.S.*, III, p. 107.

4　It is reproduced in R. Dunlap, *op.cit.* The manuscript includes marginal notes, in another hand from that of the synopsis, which read 'This was acted in Germany, before the Earl of Arundel, when he went to Vienna on behalf of the Palsgrave', and 'An: 1638'. Dunlap argues convincingly that these are incorrect. Several words in the manuscript are evidently errors and appear to be simple miscopyings of an 'original', possibly in a scribe's hand. In the version here, the following words are emendations: 'banns' (from 'bands'), 'vats' (from 'lasses', *via* 'fattes'), 'speeches' (from 'paces'), and 'light' (from life').

5　The 'stage directions' in the printed text are, of course, explanatory notes describing what happened (and mostly in the past tense), not instructions for repeated performances.

6　Reproduced in Orgel and Strong, *op.cit.*, II, pp.567–70.

7　Malone Society *Collections*, X, ed. R.F. Hill, 1977, p.46.

Index